Censure and Heresy
at the University of Paris
1200–1400

THE MIDDLE AGES SERIES
Ruth Mazo Karras, General Editor
Edward Peters, Founding Editor

A complete list of books in the series
is available from the publisher.

Censure and Heresy
at the University of Paris
1200–1400

J. M. M. H. Thijssen

PENN

University of Pennsylvania Press

Philadelphia

10 9 8 7 6 5 4 3 2 1

Published by
University of Pennsylvania Press
Philadelphia, Pennsylvania 19104-4011

Library of Congress Cataloging-in-Publication Data
Thijssen, J. M. M. H.
Censure and heresy at the University of Paris, 1200–1400 / J. M. M. H.
Thijssen.
    p.   cm. — (Middle Ages series)
Includes bibliographical references (p.   ) and index.
ISBN 0-8122-3318-2 (alk. paper)
    1. Université de Paris — History.   2. Church and education — France —
Paris — History.   3. Academic freedom — France — Paris — History.
4. Education, Medieval.   5. Heresies, Christian — History — Middle
Ages, 600–1500.   6. Philosophy, Medieval.   I. Series.
LF2166.T47   1998
378.44'361 — dc21   98-9766
                                                                        CIP

This one is for the two Alexes

Contents

Preface

Shortly before 1206, Master Amalric of Bène was summoned to the papal court to answer allegations of disseminating false teaching. The investigation did not turn out well for Amalric. His views were condemned by Pope Innocent III and upon his return to the University of Paris he had to recant them in front of his fellow scholars. According to one chronicle, Amalric was so affected by this humiliating experience that he died shortly afterward.[1]

Amalric's condemnation is the earliest documented case of academic censure in the history of the University of Paris. But it was by no means the last one. Toward the end of the thirteenth century various lists of theses that were censured at the University of Paris were gathered in the *Collectio errorum in anglia et parisius condempnatorum*, the "Collection of errors condemned in England and Paris," sometimes referred to as the Collection of Parisian Articles.[2] The only English censure that figures in this collection is the condemnation that was pronounced on March 18, 1277, at the University of Oxford by Robert Kilwardby, archbishop of Canterbury. The remaining theses of the collection represent false teaching that was disseminated and censured at the University of Paris. During the fourteenth century, this collection grew to approximately thirteen cases of censured teaching, depending on which of the many copies of the *Collectio* one consults.

Four of these censures have appeared prominently in the historiography of medieval philosophy: the condemnation issued by Bishop Stephen Tempier on March 7, 1277, the prohibition of the Ockhamist errors of 1340, the censure of Nicholas of Autrecourt in 1346, and the censure of John of Mirecourt in 1347. In textbooks of medieval philosophy, these condemnations have traditionally been presented as turning points in medieval thought.[3] But were they really such unique and important events in the intellectual life of the University of Paris? Historians of medieval thought have been so fascinated by the doctrinal meaning and impact of these academic condemnations that their larger historical and institutional framework has become obscured.

My major intent in this book is to examine these four *causes célèbres* in the historiography of medieval philosophy from a different angle, namely as manifestations of academic censure at the University of Paris. By academic censure I mean the prohibition or condemnation of teaching disseminated by a university-trained scholar concerning fine points of scholastic theology and philosophy. The terms used in the medieval sources for what I have designated as censures are *prohibitio*, *reprobatio*, or *condemnatio*. Strictly speaking there is a distinction between a *prohibitio* and a *condemnatio* or *reprobatio*. A *prohibitio* is a prohibition to disseminate certain views. It does not make any claims as to the truth or falsity of those views, so that in theory even Catholic views can be prohibited, if, for instance, they might cause public outcry (*scandalum*) or endanger believers. The geographical and temporal scope of a prohibition is limited. A *condemnatio*, on the other hand, is valid for every Christian at all times (*omnibus pro omni tempore*). A condemnation implies an adverse judgment on the views that are forbidden to be disseminated. In practice, however, the boundary line between these terms cannot be easily drawn. As will become clear in this study, prohibitions also appear to imply reproval of the forbidden views. Moreover, transgressions of prohibitions to disseminate certain teaching are also threatened with judicial sanctions, such as suspension of all scholarly activities, or excommunication. The medieval term *censura* (*ecclesiastica*), which also sometimes appears in university-related documents, has no bearing on academic censures. It was reserved for a spiritual punishment inflicted by an ecclesiastical judge, in particular for any of the three so-called ecclesiastical censures, that is, excommunication, interdict, or suspension.[4]

In this study I have made central what in the historiography of medieval philosophy has been regarded as of secondary importance, namely, questions that the academic censures raise concerning the judicial procedures, the agent of authority in monitoring false teaching at a university, and the effects that the condemnations had on the careers of the accused. In this respect, the present study joins a shift in attention from issues surrounding doctrines to issues of authority and freedom of thought that has begun with Josef Koch, and has been continued in more recent times by Jürgen Miethke, William Courtenay, and others.[5]

The four case studies are preceded by a chapter in which I will try to create a general perspective on the phenomenon of academic censure at the University of Paris. This survey covers the period between 1200 and 1400. The first date marks the beginning of the University of Paris, and hence the emergence of a community of academics in the true sense of the word. The end point of this study, approximately halfway through the Great Schism, is somewhat more arbitrary.

By 1380, the university of Paris was faced with two distinct papacies, one at Rome (Urban VI), and one at Avignon (Clement VII). The ensuing crisis in ecclesiastical authority had a great impact upon the community of academics.[6] On a practical level, the university had to decide to whom it should send the rolls (*rotuli*) with petitions for benefices. But the temporary uncertainty of the masters' incomes was only a minor problem compared to the subsequent difficulties. The Paris faculty of arts became internally divided over the recognition of Clement as the head of the church. The division reached its climax in the exodus from Paris of the masters of the English-German nation, many of whom came from countries whose sovereigns supported Urban VI.

In theology, the schism uprooted the traditional methods of validating orthodoxy. To whom should the theologians look for an authoritative statement concerning doctrinal matters? Now that the locus of authority in the church was seemingly divided, the theologians of Paris themselves came to play a role in restoring the universal jurisdiction of the church. This aspect is extremely well illustrated in the last academic censure of the fourteenth century pronounced at the University of Paris, that of the theologian John of Monzón. It happens to be one of the best-documented inquiries conducted at the University of Paris. At some point during the judicial proceedings, Monzón filed an appeal both at the papal court of Clement VII and at that of Urban VI. Moreover, the Monzón case generated a profound theoretical discussion of the locus of teaching authority at the University of Paris by the great theologian Pierre d'Ailly. So moving the temporal limits to 1400 has the advantage of including the Monzón censure in this study.

In Chapter 1, I examine those censures of scholars that were initiated within the university itself, in connection with one of the core activities of the curriculum—lecturing, disputing, or preaching. What these censures have in common, besides their institutional context and certain juridical aspects, to be discussed below, is that they all appear in one or another version of the *Collectio errorum*.

In general, the sources necessary for a study of university condemnations of false teaching between 1200 and 1400 are extremely partial and fragmentary. As a consequence, this material has to be complemented by documentary evidence from other types of academic censure, not so intimately connected with university activities, but still involving university-trained scholars. Good examples are the censures of the Dominican Durand of St. Pourçain and the Franciscan Peter Olivi: both these men held academic degrees, but their censures were handled entirely within their religious orders. In the cases of Meister Eckhart and Thomas Waleys, on the other hand, (respectively, Dominicans and alumni of the Universities of Paris and Oxford), the views at issue were examined in a procedure that was neither started by their religious order nor connected with any activities at the university. Even though the judicial forum could differ from case to case, the *ordo juris*, the way of proceeding against academics charged with disseminating false teaching, was basically the same in all cases. So, taken together, the surviving evidence provides a fair idea of how false teaching was suppressed at the University of Paris.

Chapter 2 discusses the condemnation of 219 propositions pronounced by Stephen Tempier, bishop of Paris, on March 7, 1277. Chapter 3 discusses the prohibition to disseminate six Ockhamist errors that was issued by the faculty of arts in 1340. Chapter 4 examines the investigations and censures of Nicholas of Autrecourt and John of Mirecourt. Chapter 5 addresses the interpretation of the phenomenon of academic censure. At first sight the medieval academic condemnations seem to exemplify the facile generalization of older textbooks that the Middle Ages were "a millenium in which reason was enchained, thought was enslaved."[7] Although probably no one any longer upholds this unbalanced view, the medieval academic condemnations do appear to the modern reader as striking manifestations of the limitations exerted by Christian faith on the thought and teaching of university scholars. Medieval scholars, however, perceived censure from a different point of view, namely as the exercise of teaching authority, rather than as a restraint on academic freedom. In the Conclusion I have attempted to provide a broad overview of some of the aspects of the phenomenon of academic censure considered in this study. The bibliography also provides an introductory essay to the sources relevant for the study of academic censures.

*   *   *

I have been interested in academic condemnations for some time. The idea, however, to bring together my material and expand it into a book-length study about academic censure and teaching authority at the University of Paris was only conceived in 1992, when I was a visiting scholar at the Institute for Interdisciplinary Studies in the Humanities and at the History Department of the University of California, Santa Barbara.

There are many people to whom I owe thanks for the help and encouragement they have given me when writing this book. First let me thank the two anonymous readers (one of whom revealed himself as William Courtenay) for the University of Pennsylvania Press. Both produced long and extremely valuable detailed reports that I have consulted many times while revising the manuscript. The shortcomings that remain are mine. I would also like to thank the following scholars who offered helpful comments on an earlier draft of particular sections of my study: Henk Braakhuis, Chris Coppens, the late Jan van Laarhoven, Marc van der Poel, and G. H. M. Posthumus Meyjes.

I owe a special debt of gratitude to Jeffrey Russell and William Courtenay. Jeff not only stimulated me to write this book, and helped me enormously by reading a first draft of the entire manuscript and in clarifying its argument, but also made me feel at home at Santa Barbara. Bill's studies on academic censure and its institutional context have been particularly important to me, as appears from the notes. Though we may disagree from time to time on points of finer detail, I am greatly indebted to him for the many thoughtful suggestions that he has selflessly shared with me on our common topic of interest.

Over the last four years, I have presented early drafts of some sections as lectures at the History Department, University of California, Santa Barbara; the History Department at the University of Southern California; the Medieval Academy, held at Knoxville; the Centrum voor Middeleeuwse Studies at the University of Nijmegen; and the Center for Semiotics, San Marino. I would like to thank the many participants of those lectures for their kind reception of my presentations, in particular H. Ansgar Kelly, who with his perceptive question about the chancellor's judicial authority opened a new (and laborious) venue of research for me.

Part of Chapter 2 apppeared in my articles "1277 Revisited: A New Interpretation of the Doctrinal Investigations of Thomas Aquinas and Giles of Rome," *Vivarium* 34 (1997), 1–29, and "What Really Happened on 7 March 1277? Bishop Tempier's Condemnation and Its Institutional Context," in *Texts and Contexts in Ancient and Medieval Science: Studies on the Occasion of John E. Murdoch's Seventieth Birthday*, ed. Edith Sylla and Michael McVaugh (Leiden, 1997), 84–114. Thanks are due to Royal Brill Publishers for permission to use this material.

Research for the first version of this book was financially supported by the Royal Netherlands Academy of Sciences and Arts. The Netherlands Organization for Scientific Research provided ideal conditions in which to finish this work. I am grateful to both organizations, *sine quibus non*.

I thank Edward Peters for his support and advice and for accepting this study in the Middle Ages series.

I

The Suppression of
False Teaching

The Notions of Heresy and Error in the World of Learning

In his *Dialogus* William Ockham explains that there are three types of heresy. One kind amounts to an almost verbatim denial of the truths of faith. Another is so obvious that "anyone who understands anything, even if illiterate," can see in what way Divine Scripture is contradicted. A third is perceptible only to the literate and learned who are well versed in Divine Scripture, after a long and subtle deliberation. These are heresies such as "Christ as a man is not something," or "two persons are present in Christ."[1] Heresies of the latter type are the concern of the present chapter, and, as a matter of fact, of the entire book. Ockham's definition brings out two important facets of the phenomenon of academic censure. First, academic censures concern university-trained scholars, involved in academic issues, that is, in fine points of scholastic theology and philosophy. Second, judicial actions that resulted in academic censure were started by accusations of heresy.

The term "heresy" was regularly used in the context of academic censure, either openly, by qualifying the suspect opinions as "heretical," or in a more implicit way. Academics were, for instance, charged with holding opinions against Catholic faith, Holy Scripture, Evangelical truth, or sound doctrine (*sana doctrina*), thus causing scandal (*scandalum*) and endangering the souls of believers, as well as the fabric of society itself.[2] The suspect doctrines were described as dangerous, or even as diseases.[3] Other documents concerning academic censure might use the standard formula "faith and good morals" (*in fide et bonis moribus*), or a variant thereof, when assessing the heretical character of suspect views, thus hinting at the moral dimension of the medieval concept of heresy, which could be expressed in immoral conduct, impiety, or the violation of sacraments.[4]

The roots of academic heresy were sought in the theologians' indulgence in vain curiosity (*vana curiositas*). The existence of a more than tenuous link between vain curiosity and heresy is made particularly clear by Jean Gerson. In his *Contra vanam curiositatem*, an eloquent fulmination against the neglect of Scripture and religious meaning in the study of theology during his lifetime, Gerson informs the reader that it was Eve's curiosity that made her err.[5] In other texts, Gerson presents *curiositas* as the daughter of pride (*superbia*).[6] Knowledge generating pride is contrasted with wisdom (*sapientia*) generating humility. Pride is the major vice of the heretic, for it is pride, rather than ignorance, that creates heretics.[7] Moreover, as medieval theory had it, pride manifested itself in heretics through many specific sins, such as pertinacity (*pertinacia*) and presumptuousness (*presumptio*), also a current theme in documents pertaining to academic censure.[8] In particular, the application of philosophy—one of the forms of speculative *curiositas*—to the interpretation of the message of Christ was a continuous source of suspicion to the guardians of orthodoxy all through the Middle Ages.[9] In many official documents and other texts, philosophers and theologians were exhorted not to cross the boundaries of their own fields—a reference to Proverbs 22:28—and not to become theologizing philosophers and philosophizing theologians.[10]

Although there is no doubt that the word "heresy" and its derivatives were employed in the context of academic censure, they were used in a rather loose sense. Strictly speaking, academic condemnations concerned false teachings and erroneous views, rather than clear-cut heresies. The difference between "untrue" (*falsus*), "erroneous" (*erroneus*), and "heretical" (*hereticus*) was clearly perceived by medieval intellectuals. The theologian Godfrey of Fontaines, for instance, observed that errors are faults that endanger our salvation; they become heresies when they are defended with pertinacity.[11] The same sentiment was expressed by the council of ten theologians who in 1320 were asked by Pope John XXII to examine whether necromancy should be considered heretical. In the learned treatises that preceded their reports, these theologians made the point that a heretic is someone who by his own will obstinately chooses to adhere to his errors.[12] And again, when Meister Eckhart was on trial, he claimed before his judges that he could be in error, but that he could not be a heretic, "for the first belongs to the intellect, the second to the will." Precisely because he did not obstinately adhere to his errors, Meister Eckhart claimed that the proceedings against him *as a heretic* were unjustified.[13] Eckhart also pointed to the canonistic roots of the connection between pertinacity and heresy in Gratian's *Decretum*.[14] Among the ancient canons collected and reconciled in the *Decretum* are two that emphasize the aspect of pertinacity, namely the Apostle Paul, Titus 3:10, and Augustine, *De civitate dei* Lib.18, c.51. Their purport is that those who stubbornly resist correction of their errors should be considered heretics.[15]

Probably the most extensive theoretical discussion of pertinacity is given by William Ockham, who may be considered a personal expert in this field, for at a certain point in his career he was summoned to the papal court in Avignon and became the subject of an investigation that took four years. In any case he covers many of the intricacies of this topic, such as the connection between pertinacity and heresy, the different kinds of pertinacity, who has the right to convict someone of pertinacity, and what are the legitimate forms of correction.[16] According to Ockham, a pertinacious person is one who persists in questioning the articles of faith, thus endangering his salvation.[17] Among other things, Ockham pointed out that a conviction of heresy required that (heretical) depravity be present not only in the error but also in the person himself who erred. The depravity in the erring consisted of pertinacity or obstinacy. Pertinacity turned a *haereticans* into a *haereticus*.[18] The idea of pertinacity was used to set apart the heretic from the innocent blunderer, who committed his errors not out of any obstinacy, but out of theological ignorance.[19]

The sharp distinction between "heresy" and "heretic" was not mere theory; it was also drawn at the judicial proceedings against erring scholars. In a document (1318) that records the votes of censure of several theologians with regard to three theses, some of the votes explicitly state that the thesis under consideration is heretical, "and that obstinate adherents should be condemned as heretics."[20] In order to find out whether the qualification "heretical" could be transferred from the doctrine to its holders, a "test of pertinacity" had to be performed. The test consisted of the *revocatio*, the solemn recantation of the erroneous and heretical opinions (of which more below). If the academic who had been accused of disseminating false views was willing to recant them, he avoided condemnation as a heretic, since he had not been pertinacious (*pertinax*).[21] In sum, pertinacity was an essential characteristic of the medieval heretic.

The second essential feature of the medieval conception of heresy was its symbiotic relationship with orthodoxy. In the words of Jeffrey Russell: "Orthodoxy defines heresy, and heresy helps define orthodoxy."[22] Application of the notion of heresy implies a standard or norm, a definition of what is orthodox doctrine.[23] But a formal definition of orthodoxy was precisely what was lacking in many cases of academic censure. Academics were not censured for disseminating views that had already been formally condemned by ecclesiastical authorities as heretical. Rather, they were engaged in a running scholastic debate during which they incurred accusations of false teaching.

This feature of heresy is made most explicit in the short treatise *De protestatione circa materiam fidei* by Jean Gerson. Since Gerson was not only a theologian but also chancellor at the University of Paris, he can be considered a well-informed source in matters of academic censure.[24] According to Gerson, those academics who fell victim to censure usually belonged to a category whose errors consisted not of a straightforward denial of any Christian doctrines, but of an adherence to views whose opposite was *implied* by faith, though not yet *explicitly* stated. According to Gerson, it was mere simplicity or ignorance (*ex sola simplicitate vel ignorantia*), rather than anything else, that had led censured theologians to contradict faith. They were not "real" heretics. Those who stuck to their errors and refused to recant were real heretics, even if at the moment of the charge it was nowhere yet *explicitly* stated that according to faith they should uphold the opposite position.[25] Gerson's account confirms that heresy was a fluid concept, intrinsically connected with orthodoxy. Most academics charged with heresy had touched upon a fringe of doctrines not strictly *de fide*, where the debate was still in progress. In 1305, when his views on the Eucharist were being examined, for example, John of Paris (Quidort) claimed that, since the church had not yet decided upon the question, his views had no bearing upon faith.[26]

Gerson's claim that ignorance was the root of suspect teaching must not be misunderstood. In a previous section of *De protestatione circa materiam fidei* Gerson had made the point that ignorance could never be an excuse for not knowing certain truths of faith. In particular doctors of theology had to know more truths contained in the Bible, and truths derived therefrom, than ordinary believers, "otherwise they would usurp the degree and name of doctor in a condemnable and inexcusable way." Prelates and doctors had to meet higher standards of theological sophistication than simple lay folk.[27] Gerson's observations raise two intriguing questions, namely, who possessed the *authority* to condemn erring academics who, strictly speaking, were not contradicting truths of faith, and who possessed the *knowledge* to do so. As we will see below, both aspects, power and knowledge, *potestas* and *scientia*, were represented in the proceedings against academics charged with disseminating false teaching.

In sum, then, the language of the documents concerning the censure of suspect teaching gives the impression that erring theologians were comparable to members of popular heretical movements. In reality, however, the notion of heresy most prominent in the world of learning was markedly different from that attributed to popular heretical movements. First, academics charged with suspect teaching did not adhere to views that overtly contradicted faith, or that had already been formally condemned. On the contrary, the erroneous character of their views came to be established only during the proceedings that resulted from the allegations of false teaching. Second, they did not stubbornly defend and disseminate their views, once their erroneous character had been pointed out to them, but were open to correction. These different conceptions of heresy, the broader and the more strict, are nicely illustrated in a brief written by the theologian Pierre d'Ailly. In this brief, d'Ailly summarized for the papal court why and in what way the faculty of theology had censured the theologian John of Monzón (Juan de Monzón). From the document it appears that, during the judicial proceedings, Monzón had insulted the bishop and the theologians by calling them Manicheans, that is, members of a formally condemned heretical sect. According to Pierre d'Ailly, however, the bishop and the theologians had never called John of Monzón a heretic, nor had they ever termed his views heretical. Yet his views were censured.[28]

Courts and Judges

As clerics, the scholars of the University of Paris enjoyed the privilege of trial the *privilegium fori*, in the ecclesiastical courts. They fell under ecclesiastical jurisdiction, and were, save for some exceptions, exempted from lay jurisdiction. In principle, proceedings against bachelors and masters charged with disseminating false teaching could involve any of the following four tribunals: the consistory of the chancellor and masters of theology of the University of Paris, the episcopal court, the papal court, and a forum of the minister general of a religious order and his advisors. Not the nature of the offense but its circumstances determined which tribunal or tribunals had jurisdiction over a specific case. In particular the following two factors were decisive: the status of the defendant and the institutional context in which the offense was committed. Even though many scholars belonged to a religious order, and the University of Paris was the *studium generale* of, among others, the Dominicans, Franciscans, and Cistercians, the tribunal of a minister general and his advisors never played a role in determining university cases of suspect teaching. Since the allegations of false teaching had arisen in the context of typical university activities, such as lecturing or disputing, the suspects were held accountable on the grounds of their membership in the university, even if they belonged to a religious order. The consistory of chancellor and masters of theology had precedence in such cases. Yet the tribunal of a minister general and his advisors deserves to be included in this discussion, because its jurisdictional powers and its way of proceeding in cases of suspect teaching were comparable to those of the consistory of chancellor and masters of theology. Put more succinctly, the consistory of the chancellor and theologians and the tribunal of the master general and his advisors exercised the same kind of jurisdiction in cases of suspect teaching, namely, disciplinary jurisdiction. The episcopal and papal courts, on the other hand, possessed criminal jurisdiction. Strictly speaking, only the latter two forums could *adjudicate* cases of false teaching, that is, decide a complaint of false teaching with judicial powers. As long as the proceedings against an erring academic were carried out before a panel of chancellor and theologians, or a tribunal of the minister general and his advisors, it was still a disciplinary case; the moment the case was moved to the episcopal or papal court, it became a criminal case. As will be elucidated below, the order and course of the disciplinary and criminal procedures were derived from Matthew 18: 15–17. The regular criminal procedure in cases of false teaching was preceded by "private" reproof, that is, by extrajudicial procedure.

THE FORUM OF A MINISTER GENERAL AND HIS ADVISORS

The examination of the teachings of the Dominican Durand of St. Pourçain probably provides the clearest example of the disciplinary character of the proceedings of the tribunal of the minister general and his advisors.[29] In 1313, Durand of St. Pourçain attracted for the first time the attention of his superiors. He had just received his appointment as master of theology at the papal *studium generale* at Avignon, a position that a few decades later came to be known as the *magister sacri palatii*. Against the order's statutes, Durand's commentary on the *Sentences* had been disseminated outside the order without his superiors' preliminary approval. Hence, Berengar of Landorra, minister general of the Dominicans, decided that Durand's views needed to be scrutinized by a commission of experts (*fratres periti*) in order to establish whether they ran against faith and morals.[30] The legislation on the prepublication scrutiny of writings was the formal reason for investigating Durand's commentary. Although Durand claimed that his writings had been taken away from him by some overeager friends before he had had a chance to correct them, one wonders whether Durand had deliberately avoided having his commentary on the *Sentences* examined before publication.[31] Durand's views were investigated a second time in 1317, this time because he had explicitly contradicted and attacked Thomas Aquinas's views in his commentary on the *Sentences*. This was in opposition to the order's decree, issued a few years earlier, that the Dominicans should lecture according to the doctrine and works of Thomas Aquinas.[32] Both censures were confirmed at the general chapters of the order that were held shortly after the minister general had decided, on the basis of the reports of the experts, that Durand's commentary indeed contained many errors.

Durand's superiors approached the suspicions of false teaching as a matter of internal discipline within the Dominican order. In their view, Durand had violated the order's regulations. The constitution that members of the order had to have their writings examined before publication originated in the 1350s and was repeated at several general chapters of the Dominicans.[33] The decree that forbade the order's teachers (*lectores*) to teach against the common doctrine of Thomas Aquinas — in addition to ordering that their teaching ought to be in agreement with the articles of faith, good morals, and the church's sacraments — was of earlier date. It was issued at the general chapter that was held at Bologna in 1315. The decree further stipulated that the provincial or the minister general should be informed about those teachers at the *studia* who had refused to correct themselves after respectful admonition.[34] In short, by disobeying the order's constitutions, to which he was bound by his vow of obedience, Durand incurred the prescribed sanction: his disobedience was brought to the attention of the minister general of his order, who now had grounds to start disciplinary proceedings against him.

The proceedings against Peter Olivi too may have been based on Franciscan legislation requiring that any works written by members of the order had to be approved prior to their publication. In any case, Olivi claimed that some of his brethren had published the *Questions on Evangelical Perfection* against his explicit wish.[35]

These two inquiries demonstrate that the superior, the minister general of the order, derived his jurisdictional basis for disciplinary actions from an infringement of regulations to which the inferiors, the members of the

orders, were bound by vows. In similar fashion, the jurisdiction of the
chancellor over the bachelors and masters of theology was based on the oaths
that bound them to obey the rules of the faculty and the University of Paris.

THE CONSISTORY OF CHANCELLOR AND
MASTERS OF THEOLOGY

In Paris, the chancellor of the cathedral chapter of Notre Dame was chancellor of the university.[36] His most important and prestigious assignment
was to grant the license to teach. The basis of the chancellor's authority was
very complex. As a dignitary of the cathedral chapter who had traditionally
been responsible for the cathedral school, he acted under the authority of
the bishop of Paris. However, he conferred the license to dispute, to read
(that is, lecture), to preach, and to exercise all magisterial acts required in
the faculty of theology "on the authority (*auctoritas*) of God, the Apostles
Peter and Paul, and the Apostolic See," that is, as a representative of the
pope and not as an official of the cathedral chapter.[37] In addition, the
chancellor appears to have been *iudex ordinarius*, ordinary judge of the
university community.[38] The chancellor's jurisdiction over the members of
the University of Paris stemmed, indirectly, from royal privileges, exempt-
ing the scholars in Paris from the jurisdiction of the provost.[39]

However, as early as the first decades of the thirteenth century, the
chancellor's judicial authority was challenged. Following papal appeals, the
masters obtained relief from the chancellor's jurisdiction to excommunicate
and imprison them.[40] The bull *Parens scientiarum* (1231) forbade the chancellor to have his own prison and determined that suspects were to be
imprisoned in the bishop's prison only.[41] The chancellor's judicial authority
was further attacked during a conflict that arose between Chancellor Philip
of Thori and the faculty of arts in 1283–84. At issue was the question who
was head of the university: the chancellor or the rector. The case was
brought before the papal court. John of Malignes, the legal representative
(*proctor*) of the arts faculty, maintained that the chancellor of Paris was
neither the ordinary nor the delegate judge of the scholars. As a consequence, he argued, scholars could not have one another cited before the
chancellor.[42] Pope Honorius IV, however, partly decided in favor of the
chancellor, and, in any case, confirmed the chancellor's right to exercise his
jurisdiction "as the custom was."[43] But this customary jurisdiction did not
include the right to proceed judicially in cases of false teaching at the univer-

sity. When dealing with cases of suspect teaching, the chancellor did not exercise the strictly judicial authority of an ecclesiastical judge, but responded with disciplinary proceedings. His authority was quasi-judicial. What was the jurisdictional basis of the chancellor's disciplinary actions?

For most university condemnations all that survive are the final lists of censured views. Sometimes, these are preceded by a few introductory lines indicating which authorities were responsible for the censure. This material suggests that, during the thirteenth century, all university cases of suspect teaching were determined in collaboration with the bishop of Paris.[44] All the evidence that the body of chancellor and masters of theology constituted the lowest level of jurisdiction in university cases of suspect teaching comes from the fourteenth century. From that period, we have a few university condemnations whose preface explicitly states that the censured scholar pronounced his recantation on the order of "the chancellor and the other masters in the faculty of theology."[45] However, only two cases really give us insight into the the way in which this body responded to allegations of false teaching, namely the inquiries against Denis of Foullechat and John of Monzón. Initially, both investigations were handled at the university level, but then, due to circumstances that will concern us below, they were transferred to another jurisdiction. It is probably for this reason that the records that were produced by the consistory of chancellor and masters have survived at all.

From this documentary evidence, the following picture emerges. The chancellor's power to handle allegations of false teaching was vested in an oath that bachelors of theology had to swear. The oath is attested in several sources, and extensively quoted in the records of the investigation of Foullechat's teaching. Before starting to lecture on the *Sentences*, a bachelor of theology was required to swear: "that he shall not say, hold or dogmatize anything in his 'principia' and lectures, nor in any of his other actions whatsoever that are against the catholic faith, or against a decision of the holy mother church, or against good morals, or in favor of articles that have been condemned at the Roman Curia or in Paris, or that sounds offensive in the ears of his audience, but that he will hold and dogmatize sound doctrine."[46] In addition, the bachelor swore "that if he has heard or knows of a bachelor, or someone else, who acts against this [oath], he shall reveal this to the lord bishop or the chancellor in office at that time, within seven days from the time he came to know these facts."[47]

Allegations of false teaching that involved members of the university community and that arose in a university context were first brought before the chancellor. He investigated the accusations by questioning witnesses and collecting material evidence.[48] In the Foullechat case, for instance, the chancellor obtained the quires of the lecture that had caused the allegations of false teaching. The records emphasize that Foullechat "spontaneously" gave this material to the chancellor.[49] This may mean that the chancellor did not have the authority to confiscate Foullechat's unpublished notes, because he was not acting as an ecclesiastical judge. At several meetings, the chancellor discussed the evidence with members of the faculty of theology. If they came to the conclusion that the allegations of false teaching were founded, as they did in the Foullechat and Monzón cases, the suspect was ordered to correct himself by recanting his erroneous views. To this purpose, the panel of chancellor and theologians prepared a document containing the erroneous statements that the suspect was supposed to recant. After the suspect had agreed to the document, a date was set for the public recantation before the entire university. The records of the inquiries against Foullechat give the distinct impression that the consistory of chancellor and masters of theology acted as a disciplinary council, rather than as a court. In none of the documents is the chancellor ever addressed as judge, nor do the descriptions of the procedures match those of court sessions with formal charges and defense.

The notion that university members denounced for disseminating false teaching were evaluated by a disciplinary tribunal would seem to find support in the case of John of Monzón. This investigation too started with meetings involving the chancellor, the masters of the faculty of theology, including the dean, and the suspect, and was later moved to another jurisdiction.[50] One of the records of the later stages of the trial mentions that Monzón had first been admonished by the dean and the masters of the faculty of theology in a private (*secrete*) and supportive (*caritative*) way, as was customary.[51] From this reference, it appears that the actions of the tribunal of chancellor and masters were based on the idea of fraternal correction and charity.[52] The idea was derived from Matthew 18:15–17, in which fraternal admonition is presented as an instrument for correcting a sinner in the community, particularly if his sins or crimes are nonpublic and, as a consequence, require a nonpublic remedy.[53] Obviously, theologians suspected of disseminating false teaching in the university hardly fell in the category of private sinners. The "nonpublic" reproof is here to be understood in a wider sense, as "among their own," as *secrete inter eos*, as the record explicitly states.[54]

In sum, it appears that, in the fourteenth century, university cases of false teaching were in the first instance started and settled by the masters of theology. The authority in charge was the chancellor. Only the proceedings against Monzón seem to have been chaired by the dean, usually the oldest of the regent masters of theology.[55] The position of the chancellor, John of Guignicourt, must have been weak. He was only a bachelor of theology, whereas the suspect, John of Monzón, was a master of theology. Moreover, Guignicourt's prestige among the masters may have been low anyway, because he was the pope's choice, not theirs, as the successor of John Blanchard, who had been deposed under pressure from the Parisian masters.[56] Guignicourt remained in office only for three years and was then succeeded by Pierre d'Ailly. But this merely adds a shade to the overall picture of the adjudication of false teaching at the University of Paris.

It is important that the evaluation of false teaching was, in the first instance, monitored by the (regent) masters of theology. Although the chancellor was in charge of the procedures, and the method of fact-finding was similar to that used in the ecclesiastical courts, he did not act as an ordinary ecclesiastical judge. The procedure is probably best characterized as pretrial review by a disciplinary tribunal. Most cases of false teaching within a university context were settled out of court, in a procedure that did not involve formal charges and defense, but hinged on the idea of fraternal correction, rather than strictly judicial correction. Only because Denis of Foullechat and John of Monzón did not comply with the "private" reproof of their fellow scholars were their cases brought outside the university community and transferred to a real trial court.

THE EPISCOPAL COURT

The judgment of the chancellor and masters of theology did not always prove final. On the agreed-upon day, Denis of Foullechat did not pronounce his rehearsed recantation, but, instead, read another document that he had pulled from his gown. It turned out to be his appeal to the papal court. The chancellor and masters of theology perceived Foullechat's refusal to recant as an act of contempt and stubbornness. They called in the help of the episcopal court and the inquisitor of heretical depravity to enforce their decisions.[57] John of Monzón also refused to surrender to the correction of the chancellor and masters of theology.[58] As a consequence, his case was transferred to the bishop of Paris, "the ordinary judge in this location." The faculty and university handed the bishop the dossier of the Monzón case and begged him to proceed judicially against the defendant "as is the custom in similar cases."[59] The transfer of university cases of false teaching to the episcopal court was a logical step. The fraternal admonition — that is, the extrajudicial disciplinary proceedings — had failed, and now it was time to enter the case in a regular ecclesiastical court. Since members of the university were, both by clerical status and residence at Paris, under the jurisdiction of the bishop of Paris, the episcopal court was the appropriate forum.

Unlike the tribunal of the chancellor and theologians, the episcopal court was a real trial court, or court of first instance. Presumably, the bishop, as *iudex ordinarius*, rendered his judgment on the basis of the dossier collected when the case was still under arbitration within the university itself. We cannot be certain, however, how the episcopal court operated in practice. The case of Denis of Foullechat did not go through trial at the episcopal court. Foullechat's appeal to the papal court put a stop to the judicial actions at that level. John of Monzón's case, which did go to the episcopal court, did not generate any records that inform us about the adjudication of false teaching at the episcopal court. Monzón had fled; so in the absence of a defendant, the case never came to a real trial. In any case, the record indicates that the dossier received by the faculty of theology, the *schedula facultatis theologie*, was carefully re-examined by the bishop, with the assistance of theologians and canonists.[60] The bishop took over the condemnation of the fourteen erroneous statements by the consistory of masters of theology, and forbade their dissemination at Paris on pain of excommunication. John of Monzón himself was prosecuted by a contempt of court procedure for nonappearance (*contumacia*). In his sentence, the bishop invoked the help of the secular arm for Monzón's arrest and stipulated that he would proceed against him in the ordinary judicial way.[61]

THE PAPAL COURT

Whereas the consistory of chancellor and masters turned to the episcopal court for assistance, the defendants Denis of Foullechat and John of Monzón sought help at the papal court in Avignon. The papal court was a different type of judicial tribunal than the episcopal court: it was not a trial court, but an appellate court. In other words, the papal court provided a forum for review of adjudication rendered in one of the lower courts of original jurisdiction. A fuller discussion of the appellate process will be given in the next section. The papal court could, however, also be a court of first instance or trial court. In that case, judicial action against false teaching was initiated in the papal court, and its judge gathered the evidence and handed down the decision.

What role did papal jurisdiction play in the adjudication of cases of false teaching? Between 1318 and 1342, during the pontificates of John XXII and Benedict XII, the majority of cases in which academics were charged with false teaching were decided in Avignon. But what is the significance of this fact? Richard Southern and William Courtenay suggest that during this period the influence of the university in doctrinal decisions declined, and that due to papal initiative the supervision of teaching shifted from university to papal court.[62] In addition to conscious papal policy, however, there were other, even more decisive factors that help to explain why so many censures were issued in Avignon, instead of in Paris.

Before examining the role of the papal court in the decision-making process regarding cases of false teaching, two preliminary distinctions have to be made. The first is between the papal court as a court of first instance and as a court of appeal. The second rests on whether the allegations of suspect teaching arose in the institutional context of the university or in another context. These two distinctions are helpful guiding principles for analyzing the cases of false teaching that were adjudicated in Avignon in the first half of the fourteenth century.[63]

It is fairly obvious that only those cases in which the papal court was a court of first instance would substantiate the view that the correction of false teaching became concentrated in Avignon. Consequently, the processes against Meister Eckhart and Thomas Waleys do not apply. Meister Eckhart's case was tried in Avignon because he himself had appealed against the judgment of the archbishop of Cologne. During the appellate process, he stayed at the Dominican priory in Avignon, from about 1327 until his untimely death sometime before April 1328. His views were posthumously condemned.[64] The trial of Thomas Waleys, a master of theology from Oxford, was also an appellate process. Its circumstances were slightly different though. Waleys was already present in Avignon when his troubles with the ecclesiastical authorities started. In 1333, he had been so unfortunate, or so undiplomatic, as to deliver a highly controversial sermon in Avignon about the nature of the Beatific Vision. The issue of the debate was whether the saints and purified souls would see God immediately, face to face, as Waleys and many others claimed, or whether they would only see God's essence after the Last Judgment, as Pope John XXII maintained. In his sermon Waleys referred to the pope's partisans, the Franciscans, as flatterers. They immediately informed the local inquisitor for heretical depravity, who started an investigation that would drag on for almost ten years.[65] During the entire period, Thomas Waleys was held in custody, initially in the inquisitor's prison, and later in the papal prison, to which he had been duly transferred upon his appeal to the papal court.[66]

More significant for the study of the concentration of decision-making in Avignon are those inquiries in which the papal court acted as a court of first instance. Were there any cases of false teaching that were directly handled by the Apostolic See, even though they had originated in a university context? Four inquiries seem to qualify, namely those against William Ockham, Richard of Lincoln, Nicholas of Autrecourt, and John of Mirecourt.[67]

In all these cases the investigation concerned teachings that had originated in a typically university context, such as during a disputation or in a commentary on the *Sentences*, and yet there is evidence of papal involvement in deciding these cases. In 1324, William Ockham was summoned from England to Avignon and charged with over fifty errors taken from his commentary on the *Sentences*. He had to justify himself before a papal commission of theologians. In 1328, he fled to Pisa, where he sought refuge under the protection of Louis of Bavaria, and subsequently returned with him to Munich.

We do not know why Ockham's trial took place in Avignon. For a long time, the generally accepted view was, and perhaps still is, that Ockham was denounced by John Lutterell, who in 1323 had arrived in Avignon from Oxford. Presumably in order to advance his own career as theologian at the papal court, Lutterell brought with him a booklet with 56 errors derived from Ockham's commentary on the *Sentences*, which he offered to Pope John XXII.[68] William Courtenay, however, has recently suggested that Lutterell had been assigned the task of preparing an expert report on Ockham's views, and that the process against Ockham was already under way.[69] This suggestion is far more convincing than the traditional picture, the more so since Lutterell was one of the theologians in the commission of six that was charged with evaluating Ockham's views.[70] It is impossible that the accuser would end up in the commission that had to judge the defendant's charged errors. Lutterell's task probably was to conduct a preliminary investigation and to establish whether there were grounds for a charge.[71] On the basis of his report, Pope John XXII decided that it was necessary to start an inquiry, for which purpose he appointed a judge and a commission of six theologians. Lutterell would have been a logical choice, considering that he had already been involved in the preparations.

This new picture of the inquiry against Ockham in Avignon, however, still leaves unclear the role of papal initiatives. Unfortunately, the records remain silent about the origin of the allegations that Lutterell was asked to review. Even though they concerned Ockham's commentary on the *Sentences*, they probably did not arise in the context of university activities. Ockham was at the time staying in the Franciscan convent in London. Did the accusations come from within the Franciscan order, which on a previous occasion, at the provincial chapter of 1323 in Cambridge, had already examined thirteen of Ockham's views?[72] Was the inquiry conducted in the context of Franciscan regulations concerning the prepublication approval of works written by members of the order? And if this was, indeed, the case, then who had delated this investigation from the Franciscan order to the papal court in Avignon? Was it perhaps the Franciscan John of Reading, Ockham's opponent, who is generally presumed to have been in Avignon since 1323, and who knew Ockham's commentary on the *Sentences*, who lodged the complaints about false teaching at the papal court?[73]

The Cistercian Richard of Lincoln was summoned to Avignon and censured for disseminating "peculiar views" (*opiniones fantasticae*) during a disputation in Paris. He was denied access to the bachelor's and master's degrees and honors. In 1343, Clement VI granted Lincoln papal permission to read the *Sentences*.[74] The papal letter does not mention in what way his case was routed to Avignon, but only mentions that Clement's predecessor Benedict XII had taken up the case. Given the nature and context of the charges, it is likely that the accusations originated in Paris and were then filed at the papal court.

The papal inquiry against Autrecourt may have followed a similar scenario. In the letter that cites Autrecourt together with the Parisian scholars Elias of Corso, Guido of Veeli, Peter of Monteregali, John the Servite, and Henry of England to the papal court, Pope Benedict XII mentions that he is acting on information received. The subsequent trial against Autrecourt in Avignon, which lasted until 1346, was based on evidence produced in Paris.

The evidence in the Mirecourt case is frustratingly spare. It is not known how this inquiry came to be delated to the papal court, granted that it was not subject to an appellate process. Interestingly, the inquiry against Mirecourt was conducted in Paris, though not by the usual university authorities or the bishop of Paris, but by a papal-delegated judge. A fuller analysis of the role of the papal court in adjudicating the Autrecourt and Mirecourt cases will be given in Chapter 4.

In sum, it appears that attributing these four inquiries entirely to papal initiative is to ignore the importance of the denunciation, more fully discussed below, in initiating disciplinary or juridical proceedings against false teaching. As stated above, the jurisdiction of a tribunal was based on two factors: the status of the suspect and the context of the "offense." However, the choice of the tribunal was made from below. The person or persons who denounced the suspect determined which of the potentially appropriate jurisdictions was actually going to handle the case by lodging their complaints of false teaching there, rather than elsewhere. The popes handled some cases of false teaching in response to allegations that had been directly lodged at the papal court. Even so, it is remarkable that Benedict XII and Clement VI chose to assume jurisdiction in three inquiries that must have started in the institutional context of the University of Paris, instead of referring these cases back to the local authorities that had been passed over. Their actions indicate that they took an active interest in cases of false teaching, once they had been taken to their courts, even if they were rather minor and concerned what some bachelor of theology had said or written on some occasion in faraway Paris. In this respect, there is a marked contrast between these four investigations and two earlier examples of false teaching that were immediately taken to the Holy See.

The first example concerns the doctors of theology William of St. Amour, Odo of Douai, and the masters Nicholas of Bar-sur-Aube and Christian, canon of Beauvais. In 1256 Pope Alexander IV deprived them of their ecclesiastical dignities and benefices and of their magisterial office, and had them expelled from France. A few days later, the pope asked King Louis to exile the masters and to imprison "the most perverse" — William of St. Amour and Christian — so as to "teach others to live quietly and to obey the Roman Church humbly."[75] Although all these scholars were members of the University of Paris, and the discussion over the eschatological views of the Franciscan Gerard of Borgo San Donnino and the theory of Evangelical Poverty, in which they became involved, was of a doctrinal nature, they were not adjudicated by the chancellor and masters of theology, nor by the episcopal court, but by the papal court. The reason is that the dispute in which William of St. Amour and the other scholars became entangled surpassed the context of the university. It did not arise in the course of teaching activities or of ceremonial disputations at the university. Moreover, the problems at issue were as much constitutional as doctrinal, connected as they were with mendicants' teaching rights at the university.[76] Some of the errors attributed to William of St. Amour concerned the interpretation of

papal decrees. Given this context, it was logical that the mendicant opponents of William and his fellow scholars lodged their complaints of suspect
teaching directly with the papal court.

The examination of Master John of Pouilly's views in 1318 is another
example of judicial action by the papal court. According to Southern, this
case marks the beginning of the shift from university to papal court in the
decision-making process regarding cases of false teaching. The actual circumstances of the case, however, contradict this presentation. Like William
of St. Amour, John of Pouilly was an active member of the University of
Paris, and, as a consequence, fell under its jurisdiction. Yet the allegations of
false teaching were submitted directly to the curia. Pouilly had disseminated
his suspect views at a provincial chapter of the Dominicans. They concerned the right of the mendicants to hear confession and were partly based
on an interpretation of papal decrees. The mendicants felt discredited and
drew up a list of John of Pouilly's errors, which they deposited at the papal
court.[77] The list of allegations caused Pope John XXII to begin an inquiry
and summon John to Avignon.[78]

Both examples show that the denunciation was a decisive factor in
initiating papal action. But, of course, the accusers had their reasons for
filing their allegations at the papal court, instead of elsewhere. The allegations against Master John of Pouilly were heavily influenced by a political
agenda and should be seen in the light of the struggle against mendicant
privileges to hear confession. The Dominicans and Franciscans who denounced Pouilly obviously believed that the pope would be more willing to
give them a ready ear than the chancellor or the bishop of Paris. Moreover,
as in the inquiry against William of St. Amour, the Pouilly case concerned
the interpretation of papal decrees, and hence papal involvement seemed
logical. The accusers clearly had specific expectations of the papal involvement, expectations that were not disappointed by John XXII and Benedict
XII, who actively encouraged this new arrangement by the kind of response
they gave to cases of false teaching that were directly taken into their court,
thereby passing over lower jurisdictions.

This same pattern also appears in the censures of Peter Olivi and Marsilius of Padua, both issued in Avignon. Again, the doctrinal issues are
overshadowed by larger political complications. In 1318, Pope John XXII
had entrusted a cardinal with the task of examining Peter Olivi's commentary on the *Apocalypse*. Its popularity with the spiritual Franciscans had
made this work highly suspicious. On February 8, 1326, many years after
the author's death, Pope John issued a condemnation against it. Although

the censure concerned specific passages from the *Apocalypse* commentary, and was of a doctrinal nature, it should be seen in the light of the conflict within the Franciscan order between the spirituals and their leaders. John XXII sided with the Franciscan leaders and cooperated with them to suppress dissent.[79]

Political overtones are also present in the censure of the *Defensor pacis* by Marsilius of Padua. The work was finished in 1324 and condemned on October 23, 1327. Although Marsilius was a master at the arts faculty in Paris, this work did not originate in a university context. The controversies that the work raised are connected with the contest over the Imperial See, vacant since 1316. The struggle was won by Louis of Bavaria. John XXII, however, had taken sides with Louis's competitor. The ensuing problems concerning Louis's coronation eventually led to the latter's excommunication on March 23, 1324. Marsilius of Padua belonged to the Italian party that had supported Louis of Bavaria, and attacked the papal claims to supremacy in his work.[80]

The most clear-cut case of papal initiative in a doctrinal matter appears to be the inquiry against the Dominican Durand of St. Pourçain, which ran from 1331 until his death in 1334. It was started by Pope John XXII himself, though its circumstances were extraordinary. Durand served as a theological expert on the committee to which the pope had entrusted the examination of a sermon expressing his own views on the Beatific Vision. This was a topic on which Pope John XXII held strong views. John XXII was displeased with Durand's report, and so it happened that Durand himself became the target of an investigation.[81]

What conclusions can be drawn from this brief review? Even though John XXII and even more so Benedict XII probably encouraged the centralization of the examination of doctrinal orthodoxy, the significance of this "move to Avignon" should not be exaggerated.[82] It appears that papal initiatives did not play a more decisive role than other factors in adjudicating false teaching at the papal court. The fact that so many cases were decided in Avignon during the first half of the fourteenth century should not be misunderstood. Trials in which the papal court acted as an appellate court can hardly count as examples of papal initiative. Moreover, some inquiries in which the papal court was indeed involved, such as the proceedings against Mirecourt and Foullechat, were conducted in Paris.

There was never really a shift in the balance of forces from university to papacy, as Southern claims. First, several jurisdictions were competent in handling charges of false teaching. The choice of the judicial forum was determined from below, by the person or persons who informed the authorities about their suspicions. The institutional context in which the offense had occurred and the status of the accused played a decisive role in this choice. If false teaching had been disseminated during university activities, disciplinary proceedings were initiated at that level of jurisdiction. Why the inquiries against Lincoln, Autrecourt, and perhaps Mirecourt were at some point delated to the papal court is unknown, since the initial circumstances of these cases, in particular the phase during which the allegations were submitted, have not been recorded. All other cases in which the papal court assumed jurisdiction as a court of first instance were greater cases, with political and ecclesiological implications. And even in these cases, it is more accurate to speak of papal responses than of papal initiatives. Second, as Brian Tierney has shown, the Decretists of the twelfth century already acknowledged that the pope was the supreme judge in matters of faith. The view that papal pronouncements concerning the truths of faith are authoritative was never challenged during the Middle Ages, not even by William Ockham, otherwise a sharp critic of the "heretical" John XXII.[83] Consequently, Southern's view that the adjudication of false teaching in Avignon made Pope John XXII "the regent master" of Christendom and Avignon its "highest court" needs to be qualified.[84] Papal teaching authority had always been acknowledged by the masters of theology. For this reason, nobody objected to the change of venue from Paris to Avignon, whenever it did occur, certainly not as long as the masters of theology continued to play a crucial role as consultants in any academically related proceedings.[85]

The Courts at Work: The Process

There are no normative sources on the rules of disciplinary procedure against erring masters and bachelors at the University of Paris. Nor are there any treatises setting forth the rules of a disciplinary investigation in all its aspects, as the manual *Doctrina de modo procedendi contra haereticos* did for the prosecution of heresy.[86] The principles of disciplinary procedure that gradually evolved (*consuetudo*) at the University of Paris, the lowest level of jurisdiction, have to be reconstructed from casuistry, that is, from the fragmentary records of a few individual cases. This point is neatly illustrated by the inquiry against John of Monzón. Pierre d'Ailly, who handled this case on behalf of the faculty of theology, consulted the records of the Foullechat

case of thirty years earlier in order to justify how he conducted the proceedings against Monzón.[87] One might even conjecture that the striking lack of
documentary evidence concerning most of the censures that came to be
included in the *Collectio errorum* indicates that there was usually immediate
compliance with doctrinal correction by the chancellor and theologians.
These proceedings would not have left a paper trail. Only when the disciplinary proceedings had run less smoothly, such as occurred in the cases of
Foullechat and Monzón, which had to be transferred to a higher jurisdiction, did it become necessary to report about them.

In practice the disciplinary proceedings against erring scholars contained elements that were characteristic of a criminal procedure. The strict
division of the proceedings into disciplinary and criminal may have been
more logical than real. As a result, the picture of the disciplinary procedure
that emerges from the few surviving records may be complemented by what
we know of the rules of criminal procedure.

Cases of suspect teaching that reached the episcopal and papal courts
were adjudicated according to the *ordo iuris* of inquisition (*inquisitio*),
which under Pope Innocent III had become the universal method of trial
procedure in all ecclesiastical courts.[88] The rules of inquisitorial procedure
are stipulated in the decretals. On a more practical level, the *Speculum iudiciale* by William Durant is an important source for the rules of contemporary criminal procedure.[89] The work, a manual on legal procedure, was
mainly written for the practicing lawyer.

The inquisitorial procedure was developed as a response to the shortcomings of the ancient accusatorial principle. One essential feature of the
accusatorial principle was its focus on following the correct rules. A technical error would acquit the accused. The inquisitorial procedure, on the
other hand, was more interested in establishing the material truth: had
the accused committed the charged crime, or not? This difference in approach is reflected in the essentially different roles played by the judge in
the two kinds of proceedings. Generally speaking, in accusatorial proceedings the judge was conceived as an umpire who monitored the rules of
the game, whereas in inquisitorial proceedings the judge carried on the
investigation and presented the charges. An accusatorial procedure was initiated by an accuser bringing charges against a certain individual. The accuser ran the risk of retaliation if he failed to produce proof of the defendant's guilt.

The inquisitorial procedure rested on another idea. It was modeled on
the infamatory procedure, in which an inquest (*inquisitio*) was conducted

to establish whether the public rumor (*publica fama*) that a crime had been committed was true. In order to avoid public scandal in the community (*scandalum publicum*), the alleged perpetrator was expected to exonerate himself by taking a public oath (*purgatio canonica*). The inquisitorial procedure, however, went one step beyond the infamatory procedure in that it not only examined the truthfulness of public outcry, but also investigated the truth of the crime itself. In this way, public outcry came to replace the accuser of the old system. Since judicial action was initiated by *fama*, which was considered to be the "accuser," the judge was not acting as both accuser and judge.[90] In practice, public outcry manifested itself through trustworthy informants, who would enter the case only as witnesses, if at all. Their oral or written reports would first alert ecclesiastical authorities that an academic had been disseminating false teachings. The judge played a substantial role in the gathering of evidence.

At the beginning of the fourteenth century, the judicial activities aimed at establishing the truth of the information and the nature of the crime were called *inquisitio specialis*. In its preliminary phase, the judge tried to gather evidence upon which to institute further criminal proceedings. In order to avoid scandal, the preliminary inquest had to be made in a discreet manner (*secrete*).[91] If no sufficient ground for prosecution was discovered, the matter was dropped. However, if this evidence-gathering rendered positive results, it was followed by the trial of the suspect, who was now charged with the crime and whose guilt had to be proved. A case tried according to the procedure by inquisition would typically traverse the following stages: (1) the commencement of the action; (2) the preliminary inquest; (3) the citation and defense; (4) the sentence (and its execution); (5) the appeal. Most of these stages can also be identified in the disciplinary procedures by the panel of chancellor and theologians, or the tribunal of a minister general and his advisors.

COMMENCEMENT OF THE ACTION

Judicial or extra-judicial actions against a master or bachelor could start only if the proper authorities had been informed of an offense and of its author. Although rumor (*fama*) occasionally crops up in accounts of the events that led to disciplinary proceedings, denunciation played a key role in initiating investigations of false teaching.[92] This is only logical, considering the institutional context in which academic censure occurred.

Usually, an investigation started because someone from the audience of a lecture, a sermon, or a dispute denounced a bachelor or a master for disseminating views that allegedly were against faith and good morals. The records commonly emphasize that the informants were honest and trustworthy persons motivated only by the zeal of faith and not, for instance, by jealousy. The procedure of denunciation is most clearly documented in the cases of Brother Bartholomew and Denis of Foullechat. Both were bachelors of theology who were reported to the chancellor by fellow scholars.[93] As I mentioned above, the procedure of denunciation was firmly rooted in an oath, which all members of the faculty had to swear "in the hands of the chancellor."[94]

The records are silent about the circumstances under which Brother Bartholomew was denounced. We do know, however, that Foullechat's denunciation was occasioned by what he had said during his *principium* on the *Sentences*.[95] The *principium* was a solemn inaugural lecture held by a bachelor of theology before he actually started lecturing on either the Bible or the *Sentences*. The *principia* that preceded the lectures on the *Sentences* also contained a disputation. As a matter of fact, it was the first time that the new bachelor of the *Sentences* could preside over a disputation. It marked the review and approbation of a candidate as a bachelor of theology.[96]

The investigation of John of Monzón's views started according to a similar scenario, though in his case it was not his *principium*, but his vesperies (*vesperiae*) that sparked the scrutiny of the authorities.[97] The vesperies were a review that took place on the eve of the candidate's inception as a master and marked his admission into the guild of masters (*magisterium*). The candidate had already been licensed (*licenciatus*) by the chancellor, so technically speaking he had already just moved beyond the stage of bachelor. In his treatise against John of Monzón, Pierre d'Ailly refers to a solemn declaration (*protestatio*) similar in content to the oath on which the investigation of Denis Foullechat had been based, and that scholars had to read before they started lecturing.[98] So here, too, the allegations of false teaching must have originated from people attending this important academic event, as may also have been the case with the inquiries against the bachelors of theology Simon (1351), Louis of Padua (1362), and John of Calore (1363), all of which concerned their vesperies.[99] These examples of the role of denunciation in initiating disciplinary proceedings can be multiplied if one also considers cases that arose outside the context of the university. A particularly well-documented investigation is that of the Dominican Thomas Waleys. As I mentioned above, Waleys was denounced after a sermon about the Beatific Vision, which he preached in Avignon. He was arrested and held in custody on the orders of the local inquisitor for heretical depravity.[100]

The cases discussed so far have all been examples of oral denunciations. However, denunciation could also take place by writ. Enemies of Peter Olivi sent a report of specific accusations (*articuli*) to the minister general of order, who was thus obliged to start an investigation.[101] In similar fashion, the mendicant enemies of Master John of Pouilly submitted a petition to Pope John XXII, who, as a consequence, cited John to Avignon.[102] The documents related to the examinations of Peter of Tarentaise and John of Paris also hint at the fact that both academics were denounced, but neither the identity of the denouncers, nor the circumstances are further elaborated.[103]

These examples demonstrate an important point, namely that the judicial forums, whether supervised by chancellor, minister general, bishop, or pope, were reactive institutions. They hardly ever took the initiative in disciplinary or judicial proceedings concerning suspect teaching, but became involved *ex officio*, because a third party chose to notify this, rather than that, authority about his complaints. In all cases, the nature of the offense was the same, namely the dissemination of suspect teaching. Not the offense itself, however, but its institutional context and the suspect's status determined the choice of the jurisdiction.

THE PRELIMINARY INQUEST

After a scholar had been denounced for disseminating false teaching, the proper authorities could start a preliminary inquest in order to gather evidence concerning the facts of the case. The purpose of the preliminary examination was to determine whether the suspect should be held to answer. The investigation was conducted by a "judge," even though his powers were not strictly judicial, and focused on two questions, namely whether the suspect had really upheld and disseminated certain views and whether these views were erroneous.

The evidence that came under scrutiny could consist of the testimony of witnesses or of confiscated material such as the suspect's writings or even his personal notes. When Denis of Foullechat was denounced for false teaching, the chancellor not only questioned witnesses who had attended his *principium* but also examined the yet unbound quires of this lecture. In other cases too, the examination of suspect teaching concerned "unpublished" material, such as the suspect's personal notes for disputations, ser-

mons (John of Pouilly, Meister Eckhart, Thomas Waleys, Nicholas of Autrecourt), *principia* (Nicholas of Autrecourt), or vesperies (Simon, Louis
of Padua, John of Calore, and John of Monzón). In a category by themselves were the commentaries on the *Sentences* or other writings that had
been been examined in the context of legislation concerning prepublication
scrutiny (Durand of St. Pourçain, Peter Olivi, and possibly William Ockham and John of Mirecourt).[104]

The most crucial stage of the entire inquest was the evaluation of the
reported errors. This task was not carried out by the judge himself, but was
delegated to a commission of theologians.[105] The members of the commission were appointed for the term of one case. In general, local authorities at
Paris (chancellor and bishop) recruited their consultants in matters of doctrine from the body of (regent) masters of the faculty of theology. They
would be anonymously referred to in the records as *consilium doctorum sacre
scripture* or *universitas magistrorum* or words to that effect. Bachelors of
theology, however, or even bachelors of arts could also sit on a committee,
as the disciplinary proceedings against Peter Olivi, Durand of St. Pourçain,
and Raymond Lull show.[106] If an inquest concerned false opinions disseminated solely within the context of a religious order, the minister general
would fall back on experts from the order itself. The papal curia recruited its
experts from among the theologians who happened to be in residence in
Avignon at the time of the examination, or else it would summon theologians to come to Avignon for consultation.

The fragmentary evidence concerning the constitution of the commissions of experts in cases of suspect teaching shows that some names recur
time and again. One of the experts whom Pope John XXII frequently called
on was Cardinal Jacques Fournier, the future Pope Benedict XII. He was
consulted in the investigations of Eckhart, William Ockham, Peter Olivi,
and Durand of St. Pourçain, and in a case of sorcery.[107] John XXII also
ordered Pierre Roger, the future Pope Clement VI, to write on the question
"under what conditions and in what way a person becomes a heretic."[108] In
addition, Pierre Roger was a member of the committee of theologians that
was asked to give its expert opinion in the doctrinal controversy over
Thomas Waleys's views on the Beatific Vision.[109] Another theologian whose
advice was often sought was Peter of Palude. He was not only involved in the
two doctrinal investigations that were conducted within the Dominican
order against Durand of St. Pourçain but was also a member of the commissions that had to give their expert opinion in the cases against Peter Olivi
(concerning his commentary on the *Apocalypse)* and John of Pouilly.[110] John

of Naples sat together with Peter of Palude on both committees that examined Durand. Subsequently, he became a member of three other investigative commissions delegated by Pope John XXII.[111] Durand of St. Pourçain was consulted in the controversy over Evangelical Poverty and in the examinations of Ockham's and Waleys's views.[112] The Carmelite Guido Terreni participated in the examination of Olivi's commentary on the *Apocalypse* and in a consultation concerning sorcery, the same one in which Jacques Fournier had given his advice.[113]

The members of an advisory committee in an inquest on suspect teaching were expert witnesses charged with investigating and reporting on special aspects of the case. They were appointed to scrutinize the suspect's writings for errors and to assess their degree of error, if any. They reported the results of their investigation by drawing up a list of suspect statements. Josef Koch has pointed out that at the investigation of the Franciscan Peter Olivi in 1283, two important new techniques were introduced for evaluating erring academics.[114] The most important source for our understanding of the development of these new techniques is the *Apologia*, written by Olivi in 1285.[115] In this work Olivi draws attention to certain surprising aspects of the censures against him that deserve to be quoted here:

First . . . some of my [Olivi's] questions have been excerpted by yourself [Bonagratia, the General of the Franciscan order] or some of your brethern and have been collected in a roll. Some of these excerpts were, either by all of your people unanimously, or by the majority, condemned as false by a sententious decision, which was written down and indicated in the margin of the very same roll. Some were condemned as heretical, some [were regarded] as doubtful in faith, some as dangerous to our order, some as ignorant, some as presumptuously stated, and some, as I would say, [were condemned] to be crucified or marked with the sign of the cross. And, as appears from what is indicated in the margin of this roll, not only the excerpts, but also the author himself is sententiously condemned or reproved.[116]

According to Koch, the following two new methods were employed in the examination of Peter Olivi's views.[117] First, the suspect statements were no longer paraphrased, as in former lists of errors, but were now excerpted literally from the scholar's works. Second, the predicate "erroneous" in former lists of suspect propositions came to be replaced by a whole spectrum of assessments, the most important of which were "heretical" (*hereticus*), "erroneous" (*erroneus*), "untrue" (*falsus*), and "presumptuous" (*presumptuosus*).[118] Possibly, Parisian theologians on the commission that evaluated

Olivi's teaching transferred these newly developed methods from the Franciscan order to the university at large.

The theological consultants assessed the degree of error by taking votes. Not always were their decisions unanimous. Article 23, for instance, of the list of suspect views attributed to Durand of St. Pourçain was considered false by four members of the committee, but true by the other six consultants.[119] There was also disagreement over Thomas Waleys's views. One of the propositions in the list was assessed as being erroneous by some masters, as false and temerarious by other masters, and as true by still others.[120]

In those cases in which a list of charged errors already existed (such as when an informer had prepared and sent a list of suspect views to the ecclesiastical authorities or in cases of appeal), the theologians' assignment would be somewhat different. First, they would have to establish whether the views attributed to the suspect were really his, and, second, they would have to evaluate to what degree these views were really erroneous. A good illustration of this practice is provided by the commission that was charged with examining the views of William Ockham. The theologians of that commission reported: "We looked very carefully into whether the forementioned articles are contained, as they stand, in the book and in the forementioned quires, and with regard to the same articles we deliberated between us and wrote down what we thought should be done with every single one of them."[121] The theologian Peter of Palude performed a similar task when Pope John XXII received a list of thirteen allegedly false theses that were attributed to John of Pouilly. Only after Peter of Palude had given his expert opinion that the theses were, indeed, erroneous was Pouilly summoned to Avignon and formally charged.[122]

The panels of experts played a substantial role in the production of evidence. Their findings of fact determined the judge's decision to drop a case or to institute further disciplinary proceedings. If no false opinions were discovered, the case was dismissed. This happened in the inquiries against the Dominican Thomas of Naples in 1348, and probably also in the one against Peter of Tarentaise (Pope Innocent V) around 1267.[123] If, however, the commission of theologians concluded that the allegations of false teaching were true, the judge was induced to take further action.

The next logical step was to establish the charges against the accused. The charges were specified in itemized lists of articles (*articuli*). In disciplinary proceedings against false teaching, such articles would state the charged errors. In other legal cases, the *articuli* typically would contain the facts that were at issue.[124]

THE CITATION AND DEFENSE

Once the authorities had been informed about the allegations and the charges had been established, the accused was summoned to present himself before the body of the chancellor and theologians for examination and defense. The preliminary inquest was now concluded and the defensive proceedings could start.

No formal citations have been preserved at this level of jurisdiction. One may presume that suspects voluntarily surrendered to the chancellor and appeared before the panel at the required time and place. Matters were different when other levels of jurisdiction became involved. Nicholas of Autrecourt, for instance, received an official citation in which he was given a month's time to present himself at the papal court in Avignon. Since Autrecourt was in Paris, the summons was served through the bishop of Paris and, consequently, was a delegated citation.[125] As will be argued later, an initial list of errors assembled at Paris was sent with Autrecourt to Avignon after the summons.

John of Monzón was summoned three times to appear before the episcopal court. He failed to obey any of the citations. This failure resulted in his arrest warrant, and in contumacy proceedings (*contumacia*). In essence, contumacy was considered to be obstinate disobedience to an ecclesiastical court.[126] In this particular case John of Monzón was prosecuted for contempt of court and punished with excommunication, the usual penalty for contumacy in canon law.[127] Later, when his case had been transferred to Avignon, Monzón incurred contumacy because he left before the trial was finished. This time he was excommunicated by the Holy See.[128] Probably, William Ockham's excommunication too was the result of contumacy. On May 26, 1328, he fled Avignon together with Michael of Cesena and Francis of Marchia before their trial was finished. The group was chased, but not caught. Two days later, Pope John XXII remarked in a letter that Ockham's secret departure proved that he had a bad conscience, and that by leaving he had convicted himself. Ockham was never formally condemned, however.[129]

The evidence in the Monzón and Ockham cases offers another interesting aspect of proceedings against academics who had been cited to appear before the papal court. Both defendants had to hold themselves available to the judicial authorities. Monzón stayed in an inn (*albergaria*) for three months, and Ockham spent four years at the Franciscan convent in Avignon.[130] Ockham's contemporary Meister Eckhart awaited his appeal at the Dominican priory in Avignon, from his arrival in about 1327 until his death sometime before April 1328.[131] The requirement to be available probably resulted in some kind of house arrest. In any case, the suspects were not allowed to leave Avignon. But this form of pretrial custody was relatively mild when compared to the approximately ten years, from 1333 until his release in 1342, of pretrial detention that Thomas Waleys had to experience in the inquisitor's prison and the papal prison.[132] Custody, however, only came to play a role when a case was transferred from the chancellor's jurisdiction to a higher level of jurisdiction.

Academics charged with holding erroneous or heretical views were given the opportunity to defend themselves. Giles of Rome, John of Pouilly, Durand of St. Pourçain, Thomas Waleys, Meister Eckhart, and John of Mirecourt were asked to submit a written answer to the charges, although Giles and John were only allowed one day and Thomas "a very brief period" to prepare their defenses.[133] William Ockham and Nicholas of Autrecourt met personally with the commission of prelates and theologians. The defense delivered by Ockham probably raised new doctrinal questions, for the second report of the commission was more severe than the first one. Both Ockham and Autrecourt seem to have assisted in making the charges more exact.[134]

Peter Olivi, on the other hand, was deprived of his writings and the list of charges against him; thus, his defense was hindered. Only in 1285, in an *Apologia*, could he respond to the accusations of two years earlier, and even then on his own initiative.[135] Denis of Foullechat encountered a similar difficulty. The chancellor, to whom he had handed the quires of his *principium*, never returned them to him. For this reason Denis could not properly defend himself, or so he claimed.[136] From the standpoint of the judicial authorities, the writings had been confiscated and retained by the court because they constituted evidence. The defendant, however, needed his writings in order to be able to prepare a proper defense.

In defending themselves against charges of false teaching, academics used an analogous method to that used by those investigating their orthodoxy. The defendants could either deny that a specific article really stemmed from their work, or they could admit that it did, and then proceed to various complex strategies of defense, to be discussed below. Autrecourt's roll, for instance, contains one section with articles that he either flatly denied saying, or denied having said them in the way they had been put down in the roll (*sub forma qua ponuntur*).[137] A statement to the same effect was made by John of Paris at the opening of his *Excusatio*: "I did not say these articles in the way they are being interpreted . . . and if I have said or taught them, which I do not believe nor remember — on the contrary I know it — then I want them to be considered as not having been said in the way they are imposed upon me."[138] Eckhart too denied certain articles that had been excerpted from his sermons, claiming that they had been reported partially and falsely.[139] The same line was taken by John of Pouilly, whose supposedly erroneous opinions were also derived from oral material.[140]

Another strategy of defense was taken by Peter Olivi and Durand of St. Pourçain. They tried to undermine the status of the articles by pointing out, perhaps correctly, that these articles had been extracted from works that had never been intended for publication. The implication was that the commission was actually dealing with private opinions, instead of with doctrines meant to be publicly disseminated that, as a consequence, had to follow the order's regulations on prepublication permission. In the *Apologia*, Olivi maintained that the works excerpted in the articles against him had been published against his explicit wish by other Franciscans.[141] Durand of St. Pourçain declared in a postscript that his commentary on the *Sentences*, from which ninety-three articles had been excerpted for further examination by the Dominican order, had been taken away from him and disseminated against his will.[142]

If the defendants recognized the articles as their own, they could either confess error or advance a defense. If the academics chose to defend the correctness of the excerpted articles, the defense focused on their meaning (*sensus*). The academics would claim that the accusers had understood an excerpt in a different way than intended. This strategy of defense can be illustrated by many examples. Peter Olivi, for instance, reports in the *Apologia* that he had to agree to a document called *The Letter of the Seven Seals*, which was composed of positive statements in opposition to his censured views. Olivi clearly understood the implications of his assent: "It would seem as if I confessed that I had written the articles that were excerpted from my works with a different meaning and intention than I really did, and, what is worse, I would seem to concede, and this falsely and against my conscience, that I had said those articles with the erroneous or heretical meaning that had been imposed upon me."[143]

The crux of Olivi's complaint, and of other defendants whose views were being examined, was that the accusers did not take the defendants to mean what they actually meant. I shall illustrate this with two more examples. In his appeal to the pope, Arnold of Villanova stated that "the articles you made me read, which you excerpted from my works, did not have the meaning I intended when I wrote them because you took them out context."[144] John of Mirecourt discusses in his *Apology* the manifold senses of

the articles attributed to him and concludes that he holds to certain interpretations, but not to others. Moreover, he invites the masters to state
whether they intend to condemn these articles in all their senses.[145] The
strongest opposition, perhaps, against the flaws of the method of extracting
articles was voiced by Meister Eckhart. Throughout the *Rechtfertigungsschrift* he never wearies of pointing out to his judges that the articles "touch
the truth, which can be sustained with true and sound understanding," or
that the articles "are, as it were, false or erroneous in the sense attributed to
them by those who oppose them."[146] His judges err, Eckhart says, in believ-
ing that everything that they do not understand is an error.[147] "What can I
do, if somebody does not understand?" Eckhart asks himself, and in a
response to one of the articles, he puts it this way: "The whole of what was
said is false and absurd according to the imagination of my opponents, but
it is true according to true understanding."[148]

Similarly, defendants would invoke an *assertive-disputative* distinction
in order to claim that charges did not accurately represent their views. They
pointed out that a defendant had not made the suspect statements asser-
tively (*assertive*) — that is, as representing his own authoritative views — but
only disputatively (*disputative*) — that is, for the sake of the discussion —
or recitatively (*recitative*) — that is, in quoting other persons' opinions.[149]
In other words, a defendant argued that the suspect views did occur in
his text, but maintained that they were not part of his own argument, but
had been used only for purposes of disputation and analysis. The *assertive-
disputative* distinction can also be found in scholastic texts that were never
investigated for false teaching, as a kind of precaution against charges of
false teaching.[150]

True understanding was the central issue in the defense of accused
academics. The defendants felt that they, as authors, were the best-qualified
interpreters of the suspect statements: they knew what they had meant. And
if the judge or the expert witnesses, either out of malice or out of ignorance,
misrepresented their views, they had to be corrected, for example by making distinctions and by specifying in what sense an allegedly suspect statement should be taken.[151]

This approach, however, did not quite correspond with the approach
taken by the investigators of suspect teaching. The latter had as their point
of departure the old notion that "whatever is received, is received according
to the manner of the recipient."[152] Consequently, they evaluated the articles
"as they sound" (*prout sonant*), or "as they stand" (*prout iacent*).[153] The
very fact that a defendant would need to make long explanations about the

true meaning of what he had maintained made his views look suspicious. The primary concern, real or simulated, of the ecclesiastical authorities, was the care of souls. They wanted to protect the pious ears of the learned in the audience against error and heresy. False teaching did not have a right to be heard; therefore, some of the subtlety of the academics had to be sacrificed.[154] The bull in which Eckhart was condemned (1329) stated that various of the articles extracted from his writings and sermons were heretical both as they sounded and in their context. Other articles were merely suspect, but with many explanations and additions a catholic sense could be construed. Nevertheless, all the articles were condemned, because they could lead the minds of the faithful to a heretical or erroneous interpretation. Hence, Eckhart had to recant these articles as far as concerned this sense.[155] In sum, ecclesiastical authorities demanded that theologians not express themselves in an ambiguous way. They *would* allow the academic to explain himself through additions and distinctions. This method, however, would only prevent an article from being assessed as erroneous or heretical; the article would still be false "as it sounds," or ill-sounding (*male sonat*), or offensive to pious ears.

The defenses, apologies, excusations, and recantations demonstrate that judges and defendants were entangled in a complicated hermeneutical game. The judge and his consultants thought that they as readers determined the meaning of the charges (*articuli*) derived from the defendant's works, whereas the defendant thought that he, as author, owned this privilege. The defendants focused on the intention of their words; the judge and his consultants, on the other hand, were concerned with the potential effect of the defendant's words on the audience. By appealing to what they "really" meant, the defendants were ignoring the *prout sonat* principle, and hence were missing the point of their investigators.[156] By narrowing down the discussion to excerpts, on the other hand, the investigators were talking past the defendants. Whereas the defendant insisted on context and on meaning, his opponents focused on singled-out excerpts "as they stand."

Nevertheless, the academic's strategy probably was the only way to escape the inherent arbitrariness of the *prout sonat* principle. The principle rested upon the disputable assumption that statements "as they stand" have an obvious sense that can be distinguished from a less obvious sense, whereas as a matter of fact the examiners themselves assigned this sense to the articles. Supported by the axiom that whatever is received is received according to the manner of the recipient, those who applied the *prout sonat* principle were by definition always right. The judge and his consultants decided what the articles meant if taken at face value. They decided whether the words as they sounded had a good and appropriate meaning.[157] Although they had to prove in which sense the articles were wrong, they never had to prove that this wrong sense was the sense in which the defendant had intended his own statements.

The *prout sonat* principle was the hermeneutical principle that was reserved for the interpretation of contemporary authors suspected of false teaching. Other authors required other heremeneutics. In particular, *auctoritates*, that is, writers with authority whose texts constituted the curriculum of a medieval university, were interpreted according to rules that were diametrically opposed to the *prout sonat* principle. Authoritative texts were explained according to the methodological principle that "words have to be interpreted in the sense in which they are made (*fiunt*), not in the sense they make (*faciunt*)."[158] In other words, the interpreter made a distinction between the literal sense of statements and the author's intention. Whenever the literal sense was thought to conflict with doctrinal considerations, the interpreter would start clarifying an authoritative text "according to the writer's intention," thus contributing to its respectful and benevolent explanation (*reverenter exponere*). This hermeneutical approach, however, was ruled out under the *prout sonat* principle, reserved for lesser souls, who had better make sure to say what they mean.

Scholastic authors were fully aware of the arbitrariness of the *prout sonat* principle and even ridiculed it. Particularly illuminating in this respect is a passage from *Quodlibet* XII q.5 by the theologian Godfrey of Fontaines, written in 1296 or 1297.[159] Godfrey maintains that the condemnation of certain articles issued by Bishop Tempier in 1277 is "incomprehensible, untrue, and impossible." Among other things he points out that some of the articles are contradictory and totally impossible if taken literally, and cannot be rationally sustained unless they are explained in some way other than "the surface of the letter as it stands," that is, if they are taken in a nonliteral sense. According to Godfrey, Tempier's condemnation may cause scandal (*scandalum*) because some of the articles need to be expounded in a way that runs not so much against the truth, or against the intention of the editors of the articles, but against what seems to be the literal sense of these articles. Consequently, people who are less well versed in the techniques of interpretation think that the interpreters are excommunicated and that their views are incorrect. And these simple-minded people, Godfrey continues, denounce good and authoritative persons to the bishop or chancellor as if they were marked for excommunication and error. This in turn may cause much inconvenience for scholars and even produce sects among them.[160] Godfrey's reproach that Tempier's articles appear irrational, if taken at the face value of their wording (*superficies literae sicut iacet*) is a double entendre. Godfrey is applying the vocabulary of the issuers of academic condemnations to the issuers themselves. Also Godfrey's claim that Tempier's condemnation gives rise to *scandalum* among the learned and leads to the formation of sects should be seen in the light of this "reversed rhetoric." For it was precisely the heretics, academic or otherwise, who were charged with causing scandal and for this reason became the subject of an inquisition.[161]

THE SENTENCE AND ITS EXECUTION

On the basis of the evidence produced in the report of the committee of experts and the defendant's own response to it, the supervising authority rendered a decision, the sentence. The sentence was a formal statement by which the defendant was either convicted or acquitted. Since, however, the proceedings would never have come thus far unless some incriminating facts had been discovered during the preliminary investigation, acquittal never occurred.

Academics found guilty of disseminating false teaching incurred corrective measures. They were sentenced to publicly recant the charged errors. From Jean Gerson we know that the type of recantation required of condemned academics was a so-called "particular and absolute recantation of an error" (*revocatio particularis et absoluta de errore*). In the short treatise *De protestatione circa materiam fidei*, which gives a theoretical discussion of the subject, Gerson distinguishes this type of recantation from a "conditional recantation" (*revocatio conditionalis*), to be discussed below. The latter was a formula in which a scholar declared in a more general way that he did not intend to say anything contrary to faith, and in case he did so inadvertently, he would retract his position immediately.[162]

In light of the medieval concept of heresy, it is easy to understand why courts considered the recantation of the condemned errors crucial: those who would refuse to recant proved their pertinacity and, as a consequence, became heretics and ought to be punished as heretics. They were handed over to the secular arm. Those, however, who were willing to correct themselves "would be saved by penitence." The recantation was the external sign of correction, and for this reason the theological scholars at Paris were not punished as heretics, nor noted for infamy. Scholars who failed to recant, such as John of Brescain and a Master Raymond in 1247, were punished. The papal legate Odo of Chateauroux ordered that John be expelled from the city and the diocese of Paris forever and Master Raymond be returned to his former prison. Apparently Raymond had pretended to revise his views, but, once released, had continued to spread "the virus of his former errors to certain simple-minded souls (*simplices*)," hence proving to his judges that he was contumacious.[163]

In order that the sentence obtained its effects also in the outside world, and not merely in court, an official declaration was required that it had been incurred. For this reason the enforcement of the sentence took place in public places, in the presence of members of the academic community. In Avignon, cases of false teaching were tried in the quarters of the presiding judge of the papal court. If the scholars who were sentenced to recant were members of the University of Paris, they had to repeat their recantation *in publice* in Paris.[164]

Recantations were conducted at various locations in Paris. Foullechat was sentenced to recant *in disputatione* in the Dominican priory. This probably means that his recantation was scheduled to precede the usual disputations, which were attended by a large crowd.[165] In fact, however, he recanted in the Dominican church (*in ecclesia Predicatorum*). This was also the place where Nicholas of Autrecourt and John Guyon recanted.[166] Brother Bartholomew recanted in Saint Bernard (*apud sanctum Bernardum*), the house of the Cistercians.[167]

The essence of the ceremony was that the convicted academic read aloud his censured views one by one, adding "this is false and heretical and should be recanted" or words to that effect. He furthermore had to swear not to teach (*legere, docere, dogmatizare*) or defend (*defendere, asserere, sustinere*) the condemned views any more, secretly or in public.[168] Recantation truly must have been "a supreme form of public humiliation."[169] Since the recantations summarize in detail the charges raised against the accused, they are important sources for our knowledge of academic censures, especially in those cases where other records of the proceedings are lacking.

In the same *De protestatione* treatise mentioned above, Jean Gerson, reflecting on Parisian practice, maintains that masters who recanted the charged errors were not deprived of their (teaching) privileges.[170] The theoretical foundation of this practice is obvious. Since the convicted academic had recanted, he was not a heretic, even though some of his opinions had at one time been considered erroneous or heretical. A good case in point is Durand of St. Pourçain's career. Although ninety-three statements from his commentary on the *Sentences* were examined and condemned in 1314 by his Dominican order, he still remained lecturer in theology at the papal curia at Avignon and was made bishop of Le Puy in 1318.[171]

Yet other examples show that Gerson's observations may need to be qualified. Giles of Rome and Peter Olivi were temporarily removed from their teaching positions or were denied access to academic degrees. Giles was refused the licentiate in theology in 1277 and only obtained it in 1285.[172] Olivi was not eligible for the master's degree in theology because his works had been censured in 1283. These corrective measures must have fallen hard on them, because lecturing and studying were the core of their professional duties. Olivi's nominations in 1287 and 1290 as lecturer in Florence and Montpellier, respectively, indicate, however, that at least within the Franciscan order he was professionally rehabilitated.[173]

The discontinuation of one's academic career was a disciplinary penalty. This is most clearly demonstrated in the records of the trial against Nicholas of Autrecourt, who was not only condemned to recant his views, but was also explicitly refused the opportunity to obtain the magisterial honor and degree in theology without special permission from Rome.[174] Sometimes this permission was given, as in the cases of Giles of Rome and Richard of Lincoln, even though Giles had to wait eleven years.[175]

Apparently, some academics accused of disseminating false teaching at the faculty of theology had become unacceptable as members of the *universitas* of scholars. The reason may have been that they did not too readily comply with the fraternal correction of their peers. The juridical background of their (temporary) removal from the academic community was that they had broken their oaths, in this particular case the oath not to teach anything against faith or good morals. Any violation of these oaths constituted perjury and was punishable by excommunication and expulsion from the faculty and university.[176] Consequently, the social and professional effects of an investigation of allegations of false teaching must not be underestimated. Most likely, error and heresy were charges that were difficult to recover from. To his colleagues and peers, if not to the panel that supervised the disciplinary proceedings, a scholar charged with false teaching was presumed guilty until proven innocent. Once an accusation was made, everybody might have pulled away. To these censured academics the process itself may have seemed the punishment.

THE APPEAL

If an academic was sentenced to recant certain of his opinions, but was dissatisfied with the procedures, he could seek recourse from the decision made by the authority that had sentenced him. The most common legal method of reversing judgment was the appeal. The appeal was not specific to cases of academic censure, but was a particular stage of criminal procedure in general.

Basically, an appeal was a petition to a competent higher authority to rehear a case that had already been decided by a lower authority. An appeal was lodged if one of the parties felt grieved by the sentence of a lower jurisdiction. Its purpose was to obtain redress. In order to be accepted, an appeal had to conform to certain legal formalities. It had, for instance, to be entered within a certain period of time. An appeal had to be made in writing, although in some cases it could also be made by word of mouth. A written petition for appeal had to observe certain formulas and had to provide certain data, such as the names of the appellant and appellee, the judgment appealed from, and the grounds for the appeal. As a rule, an appeal went from a lower jurisdiction through the regular order of the higher jurisdictions, for instance, from the episcopal to the archiepiscopal court, and from this to the papal court. On the other hand, appeals to the papal court could be entered directly there.[177] The principal effect of an appeal was to suspend the sentence. The inferior court was not allowed to execute its sentence until the case under appeal was remitted. The cases of Denis of Foullechat and John of Monzón provide interesting details of the practice of an appellate trial by the papal court.

In 1364, Denis of Foullechat refused to read the recantation that was prepared by the chancellor and masters and handed over to him a few days earlier. Instead, he read another paper document (*cedula papiracea*) that contained his appeal (*appellacio seu provocacio*).[178] Usually, the appeal had to be entered with the judge or superior from whom the defendent appealed. In this case, Foullechat entered his appeal with the chancellor. However, he indicated that he wished to take his appeal directly to the Holy See. In this way, he avoided the episcopal court, which would have been the next jurisdiction in line of superiority. Probably, he feared that his appeal would not be admitted by the episcopal court, or, if admitted, that this forum might not want to modify or annul the judgment of the disciplinary tribunal of the chancellor and masters. As indicated above, the chancellor ordinarily transferred the disciplinary proceedings to the episcopal court and notified the inquisitor of heretical depravity.[179]

The text of the document by which Foullechat gave notice of his appeal was duly copied by the public officer (*notarius publicus*) in the minutes of the meeting that was supposed to be his recantation. As grounds for his appeal Foullechat claimed that he had not been offered the opportunity to defend himself properly against the charged errors, or to explain the meaning of what he had said during his *principium*. In addition, he demanded that the quires of his *principium* be returned to him immediately, on the plea that, otherwise, he would hold suspect any further judicial action by the chancellor against him.[180] Foullechat probably feared that, now that the chancellor had obtained control over the evidence, he could, in principle, be charged with any error.

Pope Urban V admitted Foullechat's appeal and had the case reviewed in Avignon in 1365. From Paris were present Denis of Foullechat, and the chancellor and the two theologians Simon Freron and Nicole Oresme, who were the appellees or respondents in this case. They met together with a number of other people from the Roman curia in the quarters (*hospicium*) of the Dominican William Romani in the priory in Avignon. Romani was the papal theologian (*lector palatii*) and probably chaired the session. From the minutes of this meeting it is clear that the review of the Foullechat case was conducted as an informal meeting, rather than as a genuine appellate process. Also, the terminology of *appellacio seu provocacio* in Foullechat's petition suggests that he was employing "appeal" in its wider sense to indicate any recourse, formal or informal. During the meeting, Foullechat became convinced that entering an appeal had been an ill-advised move. As a consequence, he withdrew his petition. The list of charged errors that had been drawn up in Paris remained in force and still had to be recanted.[181]

The matter dragged on, however. Whereas Foullechat had hoped to be treated decently by the chancellor, relations with him deteriorated. Foullechat claimed that he was prosecuted even more vigorously by the bishop and the inquisitor for heretical depravity.[182] Somehow, he succeeded in having the pope appoint delegated auditors (*auditores*), that is, judges who were charged with conducting the inquiry, not with reaching the decision, and in making a statement before them. During these inquiries, Foullechat managed to bring up errors that were even more offensive than those for which he had been censured in Paris in the first place.[183] In December 1368, finally, after the auditors' investigations had failed, the pope appointed Cardinal John Dormans to bring the Foullechat case to a final decision (*diffinitiva sententia*).[184] A week later, on January 1, 1369, the pope wrote to the bishop of Paris and the inquisitor to inform them that the case was now in the hands of the cardinal, and that they had to refrain from any further judicial action until the matter was decided.[185]

An interesting aspect of Dormans's appointment is that he was residing in Paris and was requested to determine the Foullechat case there, with the assistance of the chancellor and the masters.[186] Since Foullechat was still in Avignon, he was cited to Paris. For the appellate review, the pope had availed himself of members from the curia, but now he found it wiser to appoint a delegate judge on location.

In the Monzón case, the appeal against the disciplinary proceedings clearly was judicial. But, then, the circumstances under which the appeal was entered were quite different from those in the proceedings against Foullechat. Whereas Foullechat entered his appeal before the bishop and the inquisitor for heretical depravity became involved, Monzón petitioned his appeal only after he had already been cited to appear before the episcopal court. As mentioned earlier, Monzón refused to obey the bishop's citation and was, as a consequence, convicted in a contempt of court procedure.[187]

In Avignon, the Monzón case was reviewed by three cardinals who had been appointed as delegate judges by Pope Clement VII.[188] The cardinals delegated the inquest to an auditor (*auditor*). His duty was to collect the evidence. Review of the case was based on a dossier that was discussed at several meetings with the pope. This dossier contained Monzón's written petition to the pope (*supplicatio*), as well as briefs (*propositiones*) and motions (*requisiciones*) from the appellees, that is, the University of Paris.[189] The petition that Monzón presented to the court had to indicate the grounds for the appeal. It was also communicated to the appellees, who were given the opportunity to produce counter-evidence. The university was represented by the theologian Pierre d'Ailly, by a chief attorney (*procurator principalis*), and by several assistant attorneys (*substituti procuratores*). Monzón was offered the opportunity for oral defense.[190]

The grounds on which Monzón based his appeal were twofold. First, he rejected the prohibition of his views as incomprehensible (*irrationabiliter*). He claimed that he had merely followed Thomas Aquinas's doctrines, which were approved and recommended both by the faculty of theology and by the pope. Second, he denied that it fell within the jurisdiction of the university and the bishop to judicially condemn (*judicialiter condemnare*) views as erroneous or heretical. Only the Apostolic See possessed this authority.[191]

In brief, Monzón's appeal was based on claims of procedural errors. The same holds true for Foullechat's appeal. He too indicated in his appeal that the chancellor (the supervisor of the disciplinary proceedings), had denied him the right to be heard and had confiscated the quires of his *principium*, that is, the evidence. Consequently, when review of these cases was granted, it was aimed at establishing the truth of the appellants' claims that there had been defects in the procedure. The function of the appellate court was not to reopen the case and review the findings of fact made at the disciplinary proceedings against Foullechat and Monzón. In both cases, appellate jurisdiction was exercised by one or more cardinals who acted as judges. They based their decision on the evidence contained in the records of the disciplinary and trial proceedings, the arguments of the appellant and the respondent or their respresentatives — such as, for instance, an attorney (*procurator*) — and their own analysis of the case.

Costs of an appeal were due only after the sentence. Until then, each party paid his own costs. These could be considerable, as a document from the Monzón case demonstrates. Around the middle of May 1388 the general chapter of the Dominicans imposed a special tax of six florins on all their convents in order to cover the costs of Monzón's appeal, which were estimated at 1,500 florins. Not surprisingly, these mainly consisted of attorneys' fees.[192] Since Monzón lost his appeal by fleeing, he supposedly also had to bear those costs. It is certain that Foullechat too was backed by his order, the Franciscans, when he entered his appeal, but any details of its costs are lacking.[193]

Appealing was not only expensive, but could also take a lot of time. Five years passed between the date that Foullechat read his petition and the date that Cardinal John Dormans pronounced his final sentence.[194] Much of the delay, however, was occasioned by Foullechat himself. The first hearing of the appeal took place only two months after it had been entered, namely on January 31, 1365. In Monzón's case, about one year elapsed before the appeal was prosecuted in Avignon.[195] The appellate process itself took at least three months, but remained unfinished because Monzón fled again.[196] In Foullechat's case, this period was considerably shorter, since at the first meeting the parties had already come to a settlement, or so it seemed.[197]

The Condemnation of
March 7, 1277

The condemnation of 219 propositions in philosophy and theology by Bishop Stephen Tempier on March 7, 1277, is one of the most-studied events in the history of the University of Paris. Most of the scholarly research on this condemnation has been devoted to elucidating its doctrinal background and impact, which was already perceived by Tempier's (near) contemporaries.[1] Since Pierre Mandonnet's study in 1911, scholars have associated Tempier's condemnation with the opposition between faith and reason, caused by the introduction of newly translated philosophical sources in the Latin West, in particular of Aristotle and his commentator Averroes.[2] By uncovering many new historical details, subsequent historians have been able to correct and refine Mandonnet's interpretation. His view of Tempier's condemnation, however, has not been basically altered. On the contrary, largely due to the influential studies by his pupil Fernand van Steenberghen, Tempier's condemnation is now generally considered to be a reaction to "heterodox" or "radical" Aristotelianism at the faculty of arts, and possibly at the faculty of theology as well, that is, to those philosophical doctrines derived from Aristotle and his commentator Averroes that were in conflict with Christian belief.[3] The idea that the condemnation of 1277 was a response to challenges posed by the absorption of non-Christian philosophical learning in the West is based on Tempier's prefatory letter, in which he indicated that the scholars whose errors he condemned took their inspiration from pagan writings (*cum errores praedictos gentilium scripturis muniant*), and from specific items on Tempier's list, such as the thesis of the world's eternity, the view that there is only one intellect for all mankind, the necessity and contingency of the world, God's absolute power, and (sexual) ethics.[4]

The doctrinal significance of the condemnation has received very diverse assessments. Pierre Duhem ascribed a momentous role to Tempier's action in the field of natural philosophy and science. He believed that Tempier had liberated Christian thought from the dogmatic acceptance of Aristotelianism. Duhem singled out propositions 39 and 49 of Tempier's syllabus in support of his claim that the condemnation marked the birth of modern science.[5]

Another thesis concerning the broader doctrinal significance of 1277 was suggested by Pierre Mandonnet, Étienne Gilson, and also by Fernand van Steenberghen. In the minds of these scholars, Tempier's condemnation of radical Aristotelianism was an attempt to curb nascent rationalist currents at the University of Paris.[6] Tempier's action was a symptom of an already existing opposition to rationalism, that is, against philosophical research pursued without concern for Christian orthodoxy. These historians focused on articles 23, 37, 40, 145, 152, and 153. Other historians believed that evidence for the presence of rationalist tendencies at the University of Paris could also be derived from Tempier's prefatory letter. In this letter Tempier reproached some of the masters of arts for insisting on the distinct and autonomous nature of philosophy. According to Tempier, these scholars maintained that certain views were true according to philosophy, but not according to Catholic faith, "as if there were two contrary truths, and as if against the truth of Sacred Scripture, there is truth in the sayings of the condemned pagans."[7] On the basis of the latter statement, historians of a few generations ago believed that some masters of arts taught the so-called doctrine of the double truth, that is, the theory that two contradictory propositions — one derived from philosophical investigation, the other from Christian revelation — can both be true at the same time. Van Steenberghen, however, has convincingly shown that Tempier's remarks were intended to ridicule a certain hermeneutical practice, namely the method of assessing a doctrine from a philosophical point of view ("philosophically speaking") and from faith. As a matter of fact there were no medieval scholars who *opposed* philosophical conclusions and statements of Christian doctrine, nor did they defend an untenable theory of double truth. In cases of conflict between reason and faith, the truth was always supposed to be on the side of the faith.[8]

Tempier's Condemnation in Context

If one compares Tempier's 1277 syllabus to the other lists of errors that were censured at the University of Paris two features stand out, namely its promulgation by a bishop and its anonymity.[9] The episcopal intervention and the anonymity of the 1277 condemnation might seem small details, but, in fact, they are highly significant for what they can tell us about the procedure that Tempier followed in issuing his syllabus.

Tempier's condemnation is one of the few censures that was pronounced not by a panel of the chancellor and his theologians, but by a bishop. In the previous chapter I argued that university censures were of a disciplinary nature. Allegations of false teaching that had arisen in a typical university context were in first instance reviewed by a body composed of the chancellor and the (regent) masters of theology. Only if problems occurred in the disciplinary proceedings was a case transferred from that level of jurisdiction to the episcopal or papal courts. At that moment, the case began to have a paper trail, because only then did it become necessary to recount the events that had led to the transfer of the case to another jurisdiction. Clear examples of this procedure are the inquiries against Denis of Foulle-chat and John of Monzón. Most accused academics, however, immediately yielded to the doctrinal correction by the panel of chancellor and masters. In that case, only the final lists of censured views gathered in the *Collectio errorum* — the verdicts, so to speak — were preserved.

This way of proceeding in cases of suspect teaching at the University of Paris finds confirmation in a little-studied source from the sixteenth century. The document is a register of pronouncements and judgments by the faculty of theology, drawn up by the theologian Noël Beda. The first part of the register covers the period 1210–1523.[10] If one were to look in this register at documents concerning suspect teaching from the thirteenth and fourteenth centuries, one would find only some records pertaining to the censures of John of Brescain, Denis of Foullechat, and John of Monzón. The register does not reproduce any documents of the censures of Stephen of Venizy, Nicholas of Autrecourt, John of Mirecourt, John Guyon, Simon, Guido (Giles of Medonta?), Louis of Padua, or John of Calore. Nor does it contain Bishop Tempier's condemnations of December 10, 1270, and March 7, 1277.

What may one infer from these omissions? First, when Beda drew up his register, he completely ignored the *Collectio errorum*. Instead he relied on other documents, namely original records from the faculty's archives. Most of these records are still extant today. The three medieval inquiries that are documented in the register are the only ones that generated the type of records that Beda could retrieve from the archives of the Sorbonne, whereas the other cases did not leave such a paper trail.

Interestingly, Beda's register does not report any records pertaining to the inquiry that led to the 1277 condemnation, even though it was handled by episcopal jurisdiction, nor have any such records been found elsewhere, for that matter. From this omission I would conclude that a transfer of jurisdiction never occurred in this investigation. A scenario involving a shift from university level to the bishop's jurisdiction would have generated records, records that would surely have been included in Beda's register. From the lack of any such records it would appear that the 1277 investigation did not start at the level of the university, but at the episcopal level. Bishop Tempier was involved in the inquiry right from the start. As will become clear below, this episcopal involvement is an important factor in explaining another distinguishing feature of the 1277 condemnation, namely its anonymity.

Whereas the other university censures concern specific scholars whose names are explicitly mentioned in the records, Tempier does not specify the persons behind the false views. He merely states that the errors were disseminated by "certain scholars at the faculty of arts" (*nonnulli Parisius studentes in artibus*).[11] Why did Bishop Tempier pronounce an anonymous censure? Why were those condemned of disseminating false teaching not named explicitly, as was the case with the proponents of the other lists of censured errors? The anonymity of the 1277 condemnation becomes even more perplexing if one considers a medieval tradition, however shallow, linking the 1277 condemnation to the names of Siger (of Brabant) and Boethius (of Dacia).[12] The reliability of this tradition is partly confirmed in the study of Roland Hissette, who examined the proximate background of the 219 condemned theses. He established that thirty condemned articles, indeed, seemed to be aimed at Siger of Brabant directly, whereas thirteen seemed to have been derived from the works of Boethius of Dacia.[13] In an effort to cast some light on why the name of Siger of Brabant was omitted from Tempier's condemnation, I shall now return to the University of Paris in the years 1276 and 1277 and propose a new way of understanding some old facts.

THE EVENTS LEADING UP TO MARCH 7, 1277

The traditional picture of the events leading to Tempier's condemnation looks something like this.[14] On January 18, 1277, Pope John XXI informed Stephen Tempier, bishop of Paris, that he had heard rumors of heresy and charged him with the task of examining (*facias inspici vel inquiri*) where and by whom these errors had been disseminated.[15] On March 7, 1277, Tempier published his list of 219 articles and of some books that were condemned. Anyone teaching or listening to the listed errors would be excommunicated, unless they turned themselves in to the bishop or the chancellor within seven days, in which case the bishop would inflict proportionate penalties.[16]

Since the papal letter precedes Tempier's condemnation, it has been generally assumed that Tempier acted on papal initiative. Two claims have been built on this alleged sequence of events, which recur in almost all the literature that has been written about Tempier's condemnation. First, since the pope merely ordered Tempier to investigate rumors of erroneous teaching and then report back to him, Tempier's pronouncement of the 1277 syllabus was the action of an overzealous bishop. Tempier went far beyond his mandate when he issued his decree, which, moreover, he did not previously submit to the Holy See. For this reason, some scholars have characterized the condemnation of 1277 as a proof of the competition over the rights of jurisdiction between pope and bishop.[17] Second, since only about six weeks elapsed between the papal instructions and Tempier's condemnation, the latter's inquiry was hasty. Further proof of Tempier's haste is found in the repetitions, contradictions, and general disorderliness of the list of 219 censured propositions.

The two claims are considered established conclusions, but they are corollaries of a rather unsophisticated and unfounded *post quem propter quem* argument. The instructions in Pope John's letter are rather vague. Moreover, nowhere does the bishop mention that he is acting on papal orders; nor did he need a papal mandate to investigate allegations of false teaching at the University of Paris. In his introductory letter to the list of condemned articles Tempier merely indicates that he had received information from important people (*magnarum et gravium personarum crebra zeloque fidei accensa insinuavit relatio*). Who these "important people" may have been is a question that will be addressed below.[18]

The evidence suggests that Tempier acted independently of the pope, and that when he received the papal letter of January 18, 1277, he was already in the process of preparing his condemnation. If Tempier received this papal letter at all before March 7, 1277, it must only have encouraged him to continue what he had already been doing, namely preparing his condemnation.[19] Historians have simply been misled by the near contemporaneity of Pope John's letter and Tempier's prohibition.

The absence of any coordination between bishop and pope becomes more apparent in a second letter — *Flumen aquae vivae* — from John XXI to Bishop Tempier.[20] This letter is dated April 28, 1277, that is, more than forty days after Tempier had promulgated his list of condemned articles. Curiously enough, this letter gives no indication whatsoever that the pope knew about Tempier's action. On the contrary, the pope grants a mandate to Tempier to notify him, the pope, about new errors, and to inform him about the names of the propagators of these errors, about their followers, and about their writings. John's second letter has generally been understood as a *new* mandate, now aimed not only at persons of the arts faculty, but also at theologians: the second letter is supposed to have been induced by new (heterodox) doctrinal developments that were not covered by Tempier's condemnation of March 7, 1277.

It seems more plausible, however, to consider John's second letter as a further specification of his first.[21] In both letters Tempier is requested to give information about errors that have been newly disseminated. In the first letter this is phrased as "certain errors to the disadvantage of faith are said to have come forth anew" (*quidam errores in prejudicium eijusdem fidei de novo pullulasse dicuntur*). In the second letter the errors are described as "errors that have been newly invented or taken up again or renewed" (*errores qui de novo inventi vel resumpti seu renovati sunt*). In the first letter Tempier receives a mandate to inquire "by which persons and in which locations" in Paris these errors have been disseminated (*a quibus personis et in quibus locis*). In the second letter, the pope himself already indicates the perpetrators of the errors, namely "some scholars of arts and in the faculty of theology at Paris" (*nonnulli tam in artibus quam in theologica facultate studentes Parisius*). The second letter, finally, is more specific in stating the purpose of the bishop's investigation. The pope will use the dossier requested from the bishop to establish — with the help of an advisory committee — the nature of the errors and to decide whether they will have to be recanted or condemned and whether the University of Paris will need to be reformed.[22]

In short, the second papal letter combines the theme of the first letter with rumors of false teaching at the faculty of theology. These rumors may have originated from the inquiry against the theologian Giles of Rome.[23] This investigation took place shortly after the condemnation of March 7, 1277.[24] This papal letter *Flumen aquae vivae* must have crossed the letter in which Tempier announced the condemnation.

The problems raised by the traditional picture, which was based on the *post quem propter quem* argument, become less serious if one links Tempier's action not to the papal letter of January 18, 1277, but to events that occurred on November 23, 1276. On that date, Simon du Val, the inquisitor of France, cited Siger of Brabant together with Bernier of Nivelles and Goswin of Chapelle to appear before his court. The citation, which was published in 1947 by Antoine Dondaine, has been preserved in a manual for inquisitors.[25] The purpose of the manual was to provide examples for drawing up official documents; the example of how to compose a citation to appear before the court of an inquisitor happened to pertain to Siger of Brabant and his two fellow masters. It is surprising that this document has not been linked before to the events of March 7, 1277.[26]

In the wake of the studies of Pierre Mandonnet and Fernand van Steenberghen, it is generally thought that Siger of Brabant and Goswin of Chapelle had already fled from Paris to Italy when this citation was issued. The purpose of their flight was to appeal to the papal court, which resided in Viterbo at that time. The evidence on which this picture is built, however, is extremely tenuous. We only have a report that Siger was stabbed at the papal court in Orvieto by his own cleric. Supposedly, this cleric was Goswin of Chapelle. Siger's death must have occurred between 1281 and 1284. There are, however, no records that show that Siger *fled* to the papal court in 1277 and remained there until the 1280s, nor that he had lodged an appeal there.[27]

Apart from this lack of documentary evidence, the suggestion that Siger of Brabant ever appealed to the papal court is, in itself, highly implausible. First, the concept of appellate jurisdiction implies the review of a sentence rendered in a lower court, or, more generally, at a lower level of jurisdiction, such as an episcopal court or a disciplinary tribunal of chancellor and masters.[28] But against which sentence would Siger have appealed?[29] Since he is supposed to have fled, the citation could not even have been served and Siger and his fellow masters would have failed to appear in court. Consequently, his supposed flight would have resulted in an arrest warrant, or in a condemnation for contempt of court (*contumacia*), rather than for disseminating false teaching.[30] Furthermore, it is highly unlikely that, pending Siger's appeal, the bishop would have moved against him. An appeal to the papal court would have put a stop to the judicial actions at the inquisitorial and episcopal levels. Following papal appeal, Siger of Brabant (and the two other masters) would have obtained relief from the inquisitor's and the bishop's jurisdictions. Yet it is generally accepted that Tempier's condemnation of March 7, 1277, includes thirty propositions that were held by Siger of Brabant. In conclusion, the known facts about the events in 1277 contradict the suggestion that Siger of Brabant ever fled to the papal court to lodge an appeal.

This does not mean, however, that Siger of Brabant and the other two masters, Goswin of Chapelle and Bernier of Nivelles, were still in Paris when the summons to appear before the inquisitor was issued. René Gauthier was the first and perhaps the only scholar to challenge seriously the traditional picture of Siger of Brabant's whereabouts after 1275.[31] On the basis of textual evidence, he has suggested that the three masters were simply staying in Liège when the citation was served to appear in Saint Quentin on a fixed day.[32] According to Gauthier, the three masters had probably returned to Liège at the end of the 1275 academic year (or, in any case, no later than 1276) to resume their ecclesiastical offices.[33] Siger of Brabant was a canon at Saint Paul's, and Goswin of Chapelle and Bernier of Nivelles were canons at Saint Martin's, and these were the ecclesiastical ranks by which the inquisitor summoned them.

Siger's departure from Paris may well have been due to the aftermath of an administrative conflict in which he had been involved and which had divided the arts faculty since 1272. A minority party, led by Siger, had rejected the legitimacy of the election of Alberic of Reims as new rector of the arts faculty. On May 7, 1275, Simon of Brion, the papal legate, settled the dispute to the disadvantage of Siger's party.[34] This administrative conflict, together with the doctrinal controversies that had been raging since the beginning of the 1270s, may have induced Siger to return to his country of origin in 1275–76, never to set foot in Paris again. This suggestion is based on conjecture, but it is consistent with what we know of Siger's academic career. The *Quaestiones super librum de causis*, Siger's last known work, was written in 1275–76.[35]

But if Siger and the other suspects received the summons in Liège, what was their response? Did they obey the citation and really go to Saint Quentin, which lies halfway between Paris and Liège? Gauthier thinks that Siger and the two other masters appeared before the inquisitor's tribunal on the stipulated day, but that they were acquitted. He bases this conclusion mainly on the fact that there is no documentary evidence about any conviction for heresy. After the reference in the inquisitor's document, Goswin of Chapelle completely disappears from the picture.[36] He probably remained in Liège. The names of Bernier of Nivelles and Siger of Brabant surface again only in the 1280s. Bernier of Nivelles reappears in the documents as theologian and member of the Sorbonne College, to which he left a legacy of twenty-five books. In 1286 he copied Thomas Aquinas's commentary on the *Sentences*, and he bore the ecclesiastical title of curator of the Church of Saint Martin in Liège.[37] He was the only one of the three masters who resumed his studies in Paris and proceeded to the faculty of theology. Siger of Brabant probably remained in Liège, like Goswin of Chapelle, until the time an Italian poem places him at the papal court in Orvieto.[38]

This alternative picture of the events raises two new questions not discussed by Gauthier. First, for what reason had the three masters been summoned in the first place? Second, what was the relation between the inquisitor's decree and Bishop Tempier's condemnation of March 7, 1277?

We do not know in any detail the charges against the three masters.[39] Yet it seems natural to assume that they were accused of disseminating false teaching at the University of Paris. The inquisitor's document clearly states that the three masters were under grave suspicion of the crime of heresy (*de crimine heresis probabiliter et vehementer suspectos*). Apparently, the complaints of disseminating false teaching were lodged with the inquisitor, who, *ex officio*, decided to start an inquiry. Since there is some evidence that the suspects resumed their academic and ecclesiastical careers, and since there is no evidence that they were condemned or had recanted their errors, it is likely that they were acquitted.[40] This scenario finds far more support in the documentary evidence than the older scenario in which Siger of Brabant fled to the papal court to appeal.

THE DISCIPLINARY PROCEDURES

The second question, the relation between the inquisitor's summons and Tempier's condemnation, brings me to the disciplinary procedures. Since Siger had already been acquitted by the inquisitor toward the end of 1276, his views could not be censured *nominatim* by the bishop. According to the juridical principle that one cannot be tried twice for the same crime (*ne bis in idem crimen judicetur*), the bishop could not start a new inquiry against Siger for disseminating false teaching at the University of Paris.[41] Yet it seems very likely that Tempier based his own examination of Siger's views on the inquisitor's inquiry. The inquisitor of France was also located in Paris, and the summons for Siger of Brabant and the two other masters was actually issued from there. The bishop of Paris, who had jurisdiction over the University of Paris, would surely have been informed about the outcome of an inquiry against some of its members. He and the theologians who were charged with examining Siger's views may have disagreed with the outcome of the inquisitor's process and, consequently, had no other option than to censure those views by including them generally in the longer list of false propositions that had already been prepared.

This way of proceeding finds some support in Tempier's introductory letter. There Tempier indicates that he had received information from important people (*magnarum et gravium personarum crebra zeloque fidei accensa insinuavit relatio*). This means that Tempier did not take the initiative, as has been often assumed in the scholarly literature, but that he responded to allegations of suspect teaching, allegations that may have been derived from the inquisitor's dossier. The general nature of these allegations is also made more explicit in the episcopal letter than in the inquisitor's citation. The important persons on whose information Tempier acted had informed him precisely that "some scholars of arts at Paris" (*nonnulli Parisius studentes in artibus*) had been transgressing the limits of their own faculty (*proprie facultatis limites excedentes*).[42] Such a complaint must surely have come from theological circles, though probably not directly from members of the faculty of theology: in Tempier's prefatory letter the theologians are clearly distinguished, as a group, from the "important persons" who denounced the suspects of false teaching.[43]

In his introductory letter Tempier reports that he sought the advice "not only of the doctors of Sacred Scripture, but also of other wise men" (*tam doctorum sacrae Scripturae, quam aliorum prudentium virorum communicato consilio*). From other cases of suspect teaching we know that the task of the theologians was to examine certain works and draw up a list of errors. In cases where a list of alleged errors already existed, the theologians were charged with assessing the degree of error of the listed propositions. The theologian John of Pouilly reports that sixteen masters of theology were Tempier's assessors for the condemnation.[44] One of the members of the commission was Henry of Ghent, as he himself testifies in his *Quodlibet* II.[45] It is unknown when these masters met, but it must have been after Henry of Ghent had become a regent master in theology, a position that he obtained in 1276. That there were some tensions between Tempier and the theologians is attested by the theologian Giles of Rome, a contemporary witness of the events of 1277: he claimed that some articles were condemned not on the basis of the advice of the masters, but rather due to the "stubbornness of a few."[46] This observation has been taken to concern Tempier, but it might also include some of the "wise men" who had assisted him.

The identity of these other wise men is unknown. Since, however, they are so clearly distinguished from the theologians, they have to be sought

among the prelates. Of these, only the involvement of the chancellor, John
of Alleux, is directly substantiated by textual evidence: the introductory
letter to Tempier's condemnation stipulates that offenders had to turn
themselves in either to the bishop himself or to the chancellor. Other likely
candidates are Simon of Brion, the papal legate, and Ranulph of Houblonnière, Tempier's future successor as bishop of Paris.

In the present state of documentary evidence it is not possible to establish which method Tempier and his advisers used to draw up their syllabus
of 219 errors. Consequently, the generally accepted conclusion that Tempier's syllabus of condemned propositions is not very well organized and
"broad in scope to the point of confusion" appears somewhat gratuitous.[47]
The lack of doctrinal cohesion is also present in other lists of the *Collectio
errorum*, simply because the order in which the charged errors appeared on
the roll was determined by other factors — such as, for instance, the order in
which they appeared in the examined work. Shortly after 1277 the extremely long list of 219 prohibited views was reorganized, possibly to facili-
tate its use in the academic community.[48] Similarly, the theologian Hugolin
of Orvieto reorganized the list of errors recanted by John of Mirecourt.[49] At
the beginning of the twentieth century, Pierre Mandonnet once again put
Tempier's articles into a new order.[50]

WHO WAS CONDEMNED ON MARCH 7, 1277?

It is uncontested that the targets of the condemnation are unspecified members of the arts faculty in Paris: *nonnulli Parisius studentes in artibus*.[51] The
rather vague "nonnulli studentes in artibus," some people engaged in the
arts, instead of the more precise "magistri in artibus," even suggests that not
all the propagators of false views were full-fledged masters. Siger of Brabant
and Boethius of Dacia appear to have been the most prominent targets of
the 1277 censure, or, in any case, among the most easily identifiable for
modern historians. They may have been the "heresiarchs," so to speak, who
caused the crisis over the encounter between faith and reason that became
manifest in Tempier's condemnation. Yet their names appear nowhere in
the syllabus. The surviving evidence suggests a specific juridical reason,
mentioned above, why Siger's name was omitted, and why his teaching was
included in a rather general censure.

But at whom else was the censure aimed? From Hissette's own sum-
mary of the results of his careful examination of the sources it appears that

surprisingly few of the censured propositions can be identified with any degree of certainty in the known works of thirteenth-century *artistae*. Of the 219 propositions, only seventy-nine are identified, with various degrees of probability, in the works of Siger of Brabant, Boethius of Dacia, or the three anonymous writings from the arts faculty that are accessible in a modern edition. Another seventy-two propositions can be attributed only uncertainly, and sixty-eight propositions cannot be identified at all.[52] Moreover, many attributable propositions do not really represent the author's own view, but rather appear to be quotations or paraphrases from Aristotle, from Arabic philosophers, or from "the philosophers," as Hissette indicates.[53]

Hissette's examination was based on the assumption that Tempier's censure envisioned only teachings from the faculty of arts. Careful reading of the introductory letter, however, seems to contradict this assumption. There, Tempier draws an important distinction, which has not been duly recognized in the scholarly literature, between propagators and views. He accuses the members of the arts faculty of disseminating (*tractare et disputare*) manifest and damned errors (*manifesti et exsecrabiles errores*). The errors are specified in the roll or leaves connected to the introductory letter (*in rotulo seu cedulis, praesentibus hiis annexo seu annexis*). They are the 219 censured propositions. Tempier does not state, however, that the members of the arts faculty are the *authors* of these errors. Only the propagators have to be sought in the arts faculty in Paris: on pain of excommunication, they are prohibited to disseminate in any way (*dogmatizare, aut defendere seu sustinere quoquo modo*) the propositions collected by Tempier. The origin of these propositions, however, is not stated in the introductory letter. In other words, Tempier indicates that those *artistae* who were castigated for disseminating false teaching were not necessarily disseminating their *own* views. When drawing up the syllabus, Tempier and his advisers relied on more sources, written or oral, than those that were used by Hissette. Possibly, Tempier's list even includes earlier lists of suspect views.

In light of this evidence one can only conclude that research into the proximate background of the censured propositions has to be broadened. The directions that such research should take are indicated, either implicitly or explicitly, in Hissette's study and in subsequent studies, such as those by John Wippel and Calvin Normore. It is generally agreed today that a considerable number of the 219 censured propositions have a bearing on the reintroduction of pagan philosophy into the arts faculty, and on the ensuing crisis over the relations of faith and reason. Consequently, Greek or Arabic

sources may prove to be at the origin of a number of censured propositions.[54] Other propositions may well have been derived from the teaching
of theologians, such as Thomas Aquinas.[55] In this respect, the often-quoted
statement from Tempier's introductory letter that members of the arts faculty were transgressing the limits of their own faculty (*propriae facultatis
limites excedentes*) acquires new meaning. Some members of the arts faculty
were rebuked not only for teaching suspect philosophical views but also for
teaching suspect theological views.

Bishop Tempier and the Inquiries Against
Thomas Aquinas and Giles of Rome

One of the puzzles that remains is to what extent Thomas Aquinas was
directly targeted by Tempier's censure. Although Thomas did not belong to
the arts faculty, some of his contemporaries believed that certain of his opinions were included in the condemnation.[56] Godfrey of Fontaines, for example, who was a student of theology in 1277 and who was very familiar with
the writings of Thomas Aquinas, Siger of Brabant, Boethius of Dacia, and
Henry of Ghent, stated that Tempier's condemnation prevented students
from taking notice of Aquinas's "very useful" doctrine.[57] The Dominican
John of Naples even found it necessary to write an apology to the effect that
Thomas was not touched by Tempier's condemnation, and that hence it was
legitimate to teach Thomas's works at Paris without danger of excommunication.[58] Also, the revocation of Tempier's articles as far as they concerned or
were claimed to concern the doctrine of Thomas Aquinas (*quantum tangunt
vel tangere asseruntur doctrinam b. Thomae*) by Bishop Stephen of Bourret on
February 14, 1325, seems to indicate that at least some scholars felt that
Thomas had been included in Tempier's action.[59] The medieval estimates as
to how many of Tempier's articles were directed against Thomas, however,
show considerable variety. Gilson observed that "the list of the Thomistic
propositions involved in the condemnation is longer or shorter, according as
it is compiled by a Franciscan or a Dominican."[60]

In the track of Thomas's contemporaries some modern historians have
maintained that Thomas Aquinas was one of Tempier's targets.[61] Their lists
too show considerable heterogeneity. The question of whether Thomas
Aquinas was included in the condemnation cannot be solved by a comparison between supposedly Thomistic propositions from Tempier's list
and Thomas's own works. Such a comparison remains inconclusive, because the articles involved are too vague to allow us to decide whether they

were held exclusively by Thomas or could have been derived from other authors. On the basis of these results, Roland Hissette has concluded that Thomas may have been implied by Tempier's censure, but he certainly was not a direct target of it.[62] John Wippel, on the other hand, has rejected this distinction between indirect and direct targets as merely verbal. He believes that Tempier and his advisors would have known whether a particular position of the syllabus was (also) upheld by Thomas Aquinas.[63]

In addition to the ambiguity of Tempier's list, the question of Thomas' inclusion in Tempier's condemnation has also been clouded by an incorrect interpretation of evidence furnished by three of his contemporaries, Henry of Ghent, John Pecham, and William de la Mare. According to their testimonies, two theses that were clearly Thomistic — one of them concerning the controversial doctrine of the unicity of substantial form, the other the existence of matter without form — were censured in 1277. None of these views, however, appears in Tempier's list.[64] This fact led Fernand van Steenberghen to the conclusion that, in the final stage of the preparation of Tempier's list of errors, these two theses were suppressed "because of the moral authority of Thomas Aquinas."[65] Robert Wielockx, on the other hand, has argued that the two Thomistic views, together with other propositions, were the subject of a separate inquiry against Thomas Aquinas.[66] Both theses seem to exclude the notion that Thomas Aquinas was directly targeted by any of charged errors of the syllabus of March 7, 1277.

According to Wielockx, Bishop Tempier conducted three separate doctrinal investigations in 1277. The first one concerned the arts faculty and was concluded on March 7, 1277, with the issuing of the syllabus of 219 condemned propositions. The second investigation concerned the theologian Giles of Rome and was concluded before March 28, 1277, with the censure of fifty-one propositions taken from Giles's commentary on the *Sentences*. The third doctrinal inquiry was aimed against Thomas Aquinas. It was begun after Giles's censure, but still before March 28, 1277. In Wielockx's view, the inquiry against Thomas Aquinas was never completed. Basing his conclusions on evidence provided in a letter by John Pecham, Wielockx claimed that during the vacancy of the Apostolic See, sometime between May 20 and November 25, 1277, Tempier received orders from the curia to stop his investigation.[67]

Wielockx's thesis of a third and separate process against Thomas Aquinas might explain why such controversial views as the unicity of substantial form in human beings were not included in the syllabus of March 7. Yet I believe that his interpretation of the textual evidence on which this thesis is based is less compelling than generally has been assumed.[68] The testimonies

of Henry of Ghent, John Pecham, and William de la Mare may be explained
without too much difficulty as references to the inquiry against Giles of
Rome. The decisive detail in their accounts is that the 1277 inquiry about
which they report concerned *views* (*opiniones*) of Thomas Aquinas. At the
time, there was one inquiry taking place at Paris that can be accurately
characterized as an investigation of Thomistic theses, namely the process
against Giles of Rome. Since Giles of Rome was a follower of Thomas
Aquinas's doctrines, the examination of his commentary on the *Sentences*
potentially implied views of Thomas Aquinas. This is true not only for the
theses of the unicity of substantial form and of the existence of matter
without form, but also for many other errors that were attributed to Giles
of Rome in the investigation of 1277, but that also happened to be defended
by Thomas Aquinas.[69] The recognition, however, that there was no separate examination in 1277 of Thomas Aquinas's orthodoxy in Paris leads to a
substantially revised account of the examination of Giles of Rome's views.

If one takes seriously Pecham's report in a letter of December 7, 1284,
Tempier's plans to proceed against the opinions of Thomas Aquinas were
aborted through intervention by the Roman curia. If, however, it is also
true that Pecham's allusion to an investigation of Aquinas's views really
concerns the inquiry against Giles of Rome, as I have argued elsewhere,
then the conclusion emerges that *this* investigation was interrupted in
1277.[70] In the scholarly literature, however, no one has ever doubted that
Giles of Rome was censured. According to the traditional picture, Giles of
Rome was required to recant his views in 1277, but he refused and was
forced to discontinue his academic career until his rehabilitation in 1285.

There is one serious problem with this scenario. If Giles of Rome had
refused to recant, he would have been convicted as a heretic and would have
incurred the customary penalties for heretics. We know for a fact, however,
that Giles of Rome remained active in his order, the Augustinian Hermits,
even though his academic career was discontinued by the university authorities. In the period from 1281 to 1285 Giles was in Italy and was involved in
organizing the general chapter of the Augustinians in Padua and the provincial chapter in Tuscany. Such a career pattern would have been impossible
for a convicted heretic. As a heretic, Giles would have been not only a
problem for the university, but also for his order.

But if Giles of Rome refused to recant, and if, as a matter of fact, he was
not convicted, what then happened to Tempier's inquiry? There is only one
scenario I can think of that would explain this seemingly contradictory
evidence: the inquiry against Giles of Rome was not brought to completion. Giles of Rome's ecclesiastical career after he had been expelled from

the university, and the absence of his recantation in any of the versions of the Collection of Parisian Articles, strongly suggest that the case against him was suspended. In this way, John Pecham's testimony and the evidence concerning Giles of Rome's process and career are in harmony.

Perhaps Pecham was right when he reported that the Roman curia vetoed Tempier's initiative to decide upon the articles that the masters had reviewed already.[71] The reason why the papal court may have wished to interfere with the disciplinary proceedings at Paris is that a condemnation of the views of Giles of Rome would also have implied a condemnation of the views of Thomas Aquinas. As Robert Wielockx has convincingly argued, there existed a strong Dominican pro-Aquinas lobby at the curia.[72] This may have been responsible for making Bishop Tempier interrupt his investigation, an investigation that through the views culled from Giles of Rome's commentary on the *Sentences* concerned positions of Thomas Aquinas. According to this scenario, then, the views of Giles of Rome escaped a formal condemnation because of their similarity to doctrinal positions of Thomas Aquinas. Giles of Rome himself, however, had become unacceptable as a member of the *universitas* of scholars. He was denied the license to teach. The discontinuation of his academic career was a disciplinary penalty usual for those members of the academic community who had broken their oaths, in this particular case the oath not to teach anything against faith or good morals. When seen in this light, the introduction of a separate inquiry against Thomas Aquinas in 1277 appears unnecessary.

In conclusion, then, Bishop Tempier was involved in two doctrinal inquiries in 1277: one against unspecified members of the arts faculty, and one against the theologian Giles of Rome. He probably initiated neither of them, but merely responded *ex officio* to allegations of false teaching.[73] Both inquiries complemented each other in that none of the fifty-one charged errors attributed to Giles of Rome appear on the syllabus of 219 articles, nor vice versa. Only the inquiry that concerned the arts faculty was brought to completion and led to a censure. Both inquiries implied positions that were also held by Thomas Aquinas. This does not mean, however, that Tempier was conducting a posthumous inquiry against Thomas Aquinas himself. Rather, Tempier, on the advice of his theologians and some ecclesiastical officials, censured views defended by still-living contemporaries. Some of these views happened to be Thomistic.

On February 14, 1325, less than two years after Thomas Aquinas's canonization, Tempier's action was modified. Stephen of Bourret, bishop of Paris, retracted those Parisian articles that concerned or were claimed to concern the doctrine of Thomas Aquinas (*quantum tangunt vel tangere asseruntur doctrinam b. Thomae*). One might argue that Bourret's revocation implies that Aquinas's views had been censured in Paris. I think, however, that Bourret's document need not be taken that way. It is uncontested that the 1325 revocation concerned the syllabus of 219 articles that Bourret's predecessor, Stephen Tempier, had issued on March 7, 1277. The retraction ended any questions concerning whether or not Tempier's censure had envisioned Thomas Aquinas's views, questions that had been raised as early as the end of the thirteenth century. Without committing himself on this point and without becoming specific about which of the 219 articles could be read as censures of Thomistic theses, Bourret simply decreed that from now on Tempier's syllabus no longer applied to the doctrine of Thomas. His intervention prepared the way for a free discussion in the schools of all those articles of Tempier's syllabus that touched on or that were supposed to touch on the doctrine of Aquinas, that is, all those articles that possibly could be interpreted as Thomistic.[74] That is more than could be said of those articles on Tempier's syllabus that still remained in force, whichever those were.

3

False Teaching at the Arts Faculty

The Ockhamist Statute of 1340 and Its Prelude

On December 29, 1340, the masters of the faculty of arts at Paris issued a statute prohibiting the dissemination of six listed errors. Although this statute clearly concerns the prohibition of false teaching, it is atypical when compared to the academic censures discussed in the preceding chapters. The 1340 statute is the only censure of erroneous views that was issued by the arts faculty. There is no documentary evidence of the intervention of ecclesiastical authorities, nor of the involvement of the faculty of theology. Remarkably, this censure took the form of a statute and not disciplinary proceedings against one or more specific members of the faculty. Actually, the persons at whom the prohibition was aimed are not named at all. Due to circumstances whose precise nature still eludes us, this statute provides an unprecedented insight into the documentary side of the censure of false teaching at the arts faculty in Paris.

The final paragraph of the 1340 statute alludes to previous legislation concerning "the doctrine of William called Ockham" (*de doctrina Guillelmi dicti Ockham alias statuimus*). This clause has generally been understood as a reference to a statute that the arts faculty issued on September 25, 1339. Both statutes have traditionally been seen as restraining the dissemination of the thought of William Ockham at the University of Paris.[1] The interpretation of their exact nature and purport, however, has given rise to considerable scholarly debate.[2] Thanks to arguments and evidence that were introduced in the last decade, there is no serious disagreement anymore, except over nuances and details, over the general character of the statutes of September 25, 1339, and December 29, 1340. In the present understanding, the 1339 statute was aimed at members of the arts faculty who disseminated Ockham's own doctrine in Paris. Perhaps this same group was in 1340 labeled as "Ockhamists" and censured for adhering to six specific errors that allegedly had been inspired by William Ockham's views.[3] As William Courtenay has put it so succinctly, the two statutes "reflect a shift in the targeted concern, from textual source (Ockham) to contemporary practitioners (Ockhamists)."[4] This chapter explores in what way the arts faculty dealt with false teaching among its ranks. Before doing so, some introductory observations on the administrative organization of the arts faculty are required.

The Arts Faculty and Its Nations

Final authority in the arts faculty lay in the general congregation of the arts masters, presided over by the rector.[5] This congregation was itself the combination of four smaller organisms, the French, Picard, Norman, and English nations. Together, the four nations acted as the faculty of arts, providing, for instance, for the needs relative to the curriculum, the degrees, and the organization of teaching. In addition to these common duties, the nations exercised activities as separate corporate components. Each nation had its own officers, revenues, treasury, seal, patron saints, and authority to regulate its own members. Actually, even in the assemblies of the entire faculty, the nations withdrew to designated areas of their meeting place to deliberate separately.

As heads of the nations, proctors held important functions in the University of Paris. Among other things they were charged with enforcing the rules and statutes of faculty and university. One of the more important duties of the proctor consisted of summoning assemblies of the members of his nation and presiding over their meetings. These were held separately in one of the many buildings at the nations' disposal, such as the convent of the Mathurins, the church of St. Julien-le-Pauvre, the Dominican chapel in the Rue St. Jacques, the Cistercian college of the Bernardins, or elsewhere. At these meetings officers were elected, ordinances and statutes were drawn up, financial affairs such as scholarships and debts were discussed, and examinations and degrees were recorded. The entire faculty usually held its meetings at the church of St. Julien-le-Pauvre or at the convent of the Mathurins.

The proceedings of the nations were secret, and the minutes of the meetings were taken down by the proctor in the proctor's book (*liber procuratorum*).[6] Other important university registers are the Book of the Rector and the books of the nations. The Book of the Rector was a register of documents that was kept by the rector of the university and contained privileges and statutes of the university and the arts faculty. In addition to the Book of the Rector, each nation had its own register, the so-called Book of the Nation. It contained privileges and statutes of the university, the arts faculty, and the nation in question. Together with original records, these registers are the most important sources for our knowledge of the medieval University of Paris.

The Arts Statute of September 25, 1339

The 1340 statute was only one stage in a controversy over the promulgation of Ockham's philosophical views at the faculty of arts in Paris. The first stage probably occurred in the academic year 1338–39 and culminated in the statute that was issued on September 25, 1339, in a plenary session of the masters of arts in the church of St. Julien-le-Pauvre. This statute is considered the first document that testifies to the impact of Ockham's teaching on the Continent. Although it is not a censure of charged errors, it is important for the light it sheds on the background of the 1340 statute.

The 1339 statute has not been preserved as an original diploma, but as a copy both in the Book of the Rector and the Book of the Picard Nation. It comprises two separate decisions or decrees, both introduced by the clause "we decree" (*statuimus quod*). The second decree is not very problematic. It is chiefly concerned with restoring order during disputations. Masters who are disobeying the decree are suspended for three lectures. Bachelors and students are suspended for a year, during which time they may not obtain any office or degree, nor exercise in any way offices they already hold. The penalties that apply to bachelors and students are actually spelled out in the first decree (*in precedenti statuto*), to which the second decree refers.[7] Apart from this reference, the decrees are unconnected. This is also indicated at the end of the document: the meeting of the masters of arts was meant "for making statutes," that is, for settling various items of legislation. The text of the document in itself gives no reason to infer that the promulgation of Ockham's teaching, referred to in the first decree, led to the disruptions described in the second decree. The first decree solely concerns the suppression of Ockham's views.

To all who shall see the present writing, each and every single master of the four nations, namely of the French, Picard, Norman, and English [nations], an everlasting greeting in the Lord. He who is not afraid of transgressing those things that have been decreed by the ancients concerning lawful and reasonable practice seems to deviate from the path of reason and not have God before his eyes, especially since he was bound to these things by the bond of an oath. Since, now, a strict regulation has preceded from our predecessors, who were not unreasonably concerned as to the books to be read publicly or privately among us, which we have sworn to observe, and because we ought not to read certain books not admitted by them or not in common use elsewhere, and because in these times several have presumed to proclaim the doctrine of William called Ockham publicly and secretly by holding small meetings on this subject in private places (despite the fact that this doctrine had not been admitted by the regulators, nor used elsewhere, and had not been examined by us or by others to whom this might pertain, for which reason it does not seem to be free from suspicion): hence we, mindful of our salvation, and considering the oath that we made to observe the above-mentioned regulation, decree that henceforth no one shall presume to proclaim the said doctrine by listening to it or lecturing on it publicly or secretly, or by holding small meetings for disputing the said doctrine, or by referring to it in lecture or in disputations. If, however, anyone should presume to act against the above or any part thereof, him we suspend for a year, and [we decree] that during said year he may not obtain any office or degree among us, nor exercise in any way offices he held. If, however, some who are found to be against the aforesaid, are pertinacious, [them] we wish to place under the aforesaid penalties forever. . . . These [decrees] were enacted at Saint Julian in our congregation of the faculty, which was specially convoked for making decrees in the year of the Lord 1339, on the Saturday after the Feast of the blessed apostle Matthew. In witness of which we believe that our seals should be affixed with the signet of the rector.[8]

The decree mentions two reasons for prohibiting the dissemination of Ockham's teachings. First, the masters and bachelors were bound by an oath to an earlier regulation (*ordinatio*) concerning the books that were acceptable for lectures, whether public or private. And second, Ockham's books had not previously been on the curriculum, at Paris or elsewhere. The identification and analysis of the earlier ordinance by Zénon Kaluza has greatly advanced our understanding of the first decree of the 1339 statute.[9] The regulation referred to in the statute was issued by the university as a whole on September 2, 1276, to the effect that no master or bachelor of any faculty was allowed to lecture privately on books, but was only allowed to lecture in classrooms (*locis communibus*). Books on grammar and logic were exempted from the prohibition, because it was assumed that they could not contain anything presumptuous (*in quibus nulla presumptio potest esse*).

As Kaluza has pointed out, the first section of the 1339 statute is a specific application of this earlier regulation, but an application that was inappropriate: the statute forbids more than is justified on the basis of the rules laid down in the 1276 ordinance. The 1339 decree implicitly or explicitly forbids private lectures on Ockham's logic, public lectures on Ockham's works, citations of Ockham — activities that are not included in the ordinance — and this because no formal inquiry into the orthodoxy of Ockham's teachings by either the masters or "others to whom it might pertain" had taken place (*neque per nos seu alios ad quos pertineat examinata*).[10] Moreover, the statute invokes concern over "our salvation" (*nostre salutis*) for those who might have forgotten the oath in which they swore obedience to the 1276 ordinance. In short, the 1339 statute forbids the use of Ockham's *doctrina*, because it had not been examined and therefore appeared not to be free from suspicion. The statute reveals a high level of concern over Ockham's doctrine. The magisterial control over books read at the university, confirmed in the 1276 ordinance, is used as a pretext to forbid the dissemination of Ockham's views.

The statute of 1339 itself does not provide any clues as to which erroneous opinions of Ockham should not be promulgated. Since that statute was issued by the arts faculty, it is only natural to assume that it was not directly aimed at Ockham's theological views, but rather at his "scientific" views. As is well known Ockham's views on quantity, time, relation, and motion, in particular, attracted the attention of his contemporaries. Ockham's controversial treatment of these topics could be culled from his earlier works, which were all available at Paris long before 1339, such as the *Summa logicae*, the commentary on the *Physics*, *Tractatus de quantitate*, *Tractatus de corpore Christi*, and the *Tractatus de successivis* (not written by Ockham himself).[11] Hence, it seems very likely that the group of people at the arts faculty who, according to the 1339 statute, were immersed in the study of the work of Ockham were focusing on Ockham's nonstandard treatment of precisely these basic concepts of natural philosophy.

More information concerning the immediate doctrinal background of the 1339 statute can be inferred from an oath, tentatively datable to 1341.[12] In general, the purpose of oaths was to ensure explicit obedience to the faculty's statutes, for instance at the moment of inception. The oaths provided the principal sanction for the corporate association of masters and scholars. Any violation of such oaths constituted perjury and was punishable by excommunication and expulsion from the community of scholars.[13]

Bachelors of arts of the French nation were required to take the following oath before inception:

[1] Again, you shall swear that you shall observe the statutes made by the faculty of arts against the Ockhamist thought (*scientia Okamica*), and that you shall not sustain said thought and similar ones in whatever way, but [that you shall sustain] the thought (*scientia*) of Aristotle and his Commentator Averroes and the other ancient commentators and expositors of said Aristotle, except in those cases that are against faith.

[2] Again, you shall observe the decree contained in the other of the forementioned two statutes concerning the Ockhamist thought (*de scientia Okamica*), namely "that no master or bachelor or scholar should argue without permission of the master who holds the disputation, which permission he may not request orally, but only by making signs in a respectful way."[14]

In particular the first section of the oath provides some interesting information concerning the doctrinal background of the 1339 statute, granted that the oath really refers to this statute. Since the identification of the statutes mentioned in the oath has given rise to some controversy, it is useful to recapitulate briefly the main reasons why this oath should, indeed, be considered a parallel to the 1339 statute.

As I mentioned above, the 1339 statute actually consists of two separate decrees or statutes, the first one dealing with the proclaiming of Ockham's doctrine, and the second one dealing with discipline during disputations. This second decree is literally quoted in section 2 of the oath: "that no master or bachelor or scholar should argue without permission of the master who holds the disputation, which permission he may not request orally, but only by making signs in a respectful way."

Section 2 of the oath indicates that the quotation was taken from one of "the *forementioned* two statutes concerning the Ockhamist thought" (*predictorum duorum statutorum de scientia Okamica*). These two statutes had already been described, hence the "forementioned," in section 1 of the oath as "the statutes issued by the faculty of arts against the Ockhamist thought" (*statuta facta per facultatem artium contra scientiam Okamicam*). Hence, it follows that the first section of the oath also refers to the 1339 statute. More specifically, it refers to the first decree of the 1339 statute, which, indeed, deals with the dissemination of Ockham's views in the arts faculty. In sum, then, the first section of the oath refers to the first decree contained in the 1339 statute, and the second section of the oath refers to the second decree contained in the 1339 statute. The "Ockhamist *scientia*" mentioned in the oath is identical to the "*doctrina* of William called Ockham" referred to in the 1339 statute. This does not imply that the second decree of the 1339 statute was understood to be a decree *contra scientiam Okamicam*. On the contrary, it did not concern Ockham's views at all, but only happened to be located in a statute that was labeled "*de scientia Ockamica*" in the oath.[15]

What light does this oath shed on the doctrinal background of the 1339 statute? The admonition in the first section of the oath to adhere to Aristotle, his commentator Averroes, and other expositors is very significant, I think. It is not derived from the statute, but is an elaboration belonging to the oath itself. The oath demonstrates that there was resistance in the arts faculty to the practice among some of its members to attribute to Ockham the same kind of authority in interpreting Aristotle's works as was given to the approved commentators, such as Averroes, Thomas Aquinas, and Giles of Rome.[16] Apparently, Ockham's views on Aristotelian topics were considered a dangerous novelty in 1339.

The Arts Statute of December 29, 1340

On the Friday after Christmas 1340, the regent masters of the faculty of arts met in a plenary session and issued a statute in which they forbade the dissemination of six specified errors. The location of this meeting is not mentioned. Like the 1339 statute, this statute too does not survive as an original document, but as a copy in several registers, namely in the books of the English nation, the French nation, the Norman nation (still lost), and the Picard nation (the latter possessed by the English nation).[17] Here follow the most relevant passages from the 1340 statute:

To all who shall see the present writing, each and every single regent master at the faculty of arts in Paris, a greeting in the Lord. Everyone is held to oppose errors to the best of his ability and to close the road to them in every way, the more so since by these knowledge of the truth may be concealed. But since it has come recently to our attention that several in our faculty of arts, adhering to the pernicious cunning of certain men, not founded on firm rock, seeking to know more than is fitting, are striving to disseminate certain less sound views from which intolerable errors not only about philosophy but even concerning divine scripture may arise in the future, hence it is that, desiring to remedy this so pestiferous disease, we have collected their profane assumptions and errors in so far as we could, decreeing concerning them in this way: [here follow the six charged errors].

If, however, anyone shall presume to move against the preceding [articles] or any of them, him do we cut off and release from our community now and for the future, and do we wish to be considered cut off and released, saving in all respects what we have decreed elsewhere as to the doctrine of William called Ockham, which in all respects and in every way we wish to hold the firmness of authority.

Given at Paris under the seals of the four nations, namely of the French, the Picards, the Normans, and the English, together with the signet of the rector of the University of Paris, A.D. 1340, the Friday after Christmas.[18]

The statute claims that "several in our faculty of arts" (*nonnulli in nostra artium facultate*) had been disseminating the six listed errors. However, the errors themselves are attributed to the pernicious cunning "of certain men" (*quorundam*). In other words, the statute distinguishes the author or authors of the errors from those scholars who disseminated them at the arts faculty in Paris. The statute is only directed against the latter category. But who had misled them? Although the leaders may have to be sought among the members of the arts faculty itself, there are two clues that suggest that William Ockham was blamed for deceiving those who disseminated the six listed errors. The statute's final paragraph reminds the reader that "what we have decreed elsewhere as to the doctrine of William called Ockham" is still intact (*salvis in omnibus que de doctrina Guillelmi dicti Ockham alias statuimus*). Furthermore, according to its rubric, the 1340 statute concerned "certain Ockhamist errors," or "certain errors of the Ockhamists" (*Statutum facultatis de reprobatione quorundam errorum Ockhanicorum*). What is the weight of this evidence?

The final section of the 1340 statute has generally been considered a reference to the 1339 statute discussed above.[19] The meaning of the entire clause is ambiguous, however. I take it to signify that the 1340 statute, in contradistinction to that of 1339, was not directly concerned with Ockham's doctrine itself, but rather with "the less sound views" (*quedam minus sana*) disseminated by "several persons" in the faculty of arts. In other words, the clause "saving in all respects what we have decreed elsewhere as to the *doctrine* of William called Ockham" was inserted by the issuers of the 1340 statute to indicate that the prohibition of the six errors *derived* from Ockham's doctrine did not discontinue the 1339 prohibition to disseminate Ockham's *own* teaching.[20] Seen in this light, the 1340 statute ties the charged errors to Ockham, and, simultaneously, implies that they were not Ockham's own views.[21]

This interpretation seems to find support in the rubric under which the 1340 statute was inscribed in the register and that claims that the statute was aimed against "Ockhamist errors." If the rubric is correct, it was William Ockham's "pernicious cunning" (*astutiis perniciosis*) that misled several members in the faculty of arts to adhere to the charged errors. Although there is no reason to question the accuracy of the rubric, it should be noted that it may only have become attached when the 1340 statute was copied in the register.[22]

What, now, was at issue in the 1340 statute? As I have argued elsewhere, the 1340 statute addresses the scholastic method, that is, the fundamental problem of interpreting texts written by authors held in high esteem.[23] In other words, the 1340 statute represents a chapter in medieval hermeneutics. The distinction between the literal meaning of a text and the authorial intention plays a key role. Twice, the statute claims that the hermeneutics of the Parisian Ockhamists, captured in the six listed errors, will lead to erroneous interpretations of Scripture as well. But this is not the real issue of the statute. Its real issue is the teaching and interpretation of the authoritative texts of the arts curriculum.

The statute offers two incommensurate solutions to the problem of which potential meanings should be attributed to authoritative texts. The Ockhamist hermeneutics is based on the idea that texts have an objective, literal meaning, independent of the subjective intention of the author. It appears to assume that this objective literal sense of texts could be grasped by virtue of the properties of speech (*proprietates sermonis*). The authors of the 1340 statute criticize the Ockhamists for ignoring other important hermeneutical clues for interpreting texts, such as the author's intention (*intentio auctoris*) and the context of discourse (*materia subjecta*). The principal idea defended in the 1340 statute is that the literal sense also expresses the intention of the author and is partly determined by the context of the topic under discussion. In short, the Ockhamists were reproved for employing too narrow a concept of the literal sense of texts, one that suffocated the authorial meaning and neglected the context of discourse.

It is somewhat ironic that the hermeneutics attacked in the 1340 statute and attributed to the Ockhamists was the very method employed by commissions that evaluated charges of false teaching. As already indicated in Chapter 1, not the intended meaning of the suspected academics, but what they had literally said was what really mattered. If the literal reading generated an erroneous meaning, the author deserved to be corrected, even if he had intended something true. Interpreting past authorities, however, called for a completely different approach from the approach used for contemporary authors, as the 1340 statute illustrates.

The Ockhamist hermeneutical program and the one replacing it both draw heavily upon a well-developed body of concepts within semantics. In particular the notions of "virtue of speech" (*virtus sermonis*), "authorial intention" (*intentio auctoris*), "properly speaking" (*proprie loquendo*), "improperly speaking" (*improprie loquendo*), and "the context of the topic" (*materia subiecta*) play a key role in the 1340 statute. This semantic background can only be fully appreciated with the help of two more or less contemporary logical textbooks, namely William Ockham's *Summa logicae* and the *Summulae dialecticae* by John Buridan.

If one descends to the level of the semantic theories that lie behind this statute, the following picture emerges. The Ockhamist hermeneutical practices prohibited on December 29, 1340, do not converge with Ockham's own methodology. Yet there is a close resemblance to Ockham's hermeneutics. It seems that the Parisian Ockhamists had been drawing upon Ockham's views, but had been missing all those crucial details that made Ockham's method a well-balanced approach for the exegesis of past authorities. Part of the methodology attacked in the statute was in the spirit of Ockham's teachings (although not an adequate reflection of it), and for this reason there seems to be a genuine doctrinal basis to qualify the errors as Ockhamist. This, however, is a modern assessment. We do not know whether the authors of the 1340 statute labeled their opponents as Ockhamists because of doctrinal considerations such as those presented above, or whether they had still other reasons for doing so.[24]

In sum, the 1339 and 1340 statutes reflect a crisis over some aspects of Ockham's teaching in Paris. Apparently, the use of Ockham's work had two grave implications for the curriculum of the arts faculty. First, Ockham's treatment of such core issues as motion and Aristotle's categories was considered an undesirable intrusion into the teaching of Aristotle and his traditional commentators. Second, a hermeneutics that was allegedly developed on the basis of Ockham's semantic views threatened to discredit the respectful exposition of the authoritative writers in the arts curriculum. The Ockhamist hermeneutics, with its narrow concept of the literal meaning of texts, implied that a statement of an *auctoritas* could be false, even if he intended something true. The 1339 statute was issued to remedy the first effect of the introduction of Ockham's writings at the arts faculty of Paris. In 1341, members of the French nation, and possibly of the other nations as well, had to confirm by oath that they would respect this statute. The 1340 statute was designed to remedy the destructive effects of the Ockhamist hermeneutics. Although Ockham's doctrine was presented as suspect, and the six Ockhamist errors as false teaching, there is a marked difference between these two statutes on the one hand and the censures of false teaching at the theological faculty, on the other. The censure of certain Ockhamist views and practices at the arts faculty did not occur out of concern for faith and good morals. Rather, the two statutes reflect a struggle between two opposing schools of thought. One got the upper hand and made its own philosophical views exclusive by censuring the opposition.

That tempers over the Ockhamists must have run high can be inferred from another piece of legislation, which has been preserved in the Proctor's Book of the English-German Nation. This register is chronologically arranged according to the terms of the consecutive proctors, which usually lasted about one month.[25] Business that came before the nation's meetings is recorded in separate items. During the proctorship of Henry of Unna of

Denmark, which lasted from September 22 until October 20, 1341, the following decision was entered:

Again, in the same congregation [that is, of the regent and nonregent masters of the English-German Nation] it was stipulated that henceforth no one should be admitted to any juridicial actions of the said nation, without first swearing that he should disclose, if he knew any of the Ockhamist sect (*secta Occamica*) to have plotted together concerning the sect or the erroneous opinions (*opiniones erroneae*) that they foster or even to have bound themselves together by oath or to be holding secret meetings; otherwise, should he not be forthcoming under oath about his knowledge, he should then incur the penalty for perjury. And they wished this regulation to be equivalent to a statute.[26]

According to the proctor's book, the English-German nation decreed on October 19, 1341, to introduce a new oath requiring its members to reveal any knowledge they might have of Ockhamists or their meetings. The purport of this oath is clearly different from the oath registered in the Book of the French Nation, discussed above. That oath obliged the incepting bachelor of arts to observe a specific statute, namely the 1339 statute against the dissemination of Ockham's doctrine. Most of the inception oaths at the arts faculty refer in similar fashion to statutory legislation.[27] The oath issued by the English-German nation, however, is not directly based on already existent statutory legislation, even though it is, of course, related to the 1339 and 1340 statutes. The oath represents new legislation to curb Ockhamism within the English-German nation.[28] Any member who failed to denounce Ockhamists, let alone any member who himself was involved with Ockhamism, was denied access to the activities of the English-German nation.

Unfortunately, neither the decree nor the oath have been preserved. The paraphrase in the proctor's book, however, demonstrates that the English-German nation found it necessary to complement the 1339 and 1340 statutes, even though its members were bound by oath to obey them. They decreed the introduction of an additional oath, which was expected to eradicate even more rigorously Ockhamism within the English-German nation. Possibly because of Ockham's English origin, his ideas found more adherence in this particular nation than in any of the other nations of the arts faculty.

The Making of the Statute of December 29, 1340

During the term that ran from January 13 to February 10, 1341, the proctor Henry of Unna of Denmark recorded the following entry:

Further, during his [Henry of Unna's] proctorship a statute of the faculty was sealed against the new opinions (*nove opiniones*) of certain ones who are called Ockhamists (*Occaniste*), in the house of said proctor, and the same statute was published before the university in a sermon at the Dominicans [St. Jacques].[29]

If the entry in the proctor's book is accurate, a statute of the faculty of arts "against the new opinions of certain ones who are called Ockhamists" was sealed and published during Henry of Unna's term as proctor. Since the publication in 1982 of an influential article authored by William Courtenay and Katherine Tachau it has been believed that this entry, considered unproblematic until the appearance of their paper, could not be a reference to the 1340 statute.[30] Courtenay and Tachau conjecture that there must have been yet another statute, this one in fact explicitly directed against Ockhamists, promulgated between late January and early February 1341, that was "either lost or removed when the statutes were revised." In an article authored in 1990, I suggested that the discrepancy in dates assigned to the 1340 statute could be removed by assuming that somehow the several different stages of issuing a university statute had in this case been separated in time.[31]

I believe that it is not unreasonable to conclude that over the past decade essential agreement has been reached that the entry in the proctor's book is a reference to the statute of December 29, 1340.[32] Henry of Unna's description of the statute that was sealed in his house matches the rubric of the 1340 statute and further confirms its anti-Ockhamist nature. Moreover, considerable progress has been made in explaining the discrepancy between the dates of sealing mentioned in the 1340 statute itself and in the proctor's book. The most recent explanations of the assignment of two different dates on which the statute was allegedly sealed all rely upon the idea that a time interval occurred between the different stages in which this document was issued.[33]

According to medieval diplomatics, the creation of a charter usually went through the following three stages: the composition of the document (*datum*; *Beurkundung*), the juridical action to which it referred (*actum*; *Handlung*), and its validation by sealing.[34] A document could be drawn up and sealed at the same meeting at which the legislative action took place that was recorded, but this seems not to have been the case with the statute of December 29, 1340. If the proctor's testimony is correct, and was not based upon a conflation of several different events, one must conclude that the sealing of the document was postponed. The evidence of the 1340

statute and the proctor's book taken together suggest the following scenario: the decisions concerning the prohibition of the Ockhamist errors
were taken on December 29, 1340, and at the same meeting the document
was authored that recorded this legislative action. The validation by seal of
the decree issued by the masters of the arts faculty took place between
January 13 and February 10, 1341, in the house of the proctor of the
English-German nation. Sometime during that same term, the statute was
officially promulgated (*in sermone*) at St. Jacques before the entire university. Since the colophon of the statute reads "given at Paris under the seals of
the four nations, namely of the French, the Picards, the Normans and the
English, together with the signet of the rector of the University of Paris,
A.D. 1340, the Friday after Christmas" one has to assume that the document
was already prepared and dated in anticipation of its actual sealing two
weeks to a month later. This picture of the issuing of the 1340 statute,
however, still raises a few questions.

Probably the most important problem, because its solution may advance our knowledge of diplomatic practices at the University of Paris, is
whether the interval between decision and sealing was exceptional. William
Courtenay has suggested that the time span between approval and sealing
was caused by special circumstances. He believes that the sealing of the
document was delayed because there were changes and additions in the
text. Thus the statute was not only sealed but also prepared during the
meeting in the proctor's house, and it was backdated to the original meeting of the masters on December 29, 1340, that had approved the statute.[35]
In other words, the preparation of the document (*datum*; *Beurkundung*)
and its sealing took place approximately two weeks to one month after the
legislative decisions had been taken (*actum*) in 1340. As Courtenay himself
pointed out, one obstacle to his hypothesis is the absence in the 1340 statute
of any mention of a delay or of emendations in its text. Such a notice of
delayed sealing, which was caused by textual emendations, was, for instance, included in a statute of 1253. Actually, it is the only known example
of a statute in which its issuers indicated that a time interval had passed
between approval and sealing.[36]

The significance of this omission deserves closer attention. The 1340
statute represented a decision of the regent masters of the arts faculty, and it
would require the authority of this legislative body to alter the texts of the
statute that was issued in its name. If one assumes for a moment that the
regent masters were present at the meeting in the proctor's house, even
though such a meeting is not mentioned in the proctor's book, the deci-

sions taken there would constitute a *new* legislative action, a new *actum*, different from the one of December 29, 1340. Under these circumstances, one would expect either a notice of the textual emendations, or an entirely new document, issued between January 13 and February 10, 1341. Backdating the newly prepared document to a previous legislative meeting whose decrees it no longer represents seems illogical. In the absence of any proof to the contrary, it seems safest at present to conclude that the 1340 statute was sealed but not changed in the proctor's lodgings. Still, two questions remain. First, which seal was affixed to the 1340 statute? Was it only the seal of the English-German nation, or the seals of all four nations? Second, was the sealing ceremony in the proctor's house business as usual?

Zénon Kaluza believes that there was nothing unusual in a time span between the approval and sealing of documents. He conjectures that the sealing of the 1340 statute could not take place sooner because the faculty had to wait for an open Sunday at St. Jacques for the public reading of this statute. Between December 29, the day that the 1340 statute was issued, and January 13, 1341, the day on which Henry of Unna became proctor, there were only two Sundays: December 31 and January 7.[37] Apparently, these were unsuitable. Consequently, Conrad of Megenberg, the proctor who preceded Henry of Unna, noted at the end of his term, on January 12, 1341, that nothing had been fully achieved.[38] When Conrad entered this report of his activities in the proctor's book, he must already have known that the 1340 statute would only be sealed and publicly promulgated during the term of his successor, Henry of Unna. Possibly, the sealing and publication took place on the first Sunday of Henry of Unna's term as proctor, that is, on January 14, two weeks after the statute had been prepared and voted at the plenary session of the arts faculty.

Kaluza's thesis satisfactorily explains the postponement of the publication of this statute for the entire university *in sermone* at St. Jacques. Yet it does not explain the late date of sealing. Kaluza is probably right in suggesting that the sealing of the 1340 statute took place at the same day as its public reading, even though the proctor's book does not explicitly say so, namely on the first Sunday that was open at St. Jacques for such occasions. One may wonder, however, whether it was usual to postpone the sealing of statutes until the day that they could be publicly promulgated. I think not. The public reading of the document, although important for the university community, is insignificant from the point of view of diplomatics. Only the *actum*, the *datum*, and the sealing were the constitutive moments in issuing a decree. Consequently, Kaluza's thesis still leaves us with an odd delay.

Why was the 1340 statute sealed on a particular Sunday in January 1341, and not on December 29, 1340, at the legislative meeting?

I believe that there is some circumstantial evidence that suggests that the delay in sealing the 1340 statute was unusual. Seals could be lost, as happened to Henry of Unna in 1341, when he had to replace the proctor's seal (not to be confused with the seal of the nation) by a new one.[39] Or, less dramatically, the proctor of the English-German nation, Henry's predecessor, Conrad of Megenberg, simply forgot to bring the nation's seal to the plenary session of 1340.

Admittedly, both scenarios are based on conjecture. Unfortunately, the 1340 statute is one of the very rare cases that allows us a glimpse into the way by which the arts faculty prepared and sealed a statute. Yet, from legislation passed during the years 1340–42, that has not been noticed previously, it can be inferred that the English-German nation was having problems with keeping and transferring its seal. The nation's legislative activity concerning its seal started between October 27 and November 18, 1340, when it issued two statutes. In the first statute it was laid down that a chest (*cista*) had to be constructed with three keys for keeping the nation's money (and seal).[40] The second statute insisted that on the day of the election of a new proctor, the last proctor had to make sure that he brought the proctor's book, paper, the seal, and the keys of the chest, in order to hand them over to his successor.[41] However, in 1341 the nation still did not have the chest. Between June 28 and July 28 of that year, when Henry of Unna was proctor, it was decided that the next receptor had to swear that, from the first money he received, he would have a box made with three keys, into which would be placed the nation's seal and money.[42] Only on June 14, 1342, did the English-German nation finally have its box in a fixed place in St. Mathurin.[43] From these statutes it can be inferred that the English-German nation did not have one fixed place where it could keep its belongings. The seal had to be brought along whenever needed, and probably the transferral of the seal from one proctor to the next had not always been a smooth operation.

In the light of this circumstantial evidence, the sealing of the 1340 statute may have taken place according to the following scenario. On December 29, 1340, the English-German nation was somehow unable to affix its seal to the statute that had just been voted and authored. Since there was no earlier opportunity to promulgate the statute in St. Jacques than January 14, 1341, or even later, it was decided that on that occasion the English-German nation would affix its seal. This ceremony took place in the proctor's lodgings, presumably prior to the meeting in St. Jacques. Present were the proctor, who presumably kept the seal at his home since the nation still did not possess a chest, and the required witnesses.[44]

It is unlikely that the sealing ceremony in Henry's house included the proctors of all four nations. They would rather have met in one of the university buildings, as they did in 1343, when the proctors of the four nations met three times in St. Geneviève to seal seven letters.[45] In any event, the statute sealed in the lodgings of the proctor was the statute of December 29, 1340. Like some previous statutes issued by the faculty of arts, this one too left its mark in the proctor's book of the English-German nation, although a little later than one would have expected.[46]

4

Nicholas of Autrecourt and John of Mirecourt

Censure at the Faculty of Theology in the Fourteenth Century

In almost any history of medieval philosophy the censures of Nicholas of Autrecourt and John of Mirecourt in 1347 are presented as the two most important events in the intellectual history of the fourteenth century. In the perception of the historians of medieval philosophy, the views of Autrecourt and Mirecourt have become linked to allegedly critical and skeptical tendencies in scholastic thought.[1] Over the last two decades, however, our understanding of the broader intellectual and institutional context of their ideas has significantly changed. Largely due to the publications of William Courtenay, it has become apparent that the study of the thought of Autrecourt and Mirecourt has been wrongly placed in the larger context of the battle against Ockhamism at the University of Paris in the years 1339–47, and has, as a consequence, been unduly overshadowed by assumptions about its relation to the views of William Ockham.[2]

In the same vein, the status of the censures of Mirecourt and Autrecourt has been reassessed. Their condemnations were not exceptional, but should be studied against the background of the academic censures of Brother Bartholomew (1314), John of Pouilly (1321), Simon (1351), Louis of Padua (1362), John of Calore (1363), Denis of Foullechat (1364), and John of Monzón (1389) in the fourteenth century, and those of Stephen of Venizy (1241), Giles of Rome (1277), and John of Paris (Quidort) (1286/87) in the thirteenth century.[3] Two features stand out in the judicial procedures against these academics. First, in all cases the doctrinal investigation concerned lectures on the *Sentences* or other writings that originated during the suspect's academic career. Secondly, most stages of the doctrinal investigation were handled *within* the University of Paris, at its faculty of theology. The evidence that has survived from the cases of Nicholas of Autrecourt and John of Mirecourt further documents some of the stages between initial denunciation and final recantation outlined in Chapter 1, and helps to complement our picture of Parisian practice in censuring academics accused of disseminating false teaching.

Nicholas of Autrecourt

The investigation of Nicholas of Autrecourt started on November 21, 1340, when Pope Benedict XII wrote a letter to the bishop of Paris to summon Autrecourt, together with John the Servite, Elias of Corso, Guido of Veeli, Peter of Monteregali, and Henry of England, to Avignon within a month. The purpose of the summons was to find out the truth concerning statements touching questions of faith that Autrecourt and the other academics reportedly had made (*aliqua catholicam fidem tangentia sunt relata*).[4] The papal letter refers to Autrecourt and the other five scholars as masters and then further specifies their theological degrees in order of importance. Autrecourt is mentioned first, and designated as *licentiatus*. His name is followed by the names of four masters who are referred to as bachelors of theology, and finally by the name of a *scolaris* in theology, that is, of someone without a degree.[5] Since the summoned scholars were not yet masters of theology, the term "master" can only mean "master of arts." The summons demonstrates that even though Autrecourt was not a master of theology, he had already obtained the license in theology when he was cited to appear in Avignon.

An extensive, but as yet incomplete dossier of the judicial process at Avignon has been preserved in the form of an *instrumentum publicum*, or, more exactly, a draft copy thereof, which served as a model for the preparation of the official record of the process.[6] It was written by a Bernardus, notary of the judge, Cardinal William Curti.[7] This draft copy was kept at the papal archives, whereas the finished document recording Autrecourt's trial at Avignon was given to Nicholas himself with the request to hand it to the Parisian authorities.[8]

The papal dossier contains copies of a number of records that played a role during earlier stages of Autrecourt's trial and gives an account (*narratio*) of the judicial proceedings from the moment that Cardinal Curti took over the investigation. The document has been exhaustively analyzed in

Zénon Kaluza's excellent biography of Autrecourt. Although I am at variance with some of Kaluza's conclusions, the following reconstruction of Autrecourt's trial is heavily indebted to his findings.[9]

From the *instrumentum* it can be inferred that the process at Avignon consisted of three stages. The first stage ended with the death of Pope Benedict XII. Benedict was succeeded in May 19, 1342, by Pope Clement VI, who became the new judge in the process against Autrecourt. Some time before October 9, 1342, he appointed Cardinal William Curti as delegate judge, after William had reminded him of Autrecourt's trial.[10] The *narratio* of the *instrumentum* picks up at the moment that William Curti was commissioned to preside over Autrecourt's process and finishes with the verdict, pronounced some time before May 1346. The investigations seem to have been interrupted between October 9, 1342, and October 30, 1343, when Curti was in Lombardy as papal legate.

Among the records reproduced in the *instrumentum* are four lists, together totaling sixty-six erroneous propositions and articles. In the margins of all the lists were added assessments of the degree of error, such as, for instance, "false," "dangerous," "presumptuous," "suspect," "erroneous," "heretical," or any combination of those. One of the lists, the fourth, consists of articles "sent from Paris." According to Kaluza, this list raised the initial suspicion at Avignon concerning Autrecourt's teaching and induced Benedict XII to write his summons. It was the only list that was drawn up at the University of Paris. The other three lists were, according to Kaluza, prepared at Avignon, the first probably under Pope Benedict XII, and the second and third during the time that Pope Clement presided over the judicial process.[11]

But do the records reproduced in the *instrumentum* really imply this course of events? Before I present an alternative scenario of Autrecourt's process, let me review what is known about these lists. The first list is a recantation of thirty-two propositions, identified by the incipit "Ve michi." It is addressed to Pope Clement VI and was copied from another list. The recantation finishes with a standard end-clause in which the defendant declares that, since he can hardly write, someone else has taken down his statements, though exactly according to the defendant's will. Since this end-clause hardly seems appropriate in Autrecourt's case, it probably is a remnant from a formulary that was used in trials of popular heresy.[12] Zénon Kaluza has done an admirable job in identifying the sources of the errors attributed to Autrecourt.[13] From his findings it appears that the propositions of "Ve michi" were mainly derived from the so-called *Letters to Ber-*

nard, that is, to the Franciscan Bernard of Arezzo, from the first *principium* to the commentary on the *Sentences*, and from oral tradition (teaching, disputation). The second list consists of four errors to which Autrecourt had confessed in his "replies or explanations" (*responsiones seu declarationes*) before the papal commission. They were derived from the *Letters*, the *principium*, and the treatise *Exigit ordo*. The third list reproduces twenty errors, all of which stem from Autrecourt's *Exigit ordo* and from an announcement from Autrecourt's lectures on Aristotle's *Politics*. The "articles sent from Paris," finally, were culled from the first *principium*, the *Exigit ordo*, and oral tradition (teaching, disputation, sermon).

The suspect propositions that were reviewed by the papal commission were drawn from Autrecourt's entire and rather meagre academic production from many years earlier. Autrecourt's announcement of his lecture on the *Politics* dates from 1330. The *Exigit ordo* was written around 1333–35, during Autrecourt's regency in arts. The nine *Letters to Bernard*, the *principium*, and the lectures on the *Sentences* all date from the period when Autrecourt was a bachelor of theology, that is, probably from the academic year 1335–36, or perhaps 1336–37.[14] In brief, the lists of suspect propositions demonstrate that the papal commission had an intimate knowledge of the local Parisian situation. According to Zénon Kaluza, the papal commission could only have obtained its information through the assistance of sources at the university, such as the bishop of Paris and the chancellor Robert de Bardis. Moreover, the commission must have had at its disposal the *Letters to Bernard* and the *Exigit ordo*, or at least the prologue and the first chapter, which were the only published parts of this incomplete treatise.[15] Kaluza rejects, however, the suggestion that the lists of erroneous propositions were prepared at Paris. According to him, there is no documentary evidence that a commission of theologians was charged with examining Autrecourt's views at the university.[16]

The thesis that the inquiry against Autrecourt was entirely initiated and prepared by the papal court seems to be contradicted by the *instrumentum*. It indicates that Autrecourt's trial at Avignon was, in fact, preceded by an inquiry elsewhere. In his account of the juridical proceedings against Autrecourt, Cardinal Curti summarizes the records that he and his commission had examined. They examined and discussed the articles (*articuli*), the replies (*responsiones*) and explanations (*declarationes*) that followed those articles, and also "the proceedings (*processus*) obtained from elsewhere about this very same material and that were contained in two documents (*cedule*) handed over by Autrecourt himself."[17] In other words, it appears that Autrecourt brought with him a dossier from another investigation, which concerned the same articles that were at issue at the papal court in Avignon.

Curti's statement is repeated twice in the *instrumentum*. A few lines below the first mention of the activities undertaken by the papal commission, Cardinal Curti reports that the prelates and theologians examined the articles against Master Autrecourt that had been transferred and assigned to him and also the replies and explanations following those articles that Autrecourt "gave, made, ventilated, and held" before the papal courts of Pope Clement VI and of William Curti himself.[18] And toward the end of the *instrumentum*, shortly before Curti spells out the sentence against Autrecourt, he observes for the last time that he has examined "all and every single article, proposition, response, explanation, document (*cedule*) and legal proceedings (*processus*) mentioned above."[19]

It is important to note that nowhere in the *instrumentum* is it reported that the papal commision or commissions charged with investigating Autrecourt's teaching drew up lists of articles or inspected Autrecourt's writings. Their activities are always described in terms of examining and discussing material that, apparently, had already been collected. For these reasons, and because the lists of theses and articles could only have been drawn up by persons familiar with Autrecourt's teachings and early writings at Paris, I conclude that the main activity of the papal commission consisted of reviewing a dossier that had originated during a previous judicial process against Autrecourt at the University of Paris. The central pieces of this dossier were lists of suspect views that were attributed to Autrecourt. The fact that Autrecourt was ordered to repeat his Avignon recantation in Paris is further proof that the proceedings against him started in a university context.

The *instrumentum* is quite explicit about how this material arrived in Avignon. One list of articles was sent from Paris, whereas other material was brought by Autrecourt himself to Avignon in two documents (*cedule*). Moreover, from the *instrumentum* it can be inferred which material these two documents contained: (1) the articles in the "Ve michi" list, of which it is explicitly indicated that it came in a *cedula*[20] and (2) the list of twenty articles derived from the *Exigit ordo*, which are referred to as the articles "given and assigned (*dati et assignati*) against this same Master Nicholas."[21]

The only documents besides the *instrumentum* itself that originated at Avignon were the replies and explanations that Autrecourt gave before the papal commissions in response to the articles with which they confronted him. These are also mentioned in the *instrumentum*. The first is a letter (*cedula*) written at the request of the prelates (*patres*) of Pope Clement's commission. In it, Autrecourt explains his motives for conducting his correspondence with Bernard of Arezzo, from which the censured theses of "Ve michi" were derived.[22] He claims that he had agreed with Bernard of Arezzo to take certain philosophical principles as the basis of the disputation in their *principia* on the *Sentences*. To continue the debate (*causa collationis*), the same principles were taken as the point of departure in the nine letters to Bernard.[23] This kind of exchange between bachelors of theology, initiated by a *principium* and continued by rejoinders and rebuttals at other *principia* was common practice and could last an entire academic year.[24] Autrecourt's letter to the *patres* can be considered a further elaboration of a point made at the end of "Ve michi," namely that the recanted articles had been upheld for the sake of the dispute (*disputative et causa collationis*) and had not been in any way stubbornly defended.[25] The second document that originated during the trial in Avignon was a list of four articles confessed "in his [that is, Autrecourt's] replies or explanations."[26]

In conclusion, it would appear that the papal commissions of Pope Clement VI and Cardinal Curti based the Autrecourt trial on evidence that had been produced during proceedings at the University of Paris and on Autrecourt's response to this evidence. Autrecourt's writings were not (re)examined in Avignon. It was on the basis of this material that Curti reached his verdict. If this scenario of the process is correct, it raises two obvious questions, namely, why was Autrecourt's trial transferred from Paris to Avignon, and how did it start in the first place?

The answers to these questions might have been provided in the first or more of the folia that are missing from the *instrumentum*.[27] In view of the fragile evidence, I can only put forward a hypothesis about the initial phase of the inquiry. In particular, the events at the University of Paris prior to Autrecourt's summons to appear in Avignon still elude us. So much seems clear, however: the chronology of Autrecourt's career rules out that his case was similar to those of, for instance, Brother Bartholomew or Denis of Foullechat, whose investigations were initiated by what they had been saying during their *principia*. Although some of Autrecourt's condemned theses were also derived from his *principium*, he already held a license in theology at the time when Pope Benedict summoned him to appear before the curia.

But Autrecourt also does not belong in the category of other licensed theologians who were investigated for suspect teaching in the fourteenth century, such as Simon, Louis of Padua, John of Calore, and John of Monzón. Their inquiries were initiated because of statements made in their vesperies, that is, in the final stage of the road that led to the magisterial honor (see Chapter 1). In the lists of errors attributed to Autrecourt, however, there is no reference whatsoever to his vesperies. So it appears that Autrecourt's denouncement was not occasioned by any of the regular university ceremonies. Nor was it caused by the prepublication scrutiny of his commentary on the *Sentences*. Although Autrecourt gave his lectures on the *Sentences*, these were probably never written down and certainly never published.[28] In any case, they do not appear at all in the lists of charged errors.

Most likely, the inquiry against Autrecourt in Paris had its origin in the correspondence with Bernard of Arezzo. The *Letters to Bernard* are Autrecourt's most recent writings before his license in theology and before his summons to the papal curia. Moreover, they figure most prominently in the three lists of errors that were drawn up from Autrecourt's teaching. In fact, the thirty-two propositions of the "Ve michi" list are almost entirely derived from the correspondence.[29] In contradistinction to the other three lists, "Ve michi" is phrased in the language of admitted guilt, as each of the theses is introduced by the words "I have said," or "I have said and written," followed by a precise indication of the *locus* from which the thesis was taken and by an evaluation of the degree of error. It is my conjecture that the "Ve michi" list had already been prepared to be recanted in Paris and that the addressee was modified once the inquiry had been transferred to Avignon.

In their search for material evidence from which Autrecourt's views could be culled, the authorities involved in the inquiry also came up with the *Exigit ordo*. Even though the treatise dated from many years back, it provided them with a list of twenty errors. Interestingly, Autrecourt explicitly denied having held any of these errors or having held them in the alleged form, as the *instrumentum* reports.[30] Autrecourt had a point here, for although, as a matter of fact, all articles stemmed from the *Exigit ordo*, they had been stated as hypothetical theses, not as affirmative statements. This distinction, however, was ignored in the list of articles.[31]

At some point during the proceedings in Paris, the papal court got wind of the investigation. As mentioned before, Pope Benedict XII clearly indicated in his summons that he was acting on information received.[32] Possibly the list of "articles sent from Paris" first alerted Benedict to the inquiry against Autrecourt and against the other five academics, who later dropped out of sight.

Theoretically, the role of the papal court could have been that of a court of appeal. There are several reasons, however, why this was not the

case in the Autrecourt investigation. First, the summons does not state that
Autrecourt, or the other five academics, had been appealing to the papal
court. Second, the *instrumentum* does not give any indication, either explicitly, or implicitly, that the papal court was acting as appellate court.
There is, for instance, no mention of the presence of representatives of the
university or the bishop, which one would expect if Autrecourt had appealed against their jurisdictions. In this respect, the *instrumentum* stands in
marked contrast to the *instrumenta* that record the appellate processes of
Foullechat and Monzón, discussed in Chapter 1.

I think that the papal court acted as trial court or court of first instance.
Once Pope Benedict XII was informed about the inquiry against Autrecourt at the University of Paris, he became interested and decided to handle
the case himself. As ordinary judge over the whole Catholic Church, he
possessed the power to assume direct jurisdiction over any cause and to pass
over lower jurisdictions. Although other popes might have been more re-
luctant to personally conduct the proceedings in cases of false teaching at
the University of Paris, if they knew at all about it, Benedict XII, a former
inquisitor and theologian with a record of involvement in the censure of
false teaching, was an exception.[33] In this respect, the inquiry against Nicholas of Autrecourt belongs to the same category as those against Richard of
Lincoln, and possibly John of Mirecourt, which were also conducted by the
papal court. The actual handling of Mirecourt's case was delegated to the
papal nuncio in Paris.

The most informative part of the *instrumentum* is the verdict.[34] It sheds
light on the relation between judicial procedures carried out at the papal
court and those carried out at the university in cases that had been transferred from Paris to Avignon. The commission of prelates and theologians,
which under the chairmanship of Cardinal Curti had discussed all the articles attributed to Autrecourt, came to the conclusion that Autrecourt's
Letters to Bernard, and his *Exigit ordo* contained many false, dangerous, presumptuous, suspect, erroneous and heretical statements. For this reason,
these writings were condemned to be burned either at the Pré-aux-Clercs or
at the Pré-de-Saint-Germain at Paris, at a date yet to be established. Moreover, Autrecourt was ordered to publicly recant the four articles that he had
confessed and the articles contained in the list "Ve michi." Kaluza has rightly
pointed out that Autrecourt was not required to recant the other articles
mentioned in the *instrumentum*, because he had denied having held them.[35]
These articles were to be publicly declared false, suspect, and erroneous and
never to be taught again. In support of the correctness of Kaluza's observa-

tion, it should be noted that the lists that Autrecourt was expected to read clearly differentiate between the articles to be recanted and those to be declared erroneous.[36] The recantations and declarations that Autrecourt was required to make at Avignon, at the palace of Cardinal Curti (*in hospitio habitationis nostre*), had to be repeated at the University of Paris. Autrecourt's recantation at the papal court took place before May 19, 1346. The exact date is unknown, because it was left blank in the draft prepared by the notary Bernard.[37]

In addition to the recantation, Autrecourt was deprived (*deprivamus*) of the magisterial honor and disqualified from and declared unworthy of ascending to the magisterial degree in the theological faculty. Anyone in possession of the authority to present or promote Autrecourt to the magisterium of the faculty of theology was forbidden to do so. Autrecourt could obtain the "magisterial honor and degree" only after special permission from the Apostolic See.[38] Does this mean that Nicholas of Autrecourt was a full-fledged master of theology, and that his magisterium in theology was taken away from him? Most likely not. The terminology of the sentence suggests that the magisterial honor in theology was not to be accorded to Autrecourt, and it was in that sense that he was deprived of the magisterium. In other words, Autrecourt was a master of arts and a licentiate in theology when he was tried at Avignon, and he kept these degrees, but he was not allowed to progress to the inception in theology until the pope decided otherwise.[39] This reading of the sentence is supported by later references from sources that can be expected to be accurate with regard to Autrecourt's degrees. An entry in the Proctor's Book of the English-German nation reports the recantation of "Master Nicholas of Autrecourt, bachelor in theology," and a letter of August 6, 1350, by Pope Clement VI records the fact that Autrecourt, licentiate in theology (*in sacra theologia licentiatus*), was made a dean at the Cathedral of Metz.[40] His academic career, however, had abruptly come to an end.

The Parisian part of the sentence took place in 1347. The Proctor's Book of the English-German nation gives a brief account of the events.[41] On November 20, 1347, the regent and nonregent masters of the university met at the church of St. Mathurin, where papal letters and the proceedings "concerning certain articles" were read. The proceedings probably are identical to the *instrumentum*. The papal letters are unknown. This material had been brought from Avignon by Autrecourt himself.[42] Unfortunately, these documents were already lost at the beginning of the sixteenth century. When in 1523 the theologian Noël Beda drew up his register of medieval censures at the faculty of theology, he did not include any documents pertaining to the Autrecourt case because they were not extant in the archive of the faculty of theology.[43]

On November 25, 1347, Autrecourt recanted the four confessed articles and the articles from the letter "Ve michi" in the church of the Dominicans and publicly declared that the propositions contained in the other two lists were wrong. In addition, he burned these articles, together with a treatise, most likely the *Exigit ordo*. There is no mention of the *Letters to Bernard* among the material that Autrecourt was ordered to burn.[44] The public reading of the *instrumentum* and the recantation had an important purpose. It not only made the sentence effective, but also informed the scholarly community of Autrecourt's errors and of the penalties laid down in the *instrumentum* against themselves, if they were to teach the censured errors.[45] Many years later, scholars such as John Buridan, Marsilius of Inghen, and André of Neufchâteau (Andreas de Novo Castro) cited the condemned erroneous propositions as the *articuli cardinalis (albi)*.[46]

John of Mirecourt

Only one stage of the judicial proceedings against the Cistercian John of Mirecourt has been well documented, namely his defense. No less than two different written responses have survived. They are not official trial records, but have come down to us as additions to Mirecourt's commentary on the *Sentences*. Although the defenses themselves are anonymous, it is clear from manuscript evidence that they were written by John of Mirecourt.[47]

One response (*excusatio*), henceforth labeled Apologia 1, is a reply to a list of sixty-three charged errors. It is addressed to Pastor de Serrescuderio (Pasteur de Sarrats), archbishop of Embrun, of whom more later. In a brief preface, Mirecourt indicates that his "reverend masters" had extracted the theses from his *lectura* (on the *Sentences*).[48] The theses are numbered, and their location in the text is carefully indicated. The second defense (*declaratio*), henceforth labeled Apologia 2, is a reply to a list of forty-one suspect theses. It does not have an addressee. In both responses, the suspect statements are consistently designated as "propositions" (*propositiones*), never as "articles" (*articuli*), and they are not annotated with assessments of the degree of error. Only the shorter list of forty-one propositions went into the *Collectio errorum*, the Collection of Parisian Articles that circulated in the university community. As a consequence, it represents the last stage of

Mirecourt's trial and must have been preceded by the list of sixty-three articles and by Mirecourt's defense, Apologia 1.

The two defenses are not dated, but the allegations of false teaching can only have been made after 1345. The reason is that the propositions of both lists were extracted from passages in Mirecourt's *entire* commentary on the *Sentences*, which were read in the academic year 1344–45.[49] The judicial proceedings against Mirecourt must have been finished in 1347, because his condemnation usually appears under this year in the medieval copies of the *Collectio errorum*.[50] This chronology seems to rule out that Mirecourt's *principia* or vesperies induced the inquiry.

There are no indications as to the occasion and the circumstances under which the suspicions of false teaching were voiced. At first sight, Mirecourt's condemnation seems similar to the prepublication censorship of the Dominican Durand of St. Pourçain. Both Pourçain and Mirecourt belonged to a religious order, and their entire commentaries on the *Sentences* came under review. Moreover, in Mirecourt's case too, the censured propositions were later attached to his commentary on the *Sentences*. Although the Cistercians, unlike the Franciscans and Dominicans, did not have explicit legislation on the prepublication scrutiny of writings produced by their members, it seems only natural to assume that they were no less concerned about the dissemination of false teaching within their order.[51] And yet two factors seem to indicate that the institutional context of Mirecourt's censure was the university rather than the Cistercian order. First, Apologia 1 was not addressed to Mirecourt's religious superiors as one would have expected in a case handled within his own order, but to the Franciscan Pastor de Serrescuderio. This stands in marked contrast to the cases of, for instance, Durand of St. Pourçain and the Franciscan Peter Olivi. Second, we are fortunate enough to possess the introductory statement of the official promulgation of Mirecourt's condemnation.[52] From this document it appears that the chancellor Robert de Bardis and the regent masters in theology were concerned that bachelors of theology would disseminate Mirecourt's erroneous views, and hence forbade them to do so under the penalty of forgoing their academic honors. In contradistinction to the condemned views of Durand of St. Pourçain and Peter Olivi, those of John of Mirecourt were included in the *Collectio errorum*. On these grounds I conclude that the University of Paris, rather than the Cistercian order, was the institutional context of the process against Mirecourt.

Yet the inquiry against Mirecourt was no regular disciplinary proceed-

ing at the university level. This can be inferred from the involvement of
Pastor de Serrescuderio, the addressee of Apologia 1. William Courtenay
has conjectured that Serrescuderio's role was identical to the role the Cistercian Cardinal William Curti played in the proceedings against Autrecourt.[53]
In other words, Serrescuderio acted as judge in the Mirecourt case. This
suggestion certainly explains why Mirecourt addressed his first defense to
him and not to the chancellor or the bishop of Paris. It finds support in a
remark by Stephen Gaudet, a fourteenth-century scholar of the College of
Sorbonne who possessed copies of Autrecourt's *Letters* and condemnation.
He observed that some academics such as Autrecourt, Mirecourt, and
Foullechat had been condemned by cardinals especially entrusted with the
conduct of the investigations.[54] In Mirecourt's case, Gaudet may well have
been thinking of Pastor de Serrescuderio, who was bishop of Embrun and
who was made a cardinal in 1350.[55]

But why would Serrescuderio have become involved in the proceedings against Mirecourt, proceedings that were probably initiated at the
University of Paris, that concerned university teaching, and that resulted
in a formal prohibition of the uncovered errors by the chancellor and the
theologians? The only explanation that comes to mind is that the Apostolic See had appointed Serrescuderio as delegate judge and had commissioned the Mirecourt case to him. In this respect, the inquiry against Mirecourt was, indeed, not different from the proceedings against Autrecourt,
Foullechat, and Monzón, which were also eventually handled by papal
delegate judges. This case was different, however, in that it was not conducted in Avignon, but saw the pope avail himself instead of a local delegate
judge, a high-ranking official who would not impair the judicial authority
of the bishop of Paris.[56] At the time of the inquiry against Mirecourt, Pastor
de Serrescuderio was resident in Paris as papal nuncio for another matter.[57]
Unfortunately, the evidence that has survived does not reveal why the
Mirecourt case was delated to the papal court. Two obvious reasons might
be that Mirecourt had appealed directly to the pope, thereby passing over
the intermediate episcopal court, or that the pope had directly assumed his
jurisdiction in the Mirecourt case, thereby passing over the episcopal instance and the chancellor. Both scenarios had precedents in the proceedings
against Foullechat and Autrecourt, respectively.

The documentation of the process against Mirecourt is particularly
significant for the view it gives of the *modus operandi* of the committee
that evaluated Mirecourt and of the strategy and effectiveness of Mirecourt's defense.[58] The following three schemes present the results of a

close comparison between the propositions in Apologia 1 and 2, taking also into account their locations in Mirecourt's commentary on the *Sentences*. Scheme 1 represents the correspondence between the propositions of Apologia 2 and 1. It demonstrates that while many propositions from Apologia 2 are identical to those of Apologia 1, several were dropped and others were added. The propositions 2–8, 10–17, 23–28, 30–33, 41, 45, 46, 48–58, and 61–63 were removed from the first list of sixty-three. The propositions 4, 8, 9, 13, 14, 19, 20, 29, 32–36, 40, and 41 of Apologia 2 were added; they did not appear on the first list of sixty-three propositions.

SCHEME 1

Apologia 2	Apologia 1	locus
1	1	I q. 38 c. 1 ad 1
2	29	I q. 37 c. 2 ad 5
3	9	I q. 39 c. 2 ad 1 nr. 2
4	—	I q. 40 c. 2 ad 3
5	18	I q. 40 not. 1 correl. 6
6	19	I q. 40 not. 4 correl. 4
7	20	I q. 40 c. 1 (+ c. 1 prob. 3)
8	—	I q. 40 c. 1prob. 3
9	—	I q. 40 c. 1 prob 4
10	21	I q. 40 c. 2
11	22	I q. 40 c. 3
12	29 (partially)	I q. 37 c. 2 ad 5
13	—	I q. 37 c. 4 ad1
14	—	II q. 17 c. 1 ad 1
15	34	II q. 17 c. 1 ad 1prop. 4
16	35	II q. 22 c. 1 ad 1 prop. 12
17	35	II q. 22 c. 1 ad 1 prop. 14
18	35	II q. 22 c. 1 ad1 prop. 13
19	—	II q. 22 c. 1 ad 1 prop. 15
20	—	II q. 22 c. 1 ad 1 prop. 16
21	36	II q. 23 c. 4
22	37	II q. 23 c. 3
23	38	II q. 23 c. 1
24	39	II q. 23 c. 1 ad. ad inst. 2
25	40 (partially)	I q. 18 c. 6 ad 4
26	42	I q. 19 c. 6

Scheme 1 (*cont.*)

Apologia 2	Apologia 1	locus
27	43	I q. 19 c. 6 ad 5
28	44 (partially)	I q. 21 c. 3
29	—	I q. 19
30	47	II q. 2 c. 3
31	47	II q. 2 c. 3
32	—	II q. 2 c. 3
33	—	II q. 2 c. 3 prob. 2
34	—	II q. 2 c. 3 prob. 2
35	—	II q. 2 c. 3 prob. 4
36	—	II. q. 2 c. 3 prob. 5
37	59 (partially)	II q. 4 c. 1 dub. 3 prop. 1 ad 1 no. 4
38	59 (partially)	II q. 4 c. 1 dub. 3 prop. 1 ad 1 no. 5
39	60 (partially)	III q. 3 c. 1
40	—	III q. 3 c. 7 corr. 1
41	—	III q. 3 c. 7 corr. 3

Scheme 2 groups the errors listed in Apologia 1 according to their order of appearance in Mirecourt's commentary on the *Sentences*. Scheme 3 does the same for the errors listed in Apologia 2.

Scheme 2

Group	Apologia 1	locus
I	prop. 1–23	I q. 38–40
II	prop. 24–33	I q. 37
III	prop. 34–39	II q. 17–23
IV	prop. 40–44	I q. 18–21
V	prop. 45–46	I q. 2 and 10
VI	prop. 47–59	II q. 2–4
VII	prop. 60–62	III q. 3–5
VIII	prop. 63	II q. 6

Scheme 3

Group	Apologia 2	locus
I	prop. 1–11 (not 2)	I q. 38–40
II	prop. 12–13	I q. 37

SCHEME 3 (*cont.*)

Group	Apologia 2	locus
III	prop. 14–24	II q. 17–23
IV	prop. 25–29	I q. 18–21
VI	prop. 30–38	II q. 2–4
VII	prop. 39–41	III q. 3

From Schemes 2 and 3 it emerges that those who reviewed Mirecourt's commentary on the *Sentences* were very methodical. The second list of forty-one propositions maintained the same order as the first list of sixty-three propositions. In other words, the systematic order of the original list of sixty-three propositions was not disturbed by the addition and removal of propositions that resulted in the second list of forty-one propositions. The only exception seems to be article 29 of the first list, which was inserted in group I in the second list as article 2, although it was derived from *Sent.* I q. 37 and therefore belonged to group II. Probably, the ordering of the different groups resulted from a division of labor, whereby each member of the commission received a few quires of Mirecourt's commentary on the *Sentences* for scrutiny.

Apologia 1 and 2 rely on different strategies of defense. The line of defense chosen in Apologia 1 falls within any of the following categories: reaffirmation, sophistication, denial, appeal to authority, or a combination of these. In almost half of the propositions on the first list of sixty-three, Mirecourt simply reaffirms his position with characteristic phrases such as "This appears to me to be a true conclusion" (5); "I believe that this is true" (7); "I have no doubt about this" (12); "It seems to me that this must be conceded" (24), or words to that effect. In about twenty-eight replies Mirecourt qualifies his position. These replies typically focus on Mirecourt's *modus loquendi* and hinge on a differentiation between the meanings of crucial terms. They are often introduced by phrases indicating *how* Mirecourt said or understood something. About ten replies rely on an appeal to authority, for instance to Godfrey of Fontaines (14) or Peter the Lombard (19, 20). More frequently, however, Mirecourt maintains that he is not deviating from the common view of the doctors (14, 36, 42, 46, 51, 59). The remaining five replies, finally, fall within the category of flat denial (2, 3, 4, 6, 62). "I have not said this," or "It is not in my lectures" are the characteristic expressions here.

It is interesting to note that all the propositions that Mirecourt denied having held were removed from the list. Although these theses did appear in his commentary, Mirecourt successfully claimed that they did not represent his own position but were taken from other parts of the argumentation. In all the other categories of defense, Mirecourt booked a success of slightly less than 50 percent in having suspect theses removed from the original list of sixty-three. Even when Mirecourt seemed to stubbornly reaffirm a suspect thesis, this line of defense was no less successful than when he qualified it or traced it to an authoritative source.

Apologia 2 relies on a different strategy of defense. Here, Mirecourt claims to present the "common senses" of the forty-one propositions.[59] In practice, he differentiates between two or more senses of each proposition, abjuring the false sense or confirming the true sense with simple statements such as "I did not mean this," "I did not have this sense," or "And this is what I understood." An interesting exception, however, is Mirecourt's reply to the censure of proposition 9. This proposition does not occur in the original list of sixty-three but was later added. It is the only proposition in the second defense of which Mirecourt maintained that he had never said or written it: that it could occur in his quires was due either to an error of the copyists or to his own inadvertency.[60]

In 1364 the theologian Hugolin of Orvieto, who was involved in founding the theological faculty at Bologna, reproduced a list of fifty prohibited articles in its statutes, "lest they infect our University of Bologna."[61] Among them were forty articles of Mirecourt's censure in a rearranged order. Article 23 from Mirecourt's list was somehow removed from Hugolin's list. Probably, the reduction from forty-one to forty articles goes back to a defective medieval copy of the censured views that Hugolin consulted.[62] He indicates that he is familiar with three lists of articles, contained in the records of the Parisian faculty of theology, of which he only reproduces the second and third in the Bologna statute.[63] One of these lists, obviously, was drawn up for Mirecourt's censure. The origin of the other list is unknown.[64]

What happened to Mirecourt after he had delivered his defense? Even though the verdict and penalties against Mirecourt are not documented, it is certain that his views were censured. As I mentioned above, the list of forty-one theses on which Mirecourt based his second reply was included in the *Collectio errorum*. The prefatory statement that accompanies Mirecourt's list declares that some of the articles were judged erroneous, whereas others were considered suspect and ill-sounding.[65] There are no records of Mirecourt's recantation, nor of his life afterward. As a consequence, it is not possible to establish what effects the censure had on his academic and ecclesiastical career, unless one concludes that precisely this abrupt break in the information about his career attests to the effects that the censure had on Mirecourt's professional life.[66]

Conclusion

If one reviews the teachings of Autrecourt and Mirecourt that were censured, it is hard to understand why they evoked the wrath of the authorities. One might even be tempted to conclude that these two scholars became victims of the competitive trade of teaching at the University of Paris. In neither condemnation were there views at issue that seemed harmful to faith. Possibly, the inquiries against Autrecourt and Mirecourt were unduly influenced by human factors that probably played a role in any proceedings against false teaching, namely envy and incompetence. Interestingly, two late medieval theologians have made quite unique remarks. Pierre d'Ailly observed that many of Autrecourt's views were condemned out of envy, but were later publicly taught in the schools.[67] The most cynical critic of the role of such human motives in censuring academics was the Cistercian Peter of Ceffons, who lectured on the *Sentences* at Paris in 1348–49. He claimed to have witnessed profound subtlety examined by ignorant peasants and silenced as error by a judge into whose head "subtlety would have entered as easily as a fully loaded elephant could get through a finger ring." He even suggested that some would condemn all opinions unless they had already been uttered by Jerome or Augustine. Moreover, Ceffons rejected papal commissions of theological experts as nitpickers who thought they had labored in vain if they did not find fault.[68] It is not clear whether Ceffons had in mind Autrecourt's censure or that of his fellow Cistercian Mirecourt, but these words were written down with sharp memories of both. In any case, these observations make one aware that academic censures could be motivated by other than purely intellectual or religious concerns.

5

Academic Freedom and Teaching Authority

To the modern mind the disciplinary and juridical proceedings for censuring suspect teaching seem to be the most glaring signs of constraints imposed upon academic freedom.[1] The condemnations seemed to hinder medieval academics in their pursuit of intellectual investigation and in putting forward its results in public. But is the concept of "academic freedom" really adequate in interpreting these cases of censure, or would it be more fitting to approach the phenomenon of academic condemnations from the opposite direction and identify them as manifestations of teaching authority, justified by intellectual and pastoral concerns?

Academic Freedom

Viewing academic censure from the perspective of the limitation of academic freedom has an inherent attractiveness for moderns. But it also raises a number of questions. Was there, for instance, any room at the medieval university for freedom of thought and teaching? How should one rate the interior dimension of academic freedom, that is, the inner limits on scholarly inquiry caused by the acceptance of revelation as the unquestionable standard for any intellectual activities?[2] And most important, does the notion of academic freedom apply at all in the medieval context?

Although the disciplinary procedures leave the impression that medieval academics were continuously steering their way between the Scylla of self-constraint upon intellectual freedom and the Charybdis of charges of heresy, one has to remain sensitive to the danger of anachronism. After all, the modern conception of academic freedom was a creation of nineteenth-century Germany.[3] It was founded on the following three principles: freedom of learning for students, freedom to teach, and institutional freedom for the university.[4] At the medieval university, however, freedom of learning had always been negligible. The university statutes bound the students to a canon of compulsory textbooks. Furthermore, the student was required by oath to spend a set time on a specific subject, to attend various lectures, and to participate in exercises such as disputations. The whole curriculum that prepared the medieval student for his academic degree was regulated in detail and was never questioned.[5] Similarly, freedom of thought and expression did not lie heavily on the minds of medieval academics. In none of the disciplinary and juridical proceedings I have studied did academics whose doctrine came under investigation plead for academic freedom in this sense.[6] Only the freedom of the university to manage its own affairs was ever explicitly discussed in medieval documents. As Peter Classen has shown in a penetrating study, it was this freedom of the *universitas*, of the corporation of masters and students to manage its own affairs, laid down in privileges granted by, for instance, king or pope, that was labeled *libertas scholastica* in the medieval records.[7]

In sum, then, the medieval concept of academic freedom was much narrower than ours. It neither comprised the freedom of learning for students nor the freedom to teach, but was based only on the principle of the freedom of the academic institution to manage its own affairs. Moreover, the very idea that academic freedom was absolutely essential to a university was alien to the Middle Ages. A medieval university was, of course, totally different from its nineteenth-century German name-sake, as an institution, in terms both of the professional identity of the academics it produced and of the assumptions about the purpose of scholarly inquiry. For these reasons, the concept of academic freedom is of limited use in explaining the phenomenon of academic censure.

This is not to say, however, that it is totally useless. Although explicit discussions of the limits of academic freedom in the sense of freedom of teaching are hard to find in medieval authors, the following two deserve to be cited as pertinent exceptions. The first discussion appears in *Quodlibet* VII by Godfrey of Fontaines, which was held in 1290/91 or 1291/92. Godfrey was regent master in the theological faculty from 1285 until approximately 1298. He studied theology under Servais (Gervais) of Mt. St. Elias and Henry of Ghent, whose colleague he later became. As has been mentioned in Chapter 2, Godfrey's student days coincided with the activities of Siger of Brabant, Thomas Aquinas, and Bishop Tempier's censure. His most important contribution to medieval philosophy and theology are his so-called quodlibetal questions, public disputes that were held twice a year, before Easter and before Christmas, and that were attended by masters, bachelors, and students alike. During the quodlibet, anyone from the audience could ask a question about any topic to the master who conducted the session. Godfrey's *Quodlibets*, fifteen in total, were the final written solutions to the questions that had been directed to him during the solemn quodlibetal disputes.[8] Question 18 of this *Quodlibet* deals with the problem of whether a master of theology may contradict an article that has been condemned by a bishop, if he believes that the opposite is true.[9] Godfrey defends the thesis that a theologian should insist that a "wrong" condemnation — such as the condemnation of 1277 by Bishop Tempier — ought to be revoked. In his discussion Godfrey introduces an important distinction between truths that are necessary for salvation and truths that are neutral to faith, in the sense that they neither directly nor indirectly oppose faith or morals. Regarding the first category of truths, those that concern salvation, Godfrey states that a theologian should not comply with a condemnation he believes to be incorrect. If the theologian on the basis of Scripture or reason is certain of the truth of an opinion, the condemnation is unjustified and he should not feel bound by it. In that case, the theologian should speak out, even if certain people are shocked by his disobedience.[10] When it comes to indifferent truths whose condemnation is unjustified, however, the theologian should restrain himself, in particular as long as he remains within the prelate's jurisdiction (*in loco in quo praelatus habet iurisdictionem*). Since salvation is not at stake, it is not really worthwhile, according to Godfrey, to break the relation of obedience to the prelate. The theologian should, however, insist that the condemnation be revoked. One of the reasons Godfrey gives is that the condemnation prevents people from freely discussing (*libere tractare*) those truths that may perfect their rational faculties.[11] Interestingly, this theme recurs in Stephen of Bourret's 1325 revocation of Tempier's condemnation. He annulled those articles of Tempier's syllabus that concerned or were supposed to concern Thomas Aquinas henceforth, "leaving them freely to be discussed in the schools."[12]

Godfrey's statements, however, should not be misunderstood. From the context it is clear that he is not insisting on the academic's freedom of inquiry and expression, but on the idea of the pursuit of truth. The impediment to "the inquiry into and knowledge of the truth" (*inquisitio et notitia veritatis*) that is caused by a wrong condemnation only worries Godfrey with regard to subjects that concern faith. In other words, he too believes that academic discussion should not transgress the boundaries of faith.

The second discussion that touches upon the freedom of thought also hinges on the distinction between truths that are pertinent to faith and truths that are "indifferent." It is taken from the *Reprobation* by Hervaeus Natalis of Durand's *Excusation*, already mentioned above.[13] While assessing the value of Durand's defense against the accusations of false teaching brought against him, Hervaeus inserts a passage about the theologian's freedom of teaching. He observes that during a disputation theologians can be confronted with three types of theses (*articuli*): those that have already been decided on the authority of Sacred Scripture or the church; those that have not yet been explicitly decided, but for which there is a preferred solution on the basis of the doctrines of the doctors and the saints; and finally those theses whose discussion is not predetermined by any authoritative statements. When theologians encounter theses of the first kind during a disputation, they may not answer by merely reciting alternative opinions, let alone hold the opposite of such a thesis. What they should do, according to Hervaeus, is assert the determination that has been given on the authority of the Bible and ecclesiastical authority. If theologians merely give a neutral survey of possible solutions to doctrinal problems that have already been explicitly decided, they are suspect, and if they contradict these decisions, they are heretical. If theologians run into theses of the second type, that is, those that concern faith, but for which ecclesiastical authority has not yet explicitly formulated a conclusion, it is safe for them to go along with the common doctrine. It may seem presumptuous, according to Hervaeus, not to do so and to prefer one's own intellect. For theses of the third kind it really makes no difference whether one solution or its opposite is defended. No matter which side is taken by the theologian, it will not be in the way of the authority of Sacred Scripture, the church, or any good doctrine. Godfrey's and Hervaeus's discussions illustrate that the field for free intellectual discussion was restricted for those subjects that were related to faith. All issues that were either explicitly or implicitly connected to faith had to be discussed *salva fide*, that is, with Catholic dogma unharmed. And this presupposition was never questioned by any medieval scholar.

Teaching Authority at the University of Paris

The discussions of Godfrey of Fontaines and Hervaeus Natalis elucidate an important aspect of the medieval concept of intellectual freedom. The theologian dedicated to the discovery of truth without hindrance took into account supernatural revelation as well, because it was part of that truth. In other words, since revelation was generally accepted as infallible truth, the boundaries this precommitment set on academic inquiry were not felt as constraints. Propositions were censured precisely because they were contrary to faith, that is, contrary to truth. The belief that it is impossible to give a valid proof of what is contrary to the truth justified disciplinary proceedings against false teachers. False teaching was even more reprehensible if it concerned not only philosophical truths intimately linked with revelation, but even the so-called truths of faith themselves. Such teaching was a hindrance not only to discovering the truth but also to reaching salvation and had to be suppressed. When seen from this perspective, university censures appear as manifestations of teaching authority, of doctrinal supervision exercised by the masters over their own *universitas*, for the sake of truth and salvation. This teaching authority or *magisterium* at the university must now first be situated in its larger context, that of the *magisterium* of the ecclesiastical hierarchy.

From the beginning of the thirteenth century, theologians played a special role in the church. Their new position was defined by the fact that they were members of the academic community who possessed a body of specialized knowledge that was critical to fulfilling the main purpose of the church: to guide people to heaven through expounding and defending revelation. When around 1200 the University of Paris gradually emerged, its appearance marked the birth of the *studium* as a new social order alongside *regnum* and *sacerdotium*, the powers of kingship and priesthood.[14] The university gave institutional expression to the self-confidence of the corporation of masters at Paris.[15] The appearance of the *universitas* or guild of masters could not have taken place without the prior development of a common professional identity. Various suggestions have been made as to what motivated the scholars to form a guild. Was it a shared love of knowledge, or was it desire for praise and money? Although these motives must have played some role, a more satisfactory view on what may have induced scholars to assemble together into a corporation has been advanced by Stephen Ferruolo. He claims that those who formed the university defined their professional identity first and foremost in terms of their duties and responsibilities as teachers.[16] As Ferruolo points out, the first statutes of the University of Paris were primarily concerned with what should be taught, how, when, and by whom.[17]

To Ferruolo's evidence can be added the results of a lexicographical and historical study of the term "master" (*magister*) which was carried out by

Yves Congar.[18] A consequence of the rise of the university was, according to Congar, that teaching Sacred Scripture and preaching no longer exclusively belonged to the office (*officium*) of the bishops. At the opening of the thirteenth century a new group of professionals developed, the university masters, who after successful graduation were licensed "to read, dispute, deliberate and teach." When the exposition of Scripture became an increasingly complicated and technical affair, this group gained in importance. Simultaneously with the development of the university as an institution, theology emerged as a science.[19] It was no longer obvious that by the term *ordo doctorum*, the order of doctors, the bishops were meant, as had been the case since Gregory the Great. Now, it could also mean the doctors or masters of theology, in the sense of persons who had the function and the authority to teach.[20]

In other words, in addition to the Apostolic teaching of the bishops, there was the scientific teaching of the theologians. From the thirteenth century onwards, they were the professional interpreters of Scripture. Moreover, they defended the faith against unbelievers, and they trained those who exercised pastoral care.[21] The teaching of the bishops, however, was of a different order than that of the theologians. It was based upon a different source of power.

The power of the theologian was vested in his expertise manifested in an academic degree.[22] The power of the prelate, on the other hand, resided in his office. As a matter of fact, his power consisted of two separate, but integrally connected elements: sacramental power and power of jurisdiction. Bishops "possessed" sacerdotal power, received through ordination and granted by God (*ex spiritu*). Those receiving the orders were only instruments to continue Christ's work on earth. In addition, bishops possessed the power of jurisdiction, that is, the jurisdiction to rule the church. This power was received by delegation from Christ through Peter and the other Apostles and it came with the ecclesiastical office (*ex officio*). In the ecclesiastical hierarchy, the pope held the highest office. The lesser ranks, that is, the bishops and presbyters, received their authority by delegation from the pope.[23] Theologians *qua* theologians lacked the priestly powers of teaching, sanctifying, and ruling.[24]

The relationship between the power of expertise and the power of authority was most succinctly expressed in the writings of the canonists.[25] They elaborated upon the theme of the two keys, each representing a different type of power, which Gratian had incorporated in Distinction 20 of the *Decretum* in the context of a discussion over the difference between theological interpretations and judicial decisions. Basing himself upon an idea that had already become the received view by the middle of the twelfth century, Gratian maintained that Christ had given two keys to Peter, a key of knowledge (*clavis scientiae*) and a key of power (*clavis potestatis*). The expositors of divine Scripture, that is, church fathers such as Jerome and Augustine, but also theologians, merely possessed the key of knowledge. The prelates, however, possessed the key of power. Gratian and canonists after him suggested that theologians might possess the gift of knowledge to a greater degree than the prelates, the pope included. In deciding cases, however, "they [that is, the expositors of Sacred Scripture] deserve to be placed after them [that is, the pontiffs]." On the basis of Distinction 20 of the *Decretum*, the decretists attributed to the pope *qua* pope a special authority in matters of faith. The responsibility for supervising doctrinal thought in the church taken as the community of believers fell to the bishops, and in particular to the bishop of Rome. In their task of authoritatively preserving, judging, and explaining the Christian doctrine, the prelates benefited from the service of the theologians. The theologians were publicly recognized as valuable consultants in everything that concerned "faith and morals." But it was the ecclesiastical authorities who indicated the doctrinal limits within which the doctors of theology exercised their expertise in explaining and explicating faith. As Stephen of Bourret, bishop of Paris, remarked almost in passing in a letter dealing with the rehabilitation of Thomas Aquinas in 1325: he and the doctors of theology had to await what the Holy Roman Church decreed, "the Holy Roman Church, the mother and master (*magistra*) of all the faithful, to whom pertains, as the universal rule of catholic truth, the approval or reproval of doctrines, the solution of dubious points, the determination of which opinions should be held, and the silencing of errors."[26]

In conclusion, theologians, like other Christians, had to defer to the legitimate church authorities in matters of faith and to observe its constitutions and decrees. Their theological expertise and academic degrees notwithstanding, they too operated under the jurisdiction of ecclesiastical authorities, under the *magisterium* of the ecclesiastical hierarchy.[27] Yet, as academics, theologians too possessed a *magisterium*, even though it was of a different nature. The theologians possessed the teaching authority of their professional competence, which they made available to the *magisterium* of the ecclesiastical hierarchy. It was this professional authority that theologians employed within their own community, the *universitas*, to suppress false teaching. When Foullechat recanted, he nicely captured both types of teaching authority by solemnly declaring that he was the humble son of both the church and the faculty of theology in Paris (*tamquam ecclesie et dicte facultatis theologie humilis filius*).[28]

Occasionally, however, debates arose over the distribution of teaching authority. Particularly interesting contributions to these debates were made by Servais of Mt. St. Elias, Godfrey of Fontaines, William Ockham, and Pierre d'Ailly. The first three theologians expressed their views on episcopal authority in doctrinal matters and its relation to the teaching authority of theologians in the context of Tempier's censure of 1277 and similar examples of episcopal censure. Pierre d'Ailly vented his thoughts on the teaching authority of bishops and theologians in the context of the Monzón affair. Although some of the texts to be discussed shortly are well known, they have not previously been presented from the point of view adopted here.[29]

SERVAIS OF MT. ST. ELIAS ON EPISCOPAL TEACHING AUTHORITY

In *Quodlibet* VI, q.61, which originated sometime between 1287 and 1291, Servais of Mt. St. Elias offered his views on a prelate's authority in doctrinal matters. The question adressed to him was "whether, if an archbishop or bishop has illicitly condemned certain articles, their successor is bound to revoke them."[30] Although there is no reference to any historical event, it seems plausible that behind the problem lurk the condemnations issued by Bishop Tempier and Bishop Kilwardby in 1277, or those by Archbishop John Pecham in 1284 and 1286 at the University of Oxford.[31] Servais's treatment of the actual question is very brief. He merely refers to Gratian's *Decretum* I, dist. 80, c.12, which mentions that archbishops, not bishops, have to deal with matters that concern faith.[32] Hence it is not a bishop's successor, but his superior, the archbishop, who has to revoke a bishop's illicit condemnation. Servais's own view, however, is that a bishop, or even his successor, may reverse a bishop's erroneous condemnation. He resolves the apparent contradiction between his own view and Gratian's *Decretum* with the help of the *Glossa Ordinaria*, which provides the following explanation of the crucial passage about episcopal involvement in matters of faith (*agitare in fide*): Gratian was not claiming that primates had to deal with matters that pertained to faith, but that they had to deal with certain matters in a faithful way.[33]

In the remainder of Question 61, Servais provides a careful analysis of the different types of articles and statutes that a bishop may issue. His reasoning has a canonistic orientation. By way of introduction Servais discusses in what way a condemnation can be said to be erroneous. According to Servais, a condemnation can be erroneous either because of a legal error (*error iuris*) or because of a factual error (*error facti*). If a sentence is based upon a legal error, it is null and void. If, on the other hand, a condemnation contains factual errors, it needs to be revoked. This can be done either by the prelate who issued the condemnation or by his successor. This view, however, raises interesting questions concerning a prelate's authority to issue statutes in his diocese. It is in discussing these questions that Servais touches the topic of the teaching authority of a bishop.

According to Servais a bishop has the jurisdiction to issue statutes in his diocese concerning what has to be said and done.[34] In the sequel, this doctrinal authority is further analyzed. Servais takes the stance that a bishop may not define new truths of faith. Only the pope has the jurisdiction to define a position that is still disputed among scholars as an article of faith, in the sense that rejection of it would be a heresy.[35] A bishop, however, has the authority to condemn *persons* of whom it has been established that they have acted against the articles of faith and are hence heretics. This authority is, according to Servais, based upon the decretals *Ad abolendam* (1184) and *Excommunicamus* (1231), which both state, among other things, that it belongs to the responsibility of bishops to pursue the investigation of heretics within their diocese.[36] In addition, Servais acknowledges that a bishop has the power to qualify statements, not as heretical, but as erroneous (*eronee*) on the advice of the doctors (*de consilio doctorum*). Such statements are not in direct contradiction to the truths of faith, but are in some other way dangerous to faith in that they can lead persons astray. The bishop's jurisdiction in this matter is also substantiated by a reference to *Excommunicamus*. A bishop is obliged by the pope's mandate to seek out those who are accused of being heretics or those who in their lifestyle and morals are dissenting from the community of believers.

Servais adduces three more arguments for why it is reasonable that it belongs to a bishop's authority to assess statements as being erroneous. First, it seems customary, and bishops have not been punished by the pope for this kind of doctrinal action. Second, it is not explicitly forbidden, and hence it is allowed, that a bishop condemn doctrinal positions as erroneous. Third, declaring that a view is false is not as important as defining it as a truth of faith. The latter task is reserved for the pope, whereas the former, easier task may be performed by a bishop.

Thus, in Servais's view only the pope has supreme teaching authority. In support of his position, Servais adduces two crucial passages from Gratian's *Decretum*, namely C.16 q.1 c.52 ("Frater noster"), and C.24 q.1 c.12 ("Quotiens").[37] Both passages make the point that only the pope has the authority to decide over matters of faith. Bishops have a more limited doctrinal authority. Assisted by the theologians, they may condemn opinions as erroneous, though not as heretical, and they may, and even must, prosecute persons who have already been judged heretics.

In conclusion, it appears that Servais attributes to a bishop a qualified doctrinal authority. He may condemn manifest and explicit heresies that have already been condemned by the papacy, but he may not condemn implicit heresies. Bishops only possess the judicial authority to censure teaching as erroneous, not as heretical, and their doctrinal determinations may be reversed by a successor.

GODFREY OF FONTAINES ON EPISCOPAL TEACHING AUTHORITY

The issue of episcopal teaching authority was also raised by Godfrey of Fontaines, in a context that is very similar to that in which Servais of Mt. St. Elias expressed his views. Question 5 of *Quodlibet* XII, which was held in 1296 or 1297, addresses the problem of whether the bishop of Paris is in sin if he fails to restore certain articles that were condemned by his predecessor.[38] The question is clearly inspired by the historical events of 1277 and by Godfrey's conviction that the condemnation of certain articles by Tempier was "incomprehensible, untrue, and impossible." It is important to note that the articles that Godfrey has in mind are all *absque periculo fidei et morum*, that is, they do not harm faith and morals, and that his discussion is thus only partially paralleled by that in Question 18 of *Quodlibet* VII.

The entire Question 5 is devoted to proving that Tempier's condemnation deserves to be corrected. The line of reasoning is as follows. Godfrey indicates three general conditions under which erroneous condemnations of truths that do not harm man's salvation ought to be corrected, and he subsequently proves that all three conditions apply to Tempier's case. He first demonstrates that Tempier's condemnation is an impediment to the progress of students. Many of Tempier's articles concern issues on which various opinions can be held. By a priori excluding certain views, the scholarly disputation (*disputatio*) as a method of investigating the truth becomes pointless. Scholars are bound to adhere to one particular solution, to the exclusion of other plausible solutions, and in this way their intellectual development is severely hampered. Second, Godfrey claims that Tempier's condemnation causes scandal (*scandalum*), both among doctors and students. The reason is that some of Tempier's articles appear irrational if taken at the face value of their wording (*superficies litterae sicut iacet*), and hence need further explanation.[39] Those, however, who are less well versed in the techniques of interpretation may think that heresies are being disseminated, when in reality they are not, and they may go to the bishop or the chancellor to complain. This in turn may cause turmoil and produce sects, even among the students.[40] Finally, Godfrey finds Tempier's condemnation to be at the expense of the students of the very useful doctrine of Thomas Aquinas. Due to its condemnation, Aquinas's doctrine has become controversial, and this may lead many to turn away from it. According to Godfrey, this is not only unfair to Thomas's doctrine but will also harm the students, for Thomas is "the salt of the earth," and when his doctrine is taken away, the students will find the doctrines of others without much taste.[41]

At the very end of his argument, Godfrey discusses an important objection against reversing Tempier's condemnation. Since Tempier's list of articles was issued with the agreement of the learned (*de consensu sapientium*), a recantation does not seem necessary at all. In his attempt to refute this counterargument, Godfrey introduces some psychological considerations derived from Aristotle's *Ethics*.[42] It is true, he admits, that the articles were published by wise men. But still, these articles *now* seem to be in need of correction. At the time when the condemnation was issued, the learned took the right action, because *at that time* many of the faculty of arts manifested themselves as unbridled chatterers concerning certain subjects, and their statements seemed to deviate beyond measure into errors. Hence, in order to drag them away from their errors and bring them back on the right track, they had to be turned to the contrary extreme, and this was precisely the purpose of Tempier's condemnation. Since, however, the (intermediate) state of truth has *now*, in Godfrey's time, twenty years after Tempier's intervention, been reached, this condemnation should *now* be reversed.

In sum, it appears that the two reasons that Godfrey had already given in *Quodlibet* VII as to why a doctor should try to achieve the revocation of a prelate's erroneous doctrinal decision return in *Quodlibet* XII. Here, too, Godfrey argues that wrong condemnations ought to be opposed by doctors and revoked by prelates because they impede students in their search for knowledge and because they give rise to scandal. In addition, Godfrey presents in *Quodlibet* XII an apology for Aquinas, whose doctrine "seems to be the most useful and praiseworthy among all, with the exception of those of the Saints and of some writers who are considered authorities (*auctoritates*)."

WILLIAM OCKHAM ON EPISCOPAL TEACHING AUTHORITY

The two most important writings for an understanding of Ockham's views on the teaching authority of bishops and theologians and their mutual relations are the *Tractatus de corpore Christi* and the first part of the *Dialogus*. The two works represent two different stages of Ockham's scholarly career: before and after his flight from Avignon in 1328. During the period 1317–24, when resident at Oxford and at the Franciscan convent in London, Ockham wrote his extensive oeuvre in philosophy and theology to which the *Tractatus* belongs. Certain works were finished during Ockham's sojourn at Avignon. After his flight from the papal court, Ockham sought the protection of Louis of Bavaria and devoted his time to writing his political and polemical works, such as the *Dialogus*, at his court in Munich. His departure to the Continent probably was the reason why Ockham never completed his master's degree at Oxford and instead became the "Venerable Inceptor" for the rest of his life.[43]

Written shortly after 1324, the *Tractatus* is cast in the scholastic form so typical of Ockham's earlier philosophical and theological writings. In this work Ockham discusses the presence of the body of Christ during the Eucharist.[44] Because his theory deviated from the common fourteenth-century scholarly opinion on the subject, Ockham probably thought it necessary to include a chapter proving that his theory of transubstantiation was not heretical.[45] He observed that no theologian of reputation found his theory heretical, stating that even if one of them should do so, no attention should be paid to his opinion. According to Ockham, it solely belongs to the Roman Church (*Romana ecclesia*), represented by the pope, to decide over matters of faith.[46] This doctrine Ockham deduced from Gratian's *Decretum*, C.24 q.1 c.12 ("Quotiens"), where it is stated that the Holy See is the supreme authority to which all doctrinal decisions are to be referred.[47] The same view is expressed, and quoted by Ockham, in C.26 q.1 c.52 ("Frater noster").[48]

Gratian's and Ockham's view that only the pope has the authority to decide on doctrinal matters, however, seemed to be contradicted by the decretal *Ad abolendam* and by *Decretum* I, dist. 80 c.2. In confronting and reconciling these apparently conflicting texts Ockham is exploiting the

Glossa Ordinaria on C.24 q.1 c.12, as he himself indicates. According to Ockham, the decretal *Ad abolendam* signifies that a bishop may solely investigate (*inquirere*) persons who have maintained something that is manifestly (*manifeste*) heretical, and may condemn them after they have confessed or have been convicted. Bishops may not decide (*terminare*) doctrinal disputes, but may only prosecute overt heretics.[49] The apparent contradiction between C.24 q.1 c.12 and I, dist. 80 c.2 is resolved in the *Glossa Ordinaria* by a specific interpretation of the expression "intervening in faith," which is adopted by Ockham, as it had been by Servais of Mt. St. Elias, as I indicated earlier.[50]

Ockham concludes from this canonistic dialectic that it is absurd to have inquisitors, "who are not very learned persons," decide difficult and complicated theological matters and condemn a famous theologian (such as Ockham himself) if he happens to defend a position that is not conso-nant with that of the inquisitor.[51] Like Servais of Mt. St. Elias, Ockham believes that the decretal *Ad abolendam* is concerned with heretics, that is, *persons*, and does not provide any basis for the view that prelates other than the pope should judge the heretical nature of *opinions*.[52] The moment when a question addresses matters of faith that are not explicitly stated in Scrip-ture or that have not yet been determined by the Roman Church, recourse has to be taken to the pope.[53] But as long as writings in which certain views are expressed have not yet been authenticated by the Roman Church, any-one is free to take issue with these views.[54] According to Ockham, however, this point is ill understood by his contemporaries, who wish to be the only ones called "rabbi," and hence, out of envy and because they lack argu-ments, condemn any opinion that dissents from their own dogmas as dan-gerous and heretical.[55]

The other principal work in which Ockham expresses his ideas on the teaching authority of bishops and in which he also explicitly discusses Tem-pier's condemnation is the first part of the *Dialogus*, finished around 1334.[56] It was composed in the form of a dialogue between a master (*Magister*) and a pupil (*Discipulus*). The Master pretends not to take any position concern-ing the problem at hand, but just to offer a whole range of possible solu-tions to the pupil, and this style of writing makes it not always easy to establish Ockham's own position.[57] Ockham chose this particular literary form in order to hide his identity, but soon after the appearance of the first volume of the *Dialogus* everyone knew its author.[58]

The first part of the *Dialogus* was written under specific historical cir-cumstances that strongly influenced its tone and content. The point of departure of the work is Ockham's conviction that the current pope, John XXII, was a heretic, given his views both on Evangelical Poverty and on the Beatific Vision.[59] The purpose of the *Dialogus* is to provide a theoretical framework for the deposition of a heretical pope. In the seven books that make up the first part of this work, Ockham treats questions such as: To whom belongs the determination of catholic truths, the theologians or the canonists?[60] Which truths are truths of faith? Can there be error in establishing the truths of faith? What are heresies? How does one recognize heretics? Can anyone, including the pope, the college of cardinals, a general council, or even all the clergy, become heretical? How should heretics be punished? What action can be taken against a heretical pope and his followers?[61] In brief, Ockham's attempt to bring about the downfall of the "pseudo-pope" John XXII made him reconsider the notions of heresy and faith and develop an alternative ecclesiology, a new view on the structure of the church.

It is within this larger context that Ockham presents his views on episcopal teaching authority.[62] These views are basically the same as the one formulated in the *Tractatus*. But, as we shall see, its consequences were to be more far-reaching. As in the *Tractatus*, Ockham maintains in I *Dialogus* 2 that it is "totally unreasonable" (*irrationabile omnino*) for a bishop or an inquisitor, who is often inexpert in Sacred Scripture, to condemn the opinions of the doctors. According to Ockham, bishops and inquisitors may take juridical action only against those who are explicitly condemned of a heresy. The "implicit heretics" fall outside their jurisdiction. In this respect, Ockham holds the same view as Servais of Mt. St. Elias. His reasoning is based upon a distinction between explicit and implicit heresies and upon the interpretation of a number of canonistic sources.

Who are the disseminators of implicit heresies? In Ockham's view, the realm of implicit heresy is to be found in the world of the learned, the "modern doctors." Their contradictions of Scripture or of doctrines of the Universal Church can only be discovered by other learned men, on the basis of subtle reflections.[63] Their heresies are implicit, said Ockham, because they concern topics on which theologians hold contrary opinions. Since all parties involved assume that their particular view is substantiated by Scripture, and since only one of two contrary views can really be true, one view is implicitly condemned, while its opposite is implicitly approved.[64] In such cases where there are disagreements among the doctors, only the pope, a general council, or the Universal Church can decide which of the alternatives ought to be explicitly condemned as a heresy.[65] Neither a bishop, who is inferior to the pope, nor a commission, which is inferior to a general council or to the Universal Church, can condemn statements that have yet to be established as heretical.[66] In order to support his doctrine of the judicial authority of the pope in doctrinal disputes, Ockham exploits a number of canonistic texts. As a matter of fact, it is the same material that he had been using in the *Tractatus* and that had also been used by Servais of Mt. St. Elias, namely *Decretum* I dist. 80 c.2 and C.24, q.1, c.12 and the *Glossa Ordinaria* on these passages.[67]

Although Ockham pretends that his views are firmly rooted in the canonistic tradition, there are a few historical instances that seem to contradict his theory. On three occasions a bishop claimed for himself the right to decide doctrinal issues: Bishop Tempier in 1277 at the University of Paris, the Dominican Robert Kilwardby, archbishop of Canterbury, in 1277 at the University of Oxford, and the Franciscan John Pecham, also archbishop of Canterbury, who in 1284 renewed the theses of his predecessor at the University of Oxford and in 1286 condemned eight theses of the Dominican Richard Knapwell.[68] Here, I will be concerned only with Tempier's condemnation, attributed by Ockham to the University of Paris, "which has excommunicated and condemned as erroneous many opinions of many persons, and even of Thomas when he was still alive."[69] When confronted with this counterexample, the Master discusses four different solutions. In the first three solutions, the condemnation of 1277 is disqualified as being rash (*temerarius*).[70] It was rash, because there were many truths among the condemned articles. This point of view is, according to the Master, especially adopted by those who after the recantation of the condemnation of 1277 (by Bishop Stephen of Bourret on February 14, 1325, as indicated above) became followers of Thomas Aquinas.[71] Another group of scholars thinks that many articles were condemned rashly because it is not clear in what way they would contradict faith.[72] A third party describes the excommunication as rash because those who pronounced the excommunication (*excommunicantes*) lacked the power (*potestas*) to do so. They had usurped this power, and for this reason the condemnation of 1277 was rightly revoked.[73] According to the fourth solution discussed by the Master, the condemnation was a justified action: it is legitimate for a party inferior to the pope to act on papal authority and condemn a statement as heretical.[74] This solution, however, induces the Disciple to raise a problem. If a condemnation is revoked at a later stage — which happened in 1325 to Tempier's condemnation — the issuer of the erroneous condemnation would become a heretic. The Master replies that, of course, all depends upon the content of the condemned theses. If the condemned articles are really heretical and are afterward repudiated, the recanter is a heretic. If the condemned articles were catholic, the issuer of the condemnation is a heretic.[75] The Master's reply brings out the emphasis that Ockham places in his ecclesiology on the content of doctrines rather than on the authority of the body that pronounces them.

The theme of doctrinal authority returns in I *Dialogus* 4, albeit in a slightly different context. Here Ockham treats the question of who has the right to correct an erroneous person and what sort of correction should be regarded as legitimate and sufficient.[76] It is in this context that Ockham again discusses the hierarchical difference between prelates and theologians. According to Ockham, a prelate or someone else who has jurisdiction, or even any Christian, can be considered a legitimate corrector of an *errans*. However, correction by someone in authority is by rebuke and due punishment; by an ordinary Christian, by fraternal admonition.[77] Against this background, Ockham moves to the crucial question of whether the learned (*litterati*) have to recant their errors solely at the admonition of their prelates.[78] Ockham denies that they would be bound to give up their doctrinal position on the mere rebuke of an ecclesiatical superior. His argument hinges on what constitutes a *legitimate* correction and on what position the theologians in the church hold. Ockham considers a correction sufficient and legitimate if it is clearly shown (*aperte ostenditur*) to the person in error that his assertion is against Catholic *truth* in such a way that to the minds of those who understand he cannot by any evasion deny that his error indeed is incompatible with Catholic truth.[79] So, even if a doctor or an expositor of Scripture out of ignorance entertains an erroneous opinion, he does not have to yield to the prelate's correction unless it is clearly shown to him, for example with the help of Scriptural texts, that his errors conflict with orthodox truth. The reason is, according to Ockham, that theologians (*doctores*) surpass the prelates in knowledge. They have a special competence as expositors of the Bible.[80]

In order to substantiate this claim, Ockham alludes to Distinction 20 of Gratian's *Decretum*.[81] Ockham takes up two specific points by Gratian and incorporates them into his own argument. First, Gratian maintained that Church Fathers such as Jerome and Augustine, "more filled with the grace of the Holy Spirit," showed more learning and adhered more to reason than others, even pontiffs. Secondly, as has been noted before, in his explanation of the doctrine of the two keys that Peter had received from Christ, namely a "key of knowledge" and a "key of power," Gratian again seemed to suggest that the theologians (*divinarum scripturarum tractatores*) possessed the gift of knowledge in greater degree than the pontiffs, and hence had "to be preferred to the pontiffs" when it came to expounding Sacred Scripture. On the basis of these two passages, Ockham concludes "that in those matters which pertain to faith, the theologians (*doctores*) are to be preferred to the prelates, and unless they [the theologians] are corrected legitimately, in the way explained above, they are not held to recant their views, if these are erroneous."[82]

In what follows, Ockham develops his argument a bit further. The Disciple in the *Dialogus* raises an objection. He observes that Gratian in Distinction 20 was only referring to doctors approved by the church, such as the ancient Church Fathers Augustine, Jerome, Gregory, and Ambrose, and not to contemporary doctors.[83] The Master, however, who here reflects Ockham's own position, replies that Gratian is talking about "doctors" in a broad sense, just as he is talking about "pontiffs" in a broad sense. The purport of Distinction 20, according to the Master, is to make a general comparison between prelates and doctors with regard to their competence in matters that pertain to faith. As a matter of fact, so the Master continues, the term "doctor" in Gratian's text signifies anyone who is capable of explaining Divine Scripture in an understanding way, whether he be a master (*magister*) or a disciple (*discipulus*), for the latter often exceed the former in expertise.[84] In conclusion, Ockham maintains that the point Gratian is making in Distinction 20 also applies to contemporary learned persons, and that learned expositors of Scripture are to be preferred to bishops and unlearned and simple inquisitors.[85] It is the same conclusion he drew in I *Dialogus* 2 and the *Tractatus*, but the emphasis has subtly changed.

I *Dialogus* 4 illustrates the overall impact of Ockham's proper ecclesiology. Ockham is convinced that the Universal Church, as the location of infallible doctrine, can be represented by a small group of Christians, or even by one single person. The only condition is that its representatives possess true understanding (*scientia*) of Scripture and Christian tradition. This more general ecclesiological view here surfaces in Ockham's discussion of doctrinal correction by prelates. In Ockham's view, the expertise in judging the truth of doctrines is grounded in outstanding knowledge (*scientia excellens*) and a laudable life (*vita laudabilis*).[86] Although, according to Ockham, any faithful Christian must bear witness to the true doctrine as he sees it, the expert in theology has a privileged role, because of his deeper understanding of faith. Ockham's expert, however, is not necessarily endowed with an academic rank. He does not have to bear the name of "doctor." The expressions "doctors," "learned" (*eruditi*), and "skilled" (*periti*) are mutually interchangeable.

The importance that Ockham assigns in his concept of doctrinal correction to understanding the truth becomes even clearer from his insistence that the simpletons (*simplices*) who merely follow the learned and skilled (*periti*), just as any simpleton, need to be corrected in the legitimate way.[87] Ecclesiastical authorities may not impose their doctrinal views upon any Christian, but must always show the truth of these views. In this way, Ockham not only demolishes the arbitrariness of ecclesiastical superiors in exercising doctrinal control, but also posits a conceptual basis for examining and resisting authoritative pronouncements, such as those made by Pope John XXII, without presupposing their truth. The orthodoxy of doctrines is judged on the basis of their truth, not on the basis of the ecclesiastical status of the person who is expressing it.

PIERRE D'AILLY ON THE TEACHING AUTHORITY OF THE THEOLOGIAN

The preceding three theologians discussed episcopal teaching authority mainly in confrontation with the theologian's academic doctrinal authority. Ideally, prelates and doctors had a shared solicitude for the safekeeping, explication, defense, and teaching of revelation. In practice, popes and bishops always used the professional expertise of theologians in guarding sound doctrine. And yet the relationship between their respective doctrinal powers was sometimes marked by tensions. The controversial doctrinal actions of Bishop Tempier and Pope John XXII worked as catalysts for the theologians Servais of Mt. St. Elias, Godfrey of Fontaines, and William Ockham and made them voice their reflections on the two types of teaching authority.

Pierre d'Ailly, however, expressed his views on the theologian's and the prelate's teaching authorities in a completely different context, in a treatise that was the outgrowth of his activities as spokesman of the university at the papal court in the case against John of Monzón. The treatise is a revision and elaboration of d'Ailly's rebuttal of Monzón's appeal.[88] The appeal itself, which, according to d'Ailly, contained "almost as many lies as words," has not been preserved. As we have seen above, one of the grounds why Monzón appealed was that he claimed that the faculty of theology and the bishop lacked the authority to censure false teaching.

In his treatise, d'Ailly attempts to refute Monzón's position. The first of the three chapters addresses the question of the manner in which the faculty of theology and the bishop of Paris may be held competent to condemn heretical or erroneous statements made by someone in Paris. First, Pierre d'Ailly explains in six theses (*conclusiones*) his position. In the remainder of the first chapter, he applies the general argument developed in his six theses to the Monzón case.[89] This part of the chapter is divided into six articles, which are subdivided into objections and responses to objections. The structure is quite complicated, imitating that of scholastic texts. The purport, however, is always clear.

The first chapter opens with an exposition of the distinction between judicial and doctrinal authority. Judicial authority only pertains to the pope and, by delegation, to the bishops. They have the judicial powers to define truths of faith. The doctors of theology, on the other hand, possess doctrinal authority. They assert in a doctrinal or scholastic way the catholic truths contained in Sacred Scripture and, consequently, reprove their opposites as heretical or erroneous. In support of this distinction between the powers of prelates and scholars, d'Ailly refers to passages from Sacred Scripture and from canonistic sources, among which the well-known C.1 d.20.

From there, however, d'Ailly moves to the much stronger proposition that the faculty of theology also possesses some kind of judicial authority to condemn heretical or erroneous views. He first argues that it pertains to the bishop of Paris and the faculty of theology together, or separately, to condemn in the forementioned ways — that is, judicially and doctrinally, respectively — erroneous and heretical statements.[90] As proofs, d'Ailly refers to the condemnation of 1277 by Bishop Tempier, for which the advice of theologians was sought; to the *protestatio*, in which theologians declared not to say anything in favor of the articles condemned at Paris by the bishops *and* the theologians; and to the decretal *Ad abolendam* (1184), which, among other things, states that it pertains to the responsibility of the bishop, advised by his clerics, to start judicial proceedings against heretics in his diocese.[91] By "clerics" the decretal means "theologians," according to d'Ailly, because they are the experts in matters of faith and Catholic truths.

D'Ailly's next claim is that it sometimes pertains to the faculty of theology to judicially condemn in some way heretical or erroneous statements of individual masters or bachelors who are sworn members of the faculty.[92] D'Ailly specifies his conception of the judicial authority of the faculty of theology as the power to coerce masters or bachelors, under pain of a certain penalty, to publicly recant their views if these have been doctrinally condemned as erroneous.

He gives three reasons why the faculty of theology possesses this type of judicial authority.[93] First, the faculty's authority is based on divine and human law: on divine law, because of the Bible texts to which d'Ailly had already alluded in support of his claim that it pertains to the faculty to doctrinally condemn eroneous views; on human law, because of the papal privileges in which the university and each of its faculties had been granted the position of a corporation. This status implies, according to d'Ailly, a political order by virtue of which the university or the faculty can exact obedience to its statutes from its sworn members, the masters and bachelors.

Second, observed custom (*consuetudo*) proves that the theological faculty has such judicial power. This custom is grounded in public interest, which constitutes the third reason why the faculty of theology possesses the judicial power to condemn erroneous views. According to d'Ailly, the theologians have an important task within Christianity, namely the inquiry into catholic truths. Summoning theologians to the court of the bishop, their *iudex ordinarius*, every time they happen to err, would interfere too much with their scholastic tasks, exercised for the defense of faith and the public utility of the entire church. Hence, academics should be doctrinally judged and compelled to correct their errors by their own faculty. Only if they ignore the faculty's condemnations should they be summoned before the episcopal court. And if they still refuse to correct themselves, they should be shunned as heretics.

D'Ailly's sixth and last thesis is that a superior judge should not impede a process initiated by the bishop and the faculty of theology, nor accept an appeal against them without good reason and due reflection.[94] Unnecessary involvement of superior judges would discourage bishop and faculty from curbing heresy and error because they would get the impression that their efforts and expenses were in vain. Instead, superior judges should stimulate bishops and other inferior judicial authorities to proceed against heretics and suspend those who neglect this task.

Next, d'Ailly applies the general argument laid down in his six theses to the Monzón case, in order to prove that the actions of the faculty of theology and the bishop were justified. In d'Ailly's understanding, Monzón's principal argument had been that only the Apostolic See or the Supreme Pontiff has the authority to examine and decide matters of faith. According to d'Ailly, this view deserves to be recanted, and even more so did Monzón's other views, which had generated the conflict in the first place. Instead of defending the bishop's or the faculty's jurisdiction to condemn erroneous views, as one might have expected on the basis of the six theses, d'Ailly made his solution develop in another direction. It hinges on the distinction

between judicial condemnation and judicial prohibition and on his conception of the Apostolic See. According to d'Ailly, it is one thing to condemn a
view judicially (*sententialiter et judicialiter condemnare*), but quite another
thing to prohibit (*inhibere*) its dissemination (*publicatio et dogmatizatio*).[95]
In the Monzón case, the faculty of theology had merely stipulated that the
suspect statements should be publicly prohibited, if the said master refused
to obey the faculty's orders. The faculty had only offered a scholastic and
doctrinal assessment of Monzón's views, which they had the right to do. As
proof, d'Ailly quotes, among other things, from the records of the Monzón
case and points out that no judicial punishment such as suspension of all
university activities, had been imposed. The same was true of the bishop's
sentence. He had not judicially pronounced that Monzón's views were
false, heretical, or erroneous, but had forbidden anyone to publish, preach,
or dogmatize them. This leads to the conclusion, not explicitly drawn by
d'Ailly, that Monzón's complaint in his appeal at the papal court was off
the mark.

Monzón's appeal also raises questions concerning the authority of the
Apostolic See and the Supreme Pontiff in defining truths of faith. This issue
induces d'Ailly to discuss the distinction between manifest heresies and so-
called implicit heresies, that is, heresies that are still being discussed
by biblical scholars. The discussion revolves around the same canonistic
sources that were quoted by Servais of Mt. St. Elias and William Ockham:
Ad abolendam, *Decretum* I dist. 80 c.2. and the *Glossa Ordinaria* on this
passage, and C.24 q.1 c.12 ("Quotiens"), which all seem to make the point
that a bishop does not have the authority to judicially condemn teaching
against faith.[96] This view d'Ailly rejects. He makes a strong claim for the
judicial authority of a bishop and the faculty of theology, an authority to a
limited extent (*secundum quid*) to be sure, but in d'Ailly's interpretation
limited only in geographical terms. Papal doctrinal authority is supreme in
that it has universal binding force for all Christians. The doctrinal authority
of the bishop or the faculty of theology are inferior in that they only have
binding force for the bishop's subjects in his diocese or the members of the
university, respectively. Doctrinal pronouncements made by the pope are
not, however, different in kind from those made by the bishop or the faculty
of theology. Members of the university, for example, have to refrain from
disseminating views that are contrary to an academic censure.[97]

Already this brief sketch makes clear that d'Ailly does more than refute
the arguments of Monzón's appeal. The Monzón case gave d'Ailly an opportunity to present his views on the teaching authority of the faculty of

theology. He built his case on the notion of the corporate autonomy of the masters and bachelors of theology. This autonomy included, according to Ailly, the authority to censure their philosophical and theological views. When d'Ailly expressed the idea that the university or any of the individual faculties had a political order by virtue of which they could regulate themselves, he was harking back to a theme as old as the origin of the university itself. Perhaps new was d'Ailly's application of this line of thought to the justification of university condemnations; but here too, he may have been merely spelling out the theoretical basis of fourteenth-century university practice. Not only the records of the Monzón case but also d'Ailly's treatise imply that the correction of false teaching of a faculty member was viewed as a secret admonition within a privileged corporation, distinguished from the rest of the church and of society, a fraternal correction of masters and bachelors by one of their own.[98]

Conclusion

The four authors discussed above all agree that only the Apostolic See had supreme teaching authority. Yet, on the basis of some canonistic sources and on the basis of historical examples such as the actions of Bishop Tempier, they attributed judicial doctrinal authority to bishops as well. Servais of Mt. St. Elias was most careful in outlining the limits of episcopal competence. A bishop was only allowed to condemn manifest and explicit heresies that had already been condemned by the papacy. The other three theologians also saw a role for the bishop in the condemnation of so-called implicit heresies, that is false teaching that could harm the soul, but was still under discussion in the schools and had not previously been condemned as heretical.

In the final analysis, two responses can be distinguished toward episcopal intervention in doctrinal matters of this kind. Godfrey of Fontaines and William Ockham attempted to downplay episcopal authority in comparison to that attributed to theologians. The opposition between episcopal authority and theological expertise is subtly modified into an opposition between authority and truth. Tempier's pronouncements, and more generally, any prelate's doctrinal definitions, are not acceptable if they are not true. The content of the doctrine becomes the decisive criterion for its acceptance, not the authority of the promulgator. If theologians disagree with a prelate, the authority of truth itself has to be followed. The truths of faith could be established objectively with the help of Scripture, tradition, and right reason. Theologians were assumed to have a deeper understanding of these sources than bishops, and on this basis they could challenge the bishop's authority in doctrinal matters. Ockham even went two steps further in separating the truth of doctrines from any established institutions: two steps, because he believed that not even papal teaching was beyond examination, and because he suggested that deeper understanding of Christian truths was not necessarily linked to an academic degree. Only the truth has authority, and, consequently, doctrinal control has to be based on cognitive criteria, not on institutional power.

Godfrey of Fontaines and William Ockham tended to focus on the tension between the power of jurisdiction, represented by the bishop and other prelates, and the power of expertise, represented by the theologians. This tension had its origin in the inherent duality of a bishop's position in the early church, in which he united the functions of ruling the church and of preaching and teaching Scripture. In the latter area, however, the bishop had competition from a new group of professionals, the university-trained theologians, which gradually emerged at the beginning of the thirteenth century.

Pierre d'Ailly, on the other hand, emphasized the link between the offices of bishop and theologian, manifest in the term "doctor," which, in the early church, designated the bishops, but which was now reserved for theologians.[99] He attributed the same type of judicial authority in doctrinal matters to the bishop, the theologian, and the pope for that matter. There is not a difference of degree, but a difference of scope. The pope's authority pertains to all Christians, that of the bishop of Paris to the subjects in his diocese, including the university, and that of the faculty of theology to its members. But let us not forget that d'Ailly was making his strong claims for judicial autonomy of the faculty of theology at a moment when one of its members was unwilling to comply with its doctrinal determinations. Moreover, when d'Ailly presented his address before pope and curia, the university was faced with two distinct papacies, one at Rome (Urban VI), and one at Avignon, both of which sought the university's support. The ensuing crisis in ecclesiastical authority cannot be better illustrated than by the finale of the Monzón affair. After having spent more than three months at Avignon, Monzón did not await the outcome of his appeal, but secretly departed for Rome, where he also appealed.

Conclusion

The focus of attention in this book has been on academic condemnations as manifestations of teaching authority rather than as chapters in the history of medieval philosophy or the history of Christian doctrine.[1] In this study I have predominantly paid attention to the quasi-judicial proceedings that gradually evolved to curb false teaching, although I have not completely ignored the teaching itself.

At the beginning of the thirteenth century, the emergence of the faculty of theology as an academic institution and of theology as a scientific discipline went hand in hand. The professionalization of the status of theologian and the development of theology as a science significantly affected the concept of doctrinal control. Theology still had its origin in divine revelation as communicated in Sacred Scripture and tradition and had as its goal man's salvation. But its method now involved more than ever before intellectual, speculative investigation. Theology employed a scientific discourse not unlike that of other disciplines, and the doctor of theology was its trained expert. He enquired, argued and taught by rational and analytical methods.

From its very beginning, theology was characterized by an intrinsic tension between faith and reason. The history of theology could be written in terms of limitations demanded from reason to make room for faith, or employment of faith to make room for reason. But from the thirteenth century onward, the scales had been definitively tipped in favor of a rational conception of theology, as faith seeking understanding, as an investigation of the data of revelation with the help of the sources of reason.[2] This development is also reflected in the disciplinary proceedings against academics accused of disseminating false teaching.

The theologians watched that scholastic inquiry at the university did not harm the axioms of Christianity, but was carried out *salva fide*, so to speak, bringing every thought "into captivity to the obedience of Christ" (2 Corinthians 10:5).[3] Unfortunately, however, some scholars became carried away by their studies. Vain curiosity and knowledge for the sake of salvation were the two extreme poles between which scholars moved.[4] Or, these were at least the terms in which the discussion about the goals and purposes of theological inquiry was cast. Some academics were accused of *curiositas*, of desiring to know things that were not useful to know and of spending their time on futile research, such charges being all reminiscences of Bible passages such as 1 Timothy 2:14 and 5:13, Titus 3:9, and Psalms 30:7, 37:13, 39:5, and 61:10.[5] Such scholars were reproved for knowing more than was necessary (*plus sapere quam oportet*), a quotation from Romans 12:3.[6] And finally the doctrines that were the result of these efforts were characterized as "alien," a reference to Hebrews 13:9.[7]

University censures did not concern full-fledged masters of theology. John of Monzón seems to have been the only exception.[8] He was already a master of theology, but only just so, because it was the inception ceremony that induced the charges of false teaching against him. Victims of a curious mind were especially to be found among the junior faculty, that is, the bachelors of theology and the members of the inferior arts faculty. Perhaps the proneness to be unduly fascinated by their own views was particularly strong among the "youthful" bachelors and members of the arts faculty, who, in their desire for fame, may have been less careful and, as a consequence, were more in need of some fraternal correction than the more sedate masters.[9] In this respect a statute of 1366 is significant. It admonishes bachelors of theology to present their *principium* in an honorable way, without insults, and not to let themselves be carried away too much by emotions.[10] They had to investigate the truth with *cauta sollicitude*, with cautious carefulness, and in a sober way.[11]

Another factor, besides age, that helps to explain why false teaching at the university mainly concerned bachelors of theology and was corrected by disciplinary rather than judicial proceedings is that they operated under the supervision of the masters of theology. In view of their status as not yet full-fledged members of the guild of masters, as apprentices, correction seemed more appropriate than punishment. As members of the university who fell under the jurisdiction of the chancellor, a jurisdiction that was confirmed by the oaths that the young scholars had taken at each stage of their academic career, they were expected to comply with the correction of their academic superiors.[12] Moreover, it would only be natural that the solutions of any irregularities that had their origin in the context of ceremonies and activities at the university and were also confined to that closed community were initially sought within that same institutional context of the *universitas*. Hence, doctrinal correctness was not imposed through judicial authority, but through academic superiority, through the masters' professional expertise, which constituted their teaching authority.

This aspect becomes also apparent in academic censures that were pronounced outside the institutional context of the University of Paris. Theologians were deliberately involved to lend the weight of their doctrinal expertise to the authoritative decisions of minister general, bishop, or pope, although, strictly speaking, the force of their arguments was not needed to censure an erring scholar. The prelates' power of authority, their *auctoritas* or *potestas*, was sufficient. By discursive reasoning, however, it was *demonstrated* to the academic that he had erred, that his speculations had not been in keeping with revelation as held and taught by the Roman Church, or, in brief, that they did not conform to Catholic faith. The implication was that the academic had been opposing truth, and for this reason his views were disqualified as erroneous. As a scholar, the theologian was free to use the rational and analytical methods common to other scholarly disciplines, but as a theologian he had a special bond with the faith of the Catholic Church. Theologians operated within boundaries of precommitments. Since, however, revelation was generally accepted as infallible truth, this framework of higher commitments, which set the limits of academic inquiry, was not felt as a constraint. Propositions were censured as erroneous or heretical precisely because they were not in accordance with faith, that is, were contrary to truth. The university or ecclesiastical authorities felt justified in suppressing false teaching, because they rightly believed that it was impossible to give a valid proof of what was contrary to truth. In other words, the truth was on the side of the judges. It was their "objective" yardstick to measure theological opinion. Viewing medieval academic censures solely in terms of restrictions on academic freedom or the imprisonment of reason not only ignores the fact that any conception of academic freedom must be attuned to a particular academic system, but also misses the distinct *rational* aspect in the process of examining and censuring medieval academics. Academic heresies and errors were demonstrated in a process of rational discourse, by cognitive criteria that were provided by experts.

The operating procedure for censuring false teaching basically consisted of two phases, the investigation and the discussion with the author. The discussion with the author started the moment he was invited to respond to the charged errors. Of course, this discussion was not a free exchange of ideas. The purpose of the whole exercise was to ascertain most precisely the views of the person under investigation. It was an interrogation rather than a free academic discussion. The striking feature of all these answers is their apologetic tone. Even though the accused pointed out that they had not made certain statements attributed to them, or had meant something different from what their investigators had understood, they eventually all complied with the decisions of the (ecclesiastical) authorities. In this way, they could assure that the negative judgment on their theological positions did not affect their person: they could claim that they were not stubbornly defending views that had been "proven" to be wrong, or even heretical.

The central target of these investigations were doctrinal views disseminated in teaching or writing. The response to false teaching was a symbiosis between the power of authority and the power of learning. Many aspects of doctrinal investigations, in particular the crucial assessment of the orthodoxy of someone's teaching or writing, were left in the hands of the academics themselves, represented in the investigative commissions appointed by the (ecclesiastical) authorities. However, this symbiosis was not free from tensions, as became most clearly articulated in the scholarly reactions to the condemnation issued by Bishop Tempier in 1277.

Contradicting *the truth* of faith not only caused intellectual embarassment but also endangered the audience's salvation. This pastoral concern was expressed in judgments such as "ill-sounding" or "scandalous." Authorities were concerned with the effect false teaching might have on the audience. Erring academics were accused of leading believers astray with their incautious discourse (*incauta locutio*), thus endangering their salvation.[13] The dissemination of views offensive to pious ears had to be prohibited because of its harmful effects.

The context of teaching authority, justified by intellectual and pastoral concerns, within which I have placed the phenomenon of academic censure in this study, should not conceal, however, the presence of other factors in evoking academic condemnations. In particular the secular-mendicant controversy over the mendicants' rights to teach, preach, and hear confession provided one of the most important but less visible agendas in doctrinal investigations during the period 1200–1400. Political motives were also present in the academic condemnations involving the doctrine of the Beatific Vision and the debate over Christ's Poverty. In both debates, the papacy took an active part. Frequently, it was not evident at all that truths of faith were being contradicted or attacked by the accused. Rather, they had disobeyed papal decrees.

The Great Schism of 1378–1417 marks an appropriate end for this study. Without suggesting a causal connection, it is interesting to note that during these years a change took place in the exercise of doctrinal control. The modus operandi in examining suspect teaching essentially remained that of the preceding decades, but the three cases of academic heresy that took place during the schism were significantly different in other ways.

The double appeals of John of Monzón have already been noted, and also the catalytic effect this case had on the faculty of theology to put forward forceful assertions of its teaching authority. The censure of Master John of Gorel O.F.M. in 1409 of views disseminated during his vesperies was a continuation of the mendicant struggle, rather than a true doctrinal condemnation.[14] At stake were the mendicants' rights to preach, hear confession, and administer the sacraments. Pope Alexander V only interfered because the Franciscans appealed to him. The condemnation of propositions from John Petit's *Justificatio ducis Burgundiae*, finally, was linked to an important political event, namely the assassination of the duke of Orléans by partisans of John the Fearless.[15] The Council of Constance (1414–17) not only ended the Great Schism but also offered its own solution to the problem of academic heresy: Jan Hus and Jerome of Prague, neither of whom, incidentally, was connected with the University of Paris, were burned at the stake.

During the remainder of the fifteenth century and during the sixteenth century, doctrinal control at the University of Paris was exercised under a somewhat different policy. The long-standing practice of prosecuting false teaching within the faculty of theology itself was not discontinued.[16] In quantitative terms, however, there was a marked shift to consultations and inquisitorial activity involving individuals who were not, and had never been, members of the University of Paris.[17] The most spectacular consultations involved Joan of Arc (1429–31), Martin Luther (1519–21), Erasmus of Rotterdam (1525–27), and King Henry VIII (1530).[18] More frequently than ever, the Paris theologians intervened in, or were drawn into international (doctrinal) conflicts.

Abbreviations

AFH	*Archivum Franciscanum Historicum*
AHDL	*Archives d'histoire doctrinale et littéraire du moyen âge*
AUP	Emile Denifle and Heinrich Chatelain, eds. *Auctarium Chartularium Universitatis Parisiensis*. 6 vols. Paris, 1894–1964
CH	*Church History*
CHLMP	Norman Kretzmann, Anthony Kenny, and Jan Pinborg, eds. *The Cambridge History of Later Medieval Philosophy*. Cambridge, 1982
CUP	Emile Denifle and Heinrich Chatelain, eds. *Chartularium Universitatis Parisiensis*. 4 vols. Paris, 1889–91
Friedberg	E. Friedberg, ed. *Corpus iuris canonici*. 2 vols. Leipzig, 1881
FS	*Franciscan Studies*
Gerson	Jean Gerson. *Oeuvres complètes*. Introduction and notes by Mgr. P. Glorieux. 10 vols. Paris, 1962–73
Koch	Josef Koch. *Kleine Schriften*. 2 vols. Rome, 1973
Maier	Anneliese Maier. *Ausgehendes Mittelalter. Gesammelte Aufsätze zur Geistesgeschichte des 14. Jahrhunderts*. 3 vols. Rome, 1964–77
MS	*Mediaeval Studies*
PL	J. P. Migne, ed. *Patrologia Latina cursus completus*. 221 vols. Paris, 1844–64
RCSF	*Rivista critica di storia della filosofia*
RSPT	*Revue des sciences philosophiques et théologiques*
RTAM	*Recherches de théologie ancienne et médiévale*

Notes

Preface

1. This censure is discussed in J. M. M. H. Thijssen, "Master Amalric and the Amalricians: Inquisitorial Procedure and the Supression of Heresy at the University of Paris," *Speculum* 71 (1996), 43–65.

2. The Collection of Parisian Articles was used in the editions of Carolus Du Plessis d'Argentré, *Collectio judiciorum de novis erroribus*, 3 vols. (Paris, 1724–36), and Emile Denifle and Heinrich Chatelain, *Chartularium Universitatis Parisiensis*, 4 vols. (Paris, 1889–91). See also the survey of the sources at the end of this study.

3. See for example Étienne Gilson, *La philosophie au moyen âge*; 2d ed. rev. and exp. (Paris, 1947), 383–85, 558–68, 657, Julius R. Weinberg, *A Short History of Medieval Philosophy* (Princeton, N.J., 1964), 49, 171–75, 235, Frederick C. Copleston, *A History of Medieval Philosophy* (London, 1972), 63, 155, 202–9, and Michael Haren, *Medieval Thought: The Western Intellectual Tradition from Antiquity to the Thirteenth Century*, 2d ed. (Toronto, 1992), 194–211.

4. See, for instance, CUP 1: 73, and 199, and 3: 184 and 508.

5. Koch; Jürgen Miethke, "Theologenprozesse in der ersten Phase ihrer institutionellen Ausbildung: Die Verfahren gegen Peter Abaelard und Gilbert von Poitiers," *Viator* 6 (1975), 87–117; Miethke, "Papst, Ortsbischof und Universität in den Pariser Theologenprozessen des 13. Jahrhunderts," in *Die Auseinandersetzungen an der Pariser Universität im XIII. Jahrhundert*, ed. Albert Zimmermann (Berlin, 1976), 52–95; Miethke, "Bildungsstand und Freiheitsforderung (12. bis 14. Jahrhundert)," in *Die Abendländische Freiheit vom 10. zum 14. Jahrhundert*, ed. Johannes Fried (Sigmaringen, 1991), esp. 231–40; William J. Courtenay, "Inquiry and Inquisition: Academic Freedom in Medieval Universities," *CH* 58 (1989), 168–82; Courtenay, "The Articles Condemned at Oxford Austin Friars in 1315," in *Via Augustini: Augustine in the Later Middle Ages, Renaissance and Reformation*, ed. Heiko O. Oberman and Frank A. James, III (Leiden, 1991), 5–18; Courtenay, "Dominicans and Suspect Opinion in the Thirteenth Century: The Case of Stephen of Venizy, Peter of Tarentaise, and the Articles of 1270 and 1271," *Vivarium* 32 (1994), 186–95; Courtenay, "The Preservation and Dissemination of Academic Condemnations at the University of Paris in the Middle Ages," in *Les philosophies morales et politiques au Moyen Age*, ed. B. C. Bazán, E. Andújar, L. Sbrocchi, 3 vols. (New York, Ottawa, and Toronto, 1995), 3: 1659–67, and J. M. M. H. Thijssen, "Academic Heresy and Intellectual Freedom at the University of Paris, 1200–1378," *Centres of Learning in Pre-Modern Europe and the Near East*, ed. Jan-Willem Drijvers and A. A. MacDonald (Leiden, 1995), 217–228. Academic condemnations play

only a minor role in the rich study by Mary M. McLaughlin, *Intellectual Freedom and Its Limitations in the University of Paris in the Thirteenth and Fourteenth Centuries* (New York, 1977), which is a reprint of a Ph.D. dissertation of 1952. See also her "Paris Masters of the Thirteenth and Fourteenth Centuries and Ideas of Intellectual Freedom," *CH* 24 (1955), 195–211. Shortly after the manuscript was completed in 1997, two pertinent articles were published that, unfortunately, could not be taken into account here: Luca Bianchi, "Censure, liberté et progrès intellectuel à l'Université de Paris au XIIIe siècle," *AHDL* 63 (1996), 45–93 and William J. Courtenay, "Pastor de Serrescuderio (d. 1356) and MS Saint-Omer 239," *AHDL* 63 (1996), 325–356.

6. For the impact of the Great Schism on the universities see Allen E. Bernstein, *Pierre d'Ailly and the Blanchard Affair* (Leiden, 1978), esp. 28–60, R. N. Swanson, *Universities, Academics and the Great Schism* (Cambridge, 1979), Guy Fitch Lytle, "Universities as Religious Authorities in the Later Middle Ages and Reformation," in *Reform and Authority in the Medieval and Reformation Church*, ed. Guy Fitch Lytle (Washington, D.C., 1981), 79–82; and Paolo Nardi, "Relations with Authority," in *Universities in the Middle Ages*, ed. Hilde De Ridder-Symoens (*A History of the University in Europe*, vol. 1; Cambridge, 1992), 100–102.

7. This view is expressed in John B. Bury, *History of Freedom of Thought* (London, 1913), 52 and quoted and rejected in Charles H. Haskins, *The Renaissance of the Twelfth Century* (New York, 1962), 361. Other examples of negative views on the independence of medieval thought with regard to religion, theology, or faith, are given in Maurice de Wulf, *Histoire de la philosophie médiévale*, 3 vols., 6th ed. (Louvain and Paris, 1934–47), 1: 10, and 18–19.

Chapter 1. The Suppression of False Teaching

1. William Ockham, *Dialogus* (*Opera plurima*; Lyon, 1494–96; republished London, 1962), fol. 11ra. Details about this work are given in Chapter 5.

2. CUP 2: 86, 141, 148, 173, 215, 243–44, 302, 506, and also Koch, 2: 232, 233, 235, 245, 246, 254, 257 for the charge of disseminating opinions against faith, against Scripture, or against sound doctrine. For the charge of causing scandal see CUP 1: 319 and n. 92; for endangering souls see CUP 1: 319, 543 and CUP 2: 243–44.

3. The background to the metaphor of heresy as disease is provided in R. I. Moore, "Heresy as Disease," in *The Concept of Heresy*, ed. W. Lourdaux and D. Verhelst (Louvain, 1976), 1–12. Cf. the following documents: CUP 1: #59, #468, #1042, #1125. In the documents CUP 1: #176, #441, #518, #798, #864, #1124, #1125 the academic errors are presented as dangerous.

4. See Othmar Hageneder, "Der Häresiebegriff bei den Juristen des 12. und 13. Jahrhunderts," in *Concept*, ed. Lourdaux and Verhelst, 42–104, and Winfried Trusen, *Der Prozess gegen Meister Eckhart. Vorgeschichte, Verlauf und Folgen* (Paderborn, 1988), 168–71. The following documents related to academic censure allude to this moral dimension: CUP 2: #148, #173, #281, and the preface to John of

Mirecourt's condemnation, edited in William J. Courtenay, "John of Mirecourt's Condemnation: Its Original Form," *RTAM* 53 (1986), 191.

5. Gerson, 3: 337: "Ecce quod Eva idcirco erravit quia curiose concupivit fructum pulchrum visu et ad vescendum suavem." See Zénon Kaluza, *Les querelles doctrinales à Paris. Nominalistes et réalistes aux confins de XIVe et XVe siècles* (Bergamo, 1988), *passim* for a discussion of Gerson's treatise *Contra vanam curiositatem.*

6. Gerson, 3: 230. See Edward Peters, *"Libertas inquirendi* and the *vitium curiositatis* in Medieval Thought," in *La notion de liberté au moyen âge. Islam, Byzance, Occident,* ed. G. Makdisi, D. Sourdel, and J. Sourdel-Thomine (Paris, 1985), 90–92, for patristic and monastic sources that link *curiositas* to *superbia.*

7. Gerson, 3: 339. See Herbert Grundman, *Ausgewählte Aufsätze,* 3 vols. (Stuttgart, 1976–78), 3: 316 for other, earlier sources.

8. Reproval of presumptuousness can be found in the following academically related documents: CUP 1: #59, #176, #441, #468, #473, #523, #798, #864, #1023, and #1124.

9. The relation between philosophy and faith from the Church Fathers until the twelfth century—and the notion of philosophy as the root of all heresy—is sketched in Gerard Verbeke, "Philosophy and Heresy: Some Conflicts between Reason and Faith," in *Concept,* ed. Lourdaux and Verhelst, 172–98. William J. Courtenay, "Inquiry and Inquisition: Academic Freedom in Medieval Universities," *CH* 58 (1989), 169 gives the example of a medieval friar who in 1358 characterized his own university as a gymnasium for heretics (and, of course, was condemned for this opinion). For thirteenth- and fourteenth-century admonitions that theologians should not become involved in idle philosophical speculation and, in general, that theologians and *artistae* should not trangress the borders of their own fields see CUP 1: #59, #176, #441, #473, #741, #1042, #1125. See further Gerson, 3: no. 99 (*Contra curiositatem studentium*), 239–40, and 249.

10. This terminology was used in a sermon by the Dominican William of Luxi around 1270. See Louis J. Bataillon, "Les crises de l'université de Paris d'après les sermons universitaires," in *Die Auseinandersetzungen and der Pariser Universität im XIII. Jahrhundert,* ed. Albert Zimmermann (Berlin, 1976), 168. The image of "transgressing the limits set by the Fathers" is discussed in Edward Peters, "Transgressing the Limits Set by the Fathers: Authority and Impious Exegesis in Medieval Thought," in *Christendom and Its Discontents. Exclusion, Persecution, and Rebellion, 1000–1500,* ed. Scott L. Waugh and Peter D. Diehl (Cambridge, 1996), 338–62.

11. Maurice de Wulf and Auguste Pelzer, *Les quatre premiers Quodlibets de Godefroid de Fontaines* (Leuven, 1904), 208.

12. Maier, 2: 59–81. On p. 72: "ille dicitur hereticus qui animo et cum pertinacia deviat et hiis quae universalis ecclesia et omnis fidelis credere tenetur," and p. 73: "ut quis talem errorem firmata et quasi obstinata pertinacique voluntate eligat et sequatur."

13. A. Daniels, *Eine lateinische Rechtfertigungsschrift des Meister Eckhart* (Münster i. W., 1923), 2: "Errare enim possum, hereticus esse non possum, nam primum ad intellectum pertinet, secundum ad voluntatem," and p. 8: "Sola enim pertinax adhesio erronei hereticum facit." For a discussion see Bernard McGinn, "Eckhart's Condemnation Reconsidered," *The Thomist* 44 (1980), 400, and Winfried Trusen,

Der Prozess gegen Meister Eckhart. Vorgeschichte, Verlauf und Folgen (Paderborn, 1988), 94 and 164. Note that Loris Sturlese has argued that the *Rechtfertigungsschrift* is a literary product, composed by the first generation of followers of Eckhart at Cologne. See Loris Sturlese, "Die Kölner Eckhartisten. Das Studium generale der deutschen Dominikaner und die Verurteilung der Thesen Meister Eckharts," in *Die Kölner Universität im Mittelalter: Geistige Wurzeln und Soziale Wirklichkeit*, ed. Albert Zimmermann (Berlin, 1989), 192–212.

14. Daniels, *Rechtfertigungsschrift*, 13–14: "Probatur hoc ex Augustino 24 q. 3a, sicut Apostolus, 'hereticum hominem post primam et secundam correctionem devit.' 'Hereticum,' glosa, 'qui suum errorem defendit pertinaciter.' Et infra in eodem capitulo sequitur: 'Sed qui sententiam suam, quamvis falsam atque perversam, nulla pertinacia defendunt, corrigi parati, nequaquam sunt inter hereticos deputandi.' Et post ibidem 31 capitulo sic ait Augustinus: 'qui in ecclesia Christi morbidum aliquid pravumque sapiunt, si correcti resistunt contumaciter suaque pestifera et mortifera dogmata emendare nolunt, sed defensare persistunt, heretici sunt.'"

15. *Decretum*, C.24 q.3, c.29 and c.31. See also Helmut G. Walther, "Häresie und päpstliche Politik: Ketzerbegriff und Ketzergesetzgebung in der Übergangsphase von der Dekretistik zur Dekretalistik," in *Concept*, ed. Lourdaux and Verhelst, 114 and Trusen, *Prozess*, 166 and 171–73 for the canonistic background.

16. The discussion of pertinacity can be found in Ockham, I *Dialogus*, 3.4–4.14. Part of this material has been discussed in Arthur S. McGrade, *The Political Thought of William Ockham* (Cambridge, 1974), 49–57, albeit from a different perspective.

17. Ockham, I *Dialogus* 4.1, fol. 22va: "Pertinaciter dubitans contra fidem est qui persistit in dubitatione circa ea que sunt fidei, quam debet de necessitate salutis dimittere."

18. Gerson, 6: 161.

19. Ockham, I *Dialogus* 3.3, fol. 18va.

20. CUP 2: 215: "credo et dico suprascriptos articulos et eorum quemlibet esse hereticos, et pertinaces assertores eorum fore sicut hereticos condemnandos."

21. Trusen, *Prozess*, 107. See also the decretal *Ad abolendam*—translated in *Heresy and Authority in Medieval Europe: Documents in Translation*, ed. Edward Peters (Philadelphia, 1980), 171, where special arrangements are stipulated for those who abjure their error.

22. Jeffrey B. Russell, *Dissent and Order in the Middle Ages. The Search for Legitimate Authority* (New York, 1992), 4.

23. Malcolm D. Lambert, *Medieval Heresy: Popular Movements from Bogomil to Hus* (London, 1977), xii and 3–4, and especially Russell, *Dissent*, 2–5.

24. See Kaluza, *Querelles*, 27 n. 8 for Gerson's knowledge of the academic practices in his epoch.

25. Gerson, 6: 163: "Sunt alii circa fidem errantes in his quae non tenentur pro tunc explicite credere; et hoc dupliciter. Uno modo pertinaciter, quia non parati sunt corrigi; sed propter superbiam suam aut aliter proprium defendunt errorem. Altero modo dum parati sunt corrigi protinus agnita veritate; quia non pertinaci animositate defendunt errorem sed ex sola simplicitate vel ignorantia sunt in errore . . . ; tertii vero pertinaciter errant in illo cujus oppositum pro tunc non tenentur

explicita fide tenere sed implicita; sed quia renuunt corrigi dicuntur haeretici . . . At vero quarti quia non jungunt errori suo pertinaciam nunc vel antea, quamvis sint corripiendi per revocationem erroris, ipsi tamen nequaquam sunt poenis haereticorum plectendi nec infamia notandi, sicut apud scholasticos theologos in praeclara Universitate Parisiensi frequenter observatur quos protestatio generalis et conditionalis revocatio juvit ad hoc ne de pertinacia notarentur, juncta humilitate qua protinus revocant errorem nedum conditionaliter sed absolute; quae revocatio sufficit magistris ad purgationem nec ab actibus studii legitimis exercendis vel consequendis revocantes obinde repelluntur."

26. CUP 2: 120: "Dicit [John of Paris] tamen quod nullus est determinatus per ecclesiam, et ideo nullus cadit sub fide."

27. Gerson, 6: 159. Besides hierarchical position, Gerson also takes into account "natural gifts," such as intelligence, erudition, etc., in evaluating how much expertise about faith may be expected from someone.

28. CUP 3: 504: "et multa dixit injuriosa contra dictos episcopum et magistros theologice facultatis, et specialiter eos Manicheos et hereticos nominando, quod tamen ipsi in suis ordinacionibus vel sentenciis de eo non dixerant, nec aliquam suarum proposicionum hereticam nominaverant."

29. See Josef Koch, *Durandus de Sancto Porciano, O.P.* (Münster, 1927), esp. 68–72, 200–207, and 410–17.

30. Koch, 2: 130–133.

31. Koch, *Durandus*, 68: "quod in primis dictaveram et scripseram, fuit a quibusdam curiosis mihi subreptum, antequam fuisset per me sufficienter correctum."

32. Koch, 2: 410 and *Durandus*, 415–16.

33. See Alfonso Maierù, *University Training in Medieval Europe*; transl. and ed. by D. N. Pryds (Leiden, 1994), 23–25, esp. n. 105, where the relevant Dominican legislation is quoted.

34. The constitution is quoted in Koch, *Durandus*, 414 n. 21. See also CUP 2: 6 (#536) for a similar decree, dating as early as 1286.

35. See David Burr, *Olivi and Franciscan Poverty: The Origins of the Usus Pauper Controversy* (Philadelphia, 1989), esp. 38–42 and 88–93, and Koch, 2: 196 n. 18: "Et certe in quaestionibus meis plura possunt esse incorrecta, quia me nolente per aliquos communicatae fuerunt, antequam eas diligentius corexissem." The extant Franciscan documents concerning the prepublication scrutiny of writings date from the 1330s. They postdate Olivi's examination, which started shortly before 1283. See CUP 2: 470 (#1006), and Zénon Kaluza, *Nicolas d'Autrecourt: Ami de la vérité* (*Histoire littéraire de la France*, vol. 42, part 1; Paris, 1995), 61 n. 138 for the relevant documents.

36. There also was a second chancellor, connected to the abbey of St. Geneviève, but he was almost exclusively concerned with the faculty of arts and did not play a role in the adjudication of false teaching. The office of the chancellor is described in Astrik L. Gabriel, "The Conflict between the Chancellor and the University of Masters and Students at Paris During the Middle Ages," in *Die Auseinandersetzungen*, ed. Zimmermann, 106–55; Alan E. Bernstein, "Magisterium and License: Corporate Autonomy against Papal Authority in the Medieval University of Paris," *Viator* 9 (1978), 291–309, and *Pierre d'Ailly and the Blanchard Affair* (Leiden,

1978), 1–28; Jacques Verger, "Les institutions universitaires françaises au Moyen Age: Origines, modèles, évolution," in *Università in Europa. Le istituzioni universitarie dal Medio Evo ai nostri giorni, strutture, organizzazione, funzionamento*, ed. A. Romano (Catanzaro, 1995), 68.

37. CUP 2: 683. See also P. Glorieux, "L'enseignement au Moyen Age. Techniques et méthodes en usage à la faculté de théologie de Paris au XIIIe siècle," *AHDL* 43 (1968), 99, and Gabriel, "Conflict," 14.

38. See Hastings Rashdall, *The Universities of Europe in the Middle Ages*, ed. F. M. Powicke and A. B. Emden, 3 vols. (Oxford, 1987), 1: 304–5, 338–39, 398, 400, but note that his discussion is not decisive.

39. CUP 1: 60 (#1), in a charter issued around 1200, although the exemption is under certain conditions. See Gabriel, "Conflict," 108. Other documents that are relevant are CUP 1: #24 (1210–16), in which Pope Innocent III allows the University of Paris its own legal representative, the *proctor*, and CUP 1: #142 (1245) in which Innocent IV acknowledges the *privilegium fori* to the masters and scholars of Paris. But see Rashdall, *Universities*, 1: 290, which claims that the *privilegium fori* was never explicitly granted by any secular or ecclesiastical authority.

40. CUP 1: 102–4 (#45), issued in 1222. See also CUP 1: #95 (1231), #113 (1237), and #162 (1246), bulls issued to the effect that the masters and scholars at the University of Paris could only be excommunicated after a special papal license had been obtained.

41. CUP 1: 138 (#79).

42. CUP 1: 622 (#515): "Prima ratio est, quia cancellarius Parisiensis non est judex ordinarius scolarium, nec delegatus; et ideo unus de ipsis non debebat facere alterum convenire coram cancellario, nec conveniri coram eodem." The conflict itself, though not its implications for the chancellor's jurisdiction, is discussed in Gabriel, "Conflict," 136–138. See also CUP 1: 640 (#528), the papal decision on the appeal, which repeats the claims of the arts faculty and shows concern for the usurpation of the judicial powers of the chancellor by the rector, who had started to try cases that used to belong in the "forum cancelarii."

43. CUP 1: 642 (#528): "Et dictus cancellarius ac successores ipsius ecclesie Parisiensis cancellarii sua jurisdictione suoque officio utantur libere prout consuetum est hactenus, donec in hac parte per sedem eandem aliud ordinatum extiterit vel provisum."

44. This seems also true for the first case that appears in the *Collectio errorum*, namely that of Frater Stephen of Venizy, in 1241. See CUP 1: 170–72 (#128). According to some manuscripts, Chancellor Odo of Chateauroux examined Venizy's views on the orders of the bishop. The case is discussed in William J. Courtenay, "Dominicans and Suspect Opinion in the Thirteenth Century: The Case of Stephen Venizy, Peter of Tarentaise, and the Articles of 1270 and 1277," *Vivarium* 32 (1994), 186–89.

45. Konstanty Michalski, "La révocation par Frère Barthélemy, en 1316, de 13 thèses incriminées," in *Aus der Geisteswelt des Mittelalters. Studien und Texte Martin Grabmann zur Vollendung des 60. Lebensjahres*, ed. Albert Lang, Joseph Lechner, and Michael Schmaus (Münster, 1935), 2: 1097; CUP 1: 170 (#128); CUP 3: 21 (#1218), 95 (#1270), and 117 (#1298).

46. CUP 3: 120 (#1299): "jurat quod in suis principiis et lecturis, necnon et in aliis actibus quibuscumque, non dicet, tenebit, aut dogmatizabit aliquid quod sit contra fidem catholicam, aut contra determinationem sancte matris ecclesie, vel contra bonos mores, seu in favorem articulorum in Romana curia vel Parisius condempnatorum, aut quod male sonet in auribus auditorum, sed sanam doctrinam tenebit et dogmatizabit." The oath itself does not appear among the statutes of the theological faculty of Paris, but it is quoted in the recantation of Brother Bartholomew. See Michalski, "Révocation," 2: 1097: "Quia iniunctum est parisius scholaribus sub pena excommunicationis, quodsi audierint quemquam doctorem sive instruentem doctrinam, que sonat contra fidem et bonos mores, quod revelabunt infra quindenam epo parisiensi vel cancellario." See further Pierre d'Ailly, *Tractatus*, 78, text quoted in note 98, and Gerson, 5: 430, who also refers to such an oath: "et jurant baccalaurei priusquam legant Sententias in manu cancellarii Parisiensis quod si quid audierint dici in favorem articulorum Parisius condemnatorum, revelabunt infra octo dies episcopo vel cancellario Parisiensi qui erunt pro tempore."

47. CUP 3: 120: "insuper et quod si audiverit aut sciverit aliquem contrarium facientem bachellarium, vel alium, infra septem dies a tempore notitie domino episcopo aut cancellario Parisiensi, qui pro tempore fuerit, revelabit."

48. CUP 3: 121: "informationem fecimus de predictis per multos bachelarios et scolares, qui in dicto principio fuerunt presentes." See also the case of Brother Bartholomew in Michalski, "Révocation," 1097: "Et relatum est cancellario parisiensi testimonio fide dignorum et probatum per testes ydoneos."

49. CUP 3: 121: "Per proprium quaternum dicti fratris [Denis of Foullechat], in quo suum dictum principium continetur, quam nobis [the chancellor] sponte tradidit." From CUP 3: 119 it is clear that the "quaternum" was not returned.

50. CUP 3: 489–97 (#1558 and #1559).

51. CUP 3: 497 (#1560): "Hii errorum frutices ne alcius profundiusque radices agerent, et darent simplicium pedibus offendiculum, decanus singulique theologice facultatis magistri, ut de more habent, obviare curaverunt, et predictum Johannem ad se accersitum primitus secundum evangelicam doctrinam, secrete inter eos et caritative, ut ab erratis resipisceret, monuerunt."

52. CUP 3: 21 (#1218) also uses the terminology of "correction."

53. The problem of the prosecution of occult sins and crimes is discussed in H. Ansgar Kelly, "Inquisitorial Due Process and the Status of Secret Crimes," in *Proceedings of the Eighth International Congress of Medieval Canon Law*, ed. Stanley Chodorow (Vatican City, 1992), 407–27. The passage from Matthew 18: 15–17 also provided the basis for the judicial proceeding known as *denunciatio evangelica*, and is included in Gratian's *Decretum* (D.45 c.17). See Piero Bellini, *"Denunciatio evangelica" e "denunciatio judicialis privata." Un capitolo di storia disciplinare della chiesa* (Milan, 1986).

54. CUP 3: 497 (#1560).

55. CUP 3: 491 (#1559). The relation between the offices of chancellor and dean deserves further study. Sometimes their relations were strained, as in 1264, when the chancellor claimed to be *ex officio* dean of the faculty of theology, which claim was denied by the masters. See CUP 1: #399.

56. Bernstein, *Pierre d'Ailly*, esp. 79–80.

57. CUP 3: 121–22 (#1299): "Et adhuc in majorem contemptum contra prohibitionem nostram et promissum suum veniens."

58. CUP 3: 503 (#1564): "Qui ita se facturum intra terciam diem promisit; sed ipse promissum suum in hoc, sicut et in omnibus aliis, violavit."

59. CUP 3: #1559, which records the sentence of the episcopal court and reproduces the record of Monzón's condemnation by the consistory of theologians. See p. 495: "Super quibus proposicionibus sic in forma per Universitatem Parisiensem ad requestam dicte facultatis theologie reverendo in Christo patri episcopo Parisiensi, ordinario judici in hac parte, judicialiter exhibitis, factoque super hiis processu." See further CUP 3: 503 (#1564): "7a est, quod postquam Universitas et facultas antedicte quod potuerant et debuerant, quantum in ipsis erat, perfecerant, postea nunciaverunt hec omnia reverendo in Christo patri domino episcopo Parisiensi, judici ordinario in hac parte, et presentata eidem cedula facultatis predicte, sibi prout in similibus casibus fieri solitum est, requirendo supplicaverunt, quatenus super hiis vellet judicialiter procedere." This passage is taken from the brief prepared by Pierre d'Ailly, when presenting the university's case at the papal court.

60. See CUP 3: 496 (#1559), and 503 (#1564).

61. CUP 3: 496 (#1559): "Contra vero personam ipsius magistri Johannis de Montesono, si apprehendi possit, ad arrestacionem et incarceracionem et examinacionem, invocato ad hoc si opus sit auxilio brachii secularis, et alias secundum juris remedia procedemus." Pierre d'Ailly specified in his brief that the bishop had summoned Monzón four times. See CUP 3: 503 (#1564).

62. Richard W. Southern, "The Changing Role of Universities in Medieval Europe," *Historical Research* 60 (1987), 133–41; Courtenay, "Inquiry," 175–78, and William J. Courtenay, "Erfurt CA 2 127 and the Censured Articles of Mirecourt and Autrecourt," in *Die Bibliotheca Amploniana. Ihre Bedeutung im Spannungsfeld von Aristotelismus, Nominalismus und Humanismus*, ed. Andreas Speer (Berlin, 1995), 342 n. 4. Courtenay rightly emphasizes that the shift from Paris to Avignon, if it indeed occurred, had no implications for the role of the masters in evaluating false teaching, for the papal court too relied heavily on their theological expertise when making doctrinal decisions.

63. John of Pouilly, William Ockham, Peter Olivi, Marsilius of Padua, Meister Eckhart, Durand of St. Pourçain, Thomas Waleys, and Nicholas of Autrecourt were all summoned to Avignon, the latter together with Elias of Corso, Guido of Veeli, Peter of Monteregali, John the Servite, and Henry of England.

64. See Koch, 1: 333–34 and 345, and McGinn, "Eckhart's Condemnation," 396.

65. The documents are edited and studied in Thomas Käppeli, O.P., *Le procès contre Thomas Waleys, O.P.* (Rome, 1936). See further Maier, 3: 543–91, Katherine Walsh, *A Fourteenth-Century Scholar and Primate: Richard Fitzralph in Oxford, Avignon, and Armagh* (Oxford, 1981), 85–107, and William J. Courtenay, *Capacity and Volition. A History of the Distinction of Absolute and Ordained Power* (Bergamo, 1990), 152 for additional perspectives on the differing judgments in the Waleys case.

66. See note 132.

67. Courtenay, "Erfurt," 342 n.4. It is unclear whether the inquiries against the Oxford scholars Henry of Costesey and Thomas of Elmedene would fit into this

category. Their cases, if they ever came to trial, originated from their opposition to a papal decree (*Ad conditorum canonum*), rather than from disseminating false teaching in a university context. See William J. Courtenay, *Adam Wodeham. An Introduction to His Life and Writings* (Leiden, 1978), 65, and "Inquiry," 177.

68. See Fritz Hoffmann, *Die Schriften des Oforder Kanzlers Iohannes Lutterell. Texte zur Theologie des Vierzehnten Jahrhunderts* (Leipzig, 1959), 125. This interpretation is based mainly on the following passage from the introduction of Lutterell's treatise (p. 7): "Ideoque, pater sanctissime, quoniam in libro, quem de gratia vestre sanctitatis et licentia pridie tenui, conceptiones aliquas reperri, que idcirco aures multorum offendunt, . . . iuxta tenuitatem ingenii mei dictas conceptiones erroneas esse ostendens." Although Hoffmann was aware that Lutterell received Ockham's commentary on the *Sentences* from the pope, he still believed that Lutterell had brought a list of charged errors with him, because he could not believe that Lutterell's treatise was the work of one day (*pridie*), as the introduction indicates. Koch 2: 283, and Southern, "Changing Role," 146.

69. Courtney, "Erfurt," 343 n. 4.

70. Koch, 2: 286.

71. See also note 122 for the theologian Peter of Palude, who was charged with a similar task in the proceedings against John of Pouilly.

72. Girard J. Etzkorn, "Ockham at a Provincial Chapter, 1323: A Prelude to Avignon," *AFH* 83 (1990), 557–67.

73. See Courtenay, *Adam Wodeham*, 62–63 for the opposition between Reading and Ockham.

74. CUP 2: 541 (#1076): "quod licet olim felicis recordationis Benedictis papa XII predecessor noster tibi, qui apud eum de nonnullis opinionibus fantasticis quas in certis disputationibus in Parisiensi studio te tenuisse delatus fueras, tibi ad suam presenciam propterea evocato interdixisset."

75. CUP 1: 280 and 282.

76. John Moorman, *A History of the Franciscan Order. From Its Origin to the Year 1517* (Oxford, 1968), 127–31, and Marc Dufeil, *Guillaume de Saint-Amour et la polémique universitaire Parisienne, 1250–1259* (Paris, 1972).

77. CUP 2: 221 (#764)

78. Koch, 2: 405–406.

79. David Burr, *Olivi's Peaceable Kingdom: A Reading of the Apocalypse Commentary* (Philadelphia, 1993), esp. 204–6.

80. Jeannine Quillet, *Marsile de Padoue. Le defenseur de la paix* (Paris, 1968), esp. 9–19, for the historical background of this treatise.

81. Koch, *Durandus*, 168–76 and Maier, 3: 416–17, and 563–64.

82. Southern's thesis is also criticized, though from a different angle than here, in Courtenay, "Inquiry," 176. Centralistic tendencies of the papal administration in other fields are discussed in George Mollat, *Les papes d'Avignon, 1305–1378* (Paris, 1964), 482–86 and 553–54. See further Southern, "Changing Role," 139–40 and Courtenay, "Inquiry," 176.

83. Brian Tierney, *Origins of Papal Infallibility, 1150–1350* (Leiden, 1972), 42 and *passim*.

84. Southern, "Changing Role," 140.

85. Courtenay, "Inquiry," 176 has pointed out that the masters of theology were not removed from their role as examiners. For this reason there was not much resistance to be expected from these quarters to the change of venue from Paris to Avignon.

86. The standard study on this type of manuals is still Antoine Dondaine, "Le manuel de l'inquisiteur (1230–1330)," *Archivum Fratrum Praedicatorum* 17 (1947), 85–194.

87. Pierre d'Ailly, *Tractatus ex parte universitatis studii Parisiensi pro causa fidei, contra quemdam fratrem Johannem de Montesono Ordinis Praedicatorum*, published in Carolus Du Plessis d'Argentré, *Collectio judiciorum de novis erroribus*, 3 vols. (Paris, 1724–36), I, part 2: 87–88. The *Tractatus* is a revised and expanded version of the brief that d'Ailly wrote for the appellate process against Monzón. See note 189.

88. For the following very brief recapitulation of the inquisitorial method I have relied on Erwin Jacobi, "Der Prozess im Decretum Gratiani und bei den ältesten Dekretisten," *Zeitschrift der Savigny-Stiftung für Rechtsgeschichte*, Kan. Abt. 34 (1913), 223–343; Walter Ullmann, "Some Medieval Principles of Criminal Procedure," *Juridical Review* 59 (1947), 1–28; reprinted in Walter Ullmann, *Jurisprudence in the Middle Ages* (London, 1980); Edward Peters, *Inquisition* (New York, 1988), 36–37, 44–45, and 64; Winfried Trusen, "Der Inquisitionsprozess. Seine historischen Grundlagen und frühen Formen," *Zeitschrift der Savigny-Stiftung für Rechtsgeschichte*, Kan. Abt. 105 (1988), 168–230; H. Ansgar Kelly, "Inquisition and the Prosecution of Heresy: Misconceptions and Abuses," *CH* 58 (1989), 439–51; Kelley, "Inquisitorial Due Process," 409; Kelly, "The Right to Remain Silent: Before and After Joan of Arc," *Speculum* 68 (1993), 995–97; E. C. Coppens, "De inquisitoire procedure in het canonieke recht," in *Misdaad, zoen en straf: Aspekten van de middeleeuwse strafrechtsgeschiedenis in de Nederlanden*, ed. H. A. Diederiks and H. W. Roodenburg (Hilversum, 1991), 37–47.

89. William Durant (Guillaume Durand), *Speculum iudiciale*, 2 vols. (Basel, 1574; reprint Aalen, 1975).

90. See Kelly, "The Right," 995, and "Inquisitorial Due Process," 409.

91. Kelly, "Inquisitorial Due Process," 421.

92. See, for instance, CUP 3: 121 (Foullechat): "querulosis clamoribus accusatus"; CUP 3: 503 (Monzón): "ut juxta formam ipsius dictas suas asserciones, que scandalum generaverant, retractaret."

93. Michalski, "Révocation," 1097: "Et relatum est cancellario parisiensi testimonio fide dignorum et probatum per testes ydoneos, quod ego, frater Bartholomeus dixi, sustinui et docui publice in scolis aliqua hic inferius contenta, quorum aliqua sunt contra fidem, aliqua contra bonos mores et aliqua falsa evidenter secundum concors iudicium omnium venerabilium doctorum in theologica facultate."; and CUP 3: 121 (#1299): "dixit plura erronea atque falsa, super quibus per nonnullos, etiam graves personas, conscientia atque juramento premisso cogentibus, apud nos [i.e., cancellarius] delatus extitit, et querulosis clamoribus accusatus."

94. CUP 3: 121 (#1299): "Que omnia . . . expresse juravit in manu prefati cancelarii modo et forma superius annotatis."

95. CUP 3: 121 (#1299): "Nichilominus idem frater Dyonisius, fama publica referente, in suo principio Sententiarum, in scolis Minorum Parisius, dixit plura

erronea atque falsa." The investigation of the views of Nicholas of Autrecourt (1340) also concerned passages from his *principium*, though not exclusively so. The Autrecourt case is discussed in Chapter 4.

96. For the role of the *principium* and the vesperies during the study of theology (and arts) see Glorieux, "L'enseignement," 138–41, Bernard C. Bazán, *e.a.*, *Les questions disputées et les questions quodlibétiques dans les facultés de théologie, de droit et de médecine* (Turnhout, 1985), 100–105, Courtenay, *Adam Wodeham*, 175; and Olga Weijers, *Terminologie des universités au XIIIe siècle* (Rome, 1987), 413–20.

97. CUP 3: 491 (#1559): "quas magister Johannes de Montesono, Or. frat. Predicat., in suis vesperiis et in sua questione de resumpta tenuit et asseruit."

98. Pierre d'Ailly, *Tractatus*, 78: "Et etiam hoc [i.e., quod ad facultatem theologiae pertinet assertiones haereticas aut erroneas condemnare] apparet ex communi protestatione, quae solet fieri in actibus theologicis, qua scholastici protestantur nihil dicere, quod cedat in favorem articulorum Parisiis per reverendos episcopos et magistros in theologia damnatorum."

99. Courtenay, "Inquiry," 178 n. 23 was the first to notice that charges of false teaching occasionally arose in the context of *principia* or vesperies. The records of the latter three cases are not explicit on the circumstances under which these scholars drew the attention of the authorities. We have only the final lists of censured views and their dates; so we are not even sure when the investigations started.

100. See note 65.

101. Burr, *Olivi*, 40.

102. Koch, 2: 405–6.

103. For Peter of Tarentaise see R. Martin, "Notes critiques au sujet de l'Opuscule IX de Saint Thomas," in *Mélanges A. Pelzer* (Louvain, 1947), 309–10. For John of Paris see P. Glorieux, "Un mémoire justificatif de Bernard de Trilia," *RSPT* 17 (1928), 407: "Istos articulos non dixi ut mihi imponuntur, et delatores non vidi nec audivi, et depositiones petivi et non habui."

104. Koch, 2: 394–95; Daniels, *Rechtfertigungsschrift*, 31–34; Käppelli, *Procès*, 11–12, ch. 4, and nn. 33 and 35.

105. Koch, 2: 207–8 and Courtenay, "Inquiry," 176.

106. Koch, 2: 53 and 206; CUP 2: 140–42.

107. Fournier's activities as an expert in commissions are documented in Koch, 2: 367–87 and in Maier, 2: 59–81 and 3: 447–81. For his activities as an inquisitor in the Languedoc see Emmanuel Le Roy Ladurie, *Montaillou, village occitan de 1294 à 1324* (Paris, 1976).

108. Léon Baudry, *Guillaume d'Occam: Sa vie, ses oeuvres, ses idées sociales et politiques* (Paris, 1949), 97 n. 3 mentions this treatise, preserved in the manuscript Carpentras, Bibliothèque de la ville 177.

109. Käppelli, *Procès*, 25.

110. Koch, 2: 131, 263, and 404.

111. Koch, 2: 131, and Maier, 3: 481–504.

112. Koch, *Durandus*, 168–76 and Maier, 3: 416–17.

113. Koch, 2: 263 and Maier, 2: 73–74.

114. See Koch, 2: 437–38.

115. The background and course of the procedures against Olivi are described

in David Burr, "Olivi and the Limits of Intellectual Freedom," in *Contemporary Reflections on the Medieval Christian Tradition*, ed. G. H. Shriver (Durham, N.C., 1974), 186–88, and *Olivi*, esp. 88–90. These studies contain important corrections to Koch's work.

116. The text has been edited in D. Laberge, "Fr. Petri Ioannis Olivi O.F.M. tria scripta sui ipsius apologetica annorum 1283 et 1285," *AFH* 28 (1935), 132: "Duo igitur ex his mihi miranda occurrunt quae satis non sufficio admirari. Quorum primum est quia, sicut per viam valde fide dignam mihi datum est intelligi, de quibusdam scriptationibus seu quaestiunculis meis, quas ad exercitationem aliqualis intelligentiae mihi datae satis secrete conscripseram, quae per fratres praeter meam intentionem, immo contra meam voluntatem expressam sunt publicatae, quaedam sunt per vos vel aliquos vestrum excerpta, et in uno rotulo recollecta. Quorum quaedam sive ab omnibus concorditer sive a maiori parte vestrum per sententialem definitionem, datam in scriptis, et in ipso rotulo a latere consignatam, sunt iudicata falsa, quaedam vero haeretica, quaedam in fide dubia, quaedam nostro Ordini periculosa, quaedam nescia seu nescie, quaedam praesumptuose prolata, et quaedam, ut ita dicam, crucifigenda seu crucis signo signanda; et, sicut apparet ex his quae a latere sunt in ipso rotulo consignata, non solum ea quae ibi excerpta sunt, sed etiam ipse auctor est sententialiter laesus seu reprehensus." Other aspects of this text will be discussed in what follows.

117. See Koch, 2: 207–9. The passage is also discussed by David Burr, *The Persecution of Peter Olivi* (Philadelphia, 1976), 41 and 43.

118. Other qualifications one encounters are *absurdus, temerarius, periculosus*, and *frivolus*. See Koch, 2: 434–45.

119. Koch, *Durandus*, 201.

120. CUP 2: 421.

121. Jürgen Miethke, *Ockhams Weg zur Sozialphilosophie* (Berlin, 1969), 62 n. 223, and Koch, 2: 446, who also addduces the example of the examination of Olivi's *Postille*. The report of the double task of the Ockham commission reads as follows: "et ex parte eiusdem sanctitatis vestre impositum, quod [1] diligentius videremus, an prefati articuli contineantur prout iacent in libro et quaternis predictis et [2] de eisdem articulis inter nos deliberaremus et scriberemus, quod nobis videretur de singulis faciendum."

122. Koch, 2: 404–6.

123. In the case of Thomas of Naples this was explicitly stated. See CUP 2: 614–15. In the case of Peter of Tarentaise this has to be inferred from the fact that there are no documents concerning his condemnation, but only Thomas Aquinas's report on his theses. The Tarentaise case is discussed in Courtenay, "Dominicans."

124. William Durant, *Speculum iudiciale*, 1: 313–17 (*De teste*). See also CUP 3: 100 (#1272) for an example of *articuli* that do not only concern doctrinal views.

125. CUP 2: 505. See also William Durant, *Speculum iudiciale*, 1: 430–31, and 440–41, which discusses several types of citation and the time interval that should be granted to respond to the citation.

126. See F. D. Logan, *Excommunication and the Secular Arm in Medieval England* (Toronto, 1968), 44–49 for a discussion of contumacy in canon law, and also William Durant, *Speculum iudiciale*, 1: 448, which enumerates three ways of incur-

ring contumacy. In addition to the two forms discussed above, the third way to incur contumacy was by a refusal to obey a court decision.

127. CUP 3: 496 and 503.

128. CUP 3: 509.

129. For information concerning Ockham's stay at Avignon and his escape see Baudry, *Guillaume d'Occam* 1: 96 and 115–16 and Miethke, *Ockhams Weg*, 72–73.

130. CUP 3: 508 (#1567). It is not known why Monzón was housed at an inn, instead of at the Dominican convent in Avignon. Since each party in an appeal had to pay his own costs, the Dominican order probably paid for Monzón's lodging. See also note 192.

131. See Koch, 1: 333–34 and 345, and McGinn, "Eckhart's Condemnation," 396.

132. See Käppeli, *Procès*, 72–73; Beryl Smalley, *English Friars and Antiquity in the Early Fourteenth Century* (Oxford, 1960), 77–78; and also Marc Dykmans, "A propos de Jean XXII et Benoît XII: La libération de Thomas Waleys," *Archivum Historiae Pontificae* 7 (1969), 115–30, who has argued that Waleys remained in the papal prison only until 1334. Even if Dykmans's thesis is true, the documents show that Waleys must have been under some milder form of arrest for a considerable period of time.

133. Robert Wielockx, ed., *Aegidii Romani, Apologia* (Florence, 1985), 92; Koch, 2: 408 and 132; Käppeli, *Procès*, 140–141; Koch, 1: 324–325; F. Stegmüller, "Die Zwei Apologien des Jean de Mirecourt," *RTAM* 5 (1933), 46.

134. Miethke, *Ockhams Weg*, 66–67 and CUP 2: 580. Unfortunately, we do not have detailed information about their defenses.

135. Burr, *Persecution*, 37 and 42–43, and *Olivi*, 90.

136. CUP 3: 119.

137. Lambert M. de Rijk, ed. and trans., *Nicholas of Autrecourt, His Correspondence with Master Giles and Bernard of Arezzo* (Leiden, 1994), 154: "Deinde per p⟨⟨relatos ac magist⟩⟩ros discussi fuerunt alii articuli dati et assignati contra ipsum magistrum Nicolaum. Quorum aliquos simpliciter et aliquos sub forma qua ponuntur, se dixisse negavit. Qui secuntur per ordinem, sub hiis verbis."

138. Glorieux, "Mémoire," 407.

139. Daniels, *Rechtfertigungsschrift*, 12: "Porro de aliis articulis extractis ex sermonibus qui michi ascribuntur responder non haberem cum passim, et frequenter etiam a clericis, studiosis et doctis dimminute et falso que audiunt reportantur."

140. Koch, 2: 394 and 409.

141. See note 35.

142. See note 31.

143. Laberge, "Fr. Petri Ioannis Olivi," 133: "Ego vero . . . indirecte viderer confiteri illa, quae de meis scripturis excerpta fuerant, me scripsisse in alio sensu et alia intentione quam feceram, et quod peius esset, viderer per hoc concedere, et hoc mendose et contra conscientiam meam, quod ego in illo erroneo vel haeretico sensu, qui michi erat impositus ea disxissem." See Burr, *Persecution*, 42–43 for a discussion of the role of the *Letter of the Seven Seals* at Olivi's trial.

144. CUP 2: 87: "quod articulos quos mihi fecistis legi scripseram non secun-

dum intellectum quo sonabant extracti per vos ab opere meo, sed secundum intellectum quo sonabant jacentis in serie scripture."

145. Stegmüller, "Die Zwei Apologien," 192 and 204.

146. Daniels, *Rechtfertigungsschrift*, 12, l. 26–28 and 34, l. 20–25.

147. Daniels, *Rechtfertigungsschrift*, 65, l. 24–25.

148. Daniels, *Rechtfertigungsschrift*, 34, l. 36 and 54, l. 16–18. For the latter
quotation see also McGinn, "Eckhart's Condemnation," 403.

149. Nicholas of Autrecourt defended himself along this line. See de Rijk,
Nicholas, 150. This distinction was also invoked by Brother Bartholomew. See
Glorieux, "Mémoire," 408, 412–13 for clear examples.

150. Examples are provided in Konstanty Michalski, *Le criticisme et le scepticisme
dans la philosophie du XIVe siècle* (Krakow, 1927), 68–71; reprinted in Konstanty
Michalski, *La philosophie au XIVe siècle* (Frankfurt, 1969), 136–39. See also Burr,
"Olivi and the Limits," 195–96 and Courtenay, *Adam Wodeham*, 174.

151. Peter Olivi, for instance, explicitly outlines the strategy of defense he used
in this way. See Laberge, "Fr. Petri Ioannis Olivi," 134. The same method can be
inferred from other rolls with articles.

152. See McGinn, "Eckhart's Condemnation," 407 and 413 for the notion of
"quidquid recipitur, secundum modum recipientis recipitur." The notion is perhaps
connected with Gregory the Great's rule for preaching, *Pastorale*, III prol. (PL 77:
49): "Pro qualitate igitur audientium formari debet sermo doctorum . . . Quid enim
sunt intentae mentes auditorum, nisi ut ita dixerim, quaedam in cithara tensiones
stratae chordarum?" The passage is also cited by Gerson, 3: 62: "juxta mores auditorum formetur sermo doctorum." See also Aristotle, *Metaphysics* 994 b 30–995 a 2.

153. Article 211 of the 1277 condemnation is qualified as *male sonat*. See CUP
1: 555. Some other examples of articles that were condemned as they sound, are to
be found in de Rijk, *Nicholas*, 150 no. 2.8, 160 no. 16.3, and 161 no. 16.8 (Nicholas
of Autrecourt); CUP 3: 108 (John of Calore). For Durand of St. Pourçain, see
Koch, 2: 75. For Meister Eckhart see Koch, 2: 323–24 and McGinn, "Eckhart's
Condemnation," 412–14.

154. See, for instance, CUP 3: 493: "propter malum sensum, quem generare
possent in animis auditorum."

155. Laurent, "Autour du procès," 436. See also Monika Asztalos, "The Faculty
of Theology," in *Universities in the Middle Ages*, ed. Hilde De Ridder-Symoens (*A
History of the University in Europe*, vol. 1; Cambridge, 1992), 443–44.

156. The term "prout sonat principle" is derived from McGinn, "Eckhart's
Condemnation," 412. He has rightly drawn attention to the great emphasis in
Eckhart's defense on the sense of the articles.

157. See, for example, Koch, 2: 237 and 255.

158. "Verba ergo interpretanda sunt ex sensu ex quo fiunt, non ex sensu quem
faciunt." See Nikolaus M. Häring, "Commentary and Hermeneutics," in *Renaissance
and Renewal in the Twelfth Century*, ed. Robert L. Benson and Giles Constable
(Oxford, 1982), 196 for the employment of this hermeneutical principle in the
twelfth century.

159. See [Godfrey of Fontaines], *Les Quodlibets XI et XII. Les Quodlibets XIII et
XIV*; ed. J. Hoffmans (Louvain, 1932 and 1935), 100. Details about Godfrey of

Fontaines's biography and writings, as well as a more systematic analysis of his reaction to Tempier's condemnation, will be given in Chapter 5. See also John F. Wippel, *The Metaphysical Thought of Godfrey of Fontaines: A Study in Late Thirteenth Century Philosophy* (Washington, D.C., 1981), 382–84, and Stephen F. Brown, "Godfrey of Fontaines and Henry of Ghent: Individuation and the Condemnations of 1277," in *Société et église: Textes et discussions dans les universités d'Europe centrale pendant le moyen âge tardif*, ed. Sophie Wlodek (Turnhout, 1995), 193–97 for a discussion of this passage.

160. Godfrey of Fontaines, *Quodlibet XII*, 102.

161. Trusen, "Der Inquisitionsprozess," 194 and 216–17.

162. Gerson, 6: 155–56 sect. 2 and p. 164 sect. 11. The formula could run as follows: "protestor quod nihil intendo dicere nec puto dixisse contra fidem, et si oppositum contingeret vel contingisset, illud ex nunc revoco vel retracto." See also Bazán, *Questions*, 103, for a similar practice in Bologna, and Courtenay, *Adam Wodeham*, 174, for Oxford. During the sixteenth century a slightly variant formula was in use at Paris: "In primis protestor quod nichil intendo dicere quod obviet, aut sit dissonum Sacrae Scripturae, aut definitionibus sacrorum conciliorum, aut etiam determinationibus sacrae facultatis theologiae matris meae, quibus adhaereo et semper adhaerere intendo." See James K. Farge, *Orthodoxy and Reform in Early Reformation France: The Faculty of Theology of Paris, 1500–1543* (Leiden, 1985), 160.

163. CUP 1: 176.

164. Good examples are the cases of Nicholas of Autrecourt and Denis of Foullechat. See CUP 2: 586 and CUP 3: 124 (#1300).

165. CUP 3: 114 (#1298), 124 (# 1300), and 185, note.

166. Kaluza, *Nicolas*, 120 and 125–27, and CUP 2 (#1158).

167. Michalski, "La révocation," 1091.

168. CUP 1: 486, 543 and CUP 2: 244, but these examples can be multiplied.

169. John Tedeschi, *The Prosecution of Heresy. Collected Studies on the Inquisition in Early Modern Italy* (Binghamton, N.Y., 1991), 49.

170. See note 25.

171. Koch, 2: 9–15.

172. Wielockx, ed., *Aegidii Romani*, 110–11.

173. See Koch, 2: 197–98 and 211 and Burr, *Olivi*, 106–8.

174. The standard formula would run something as follows: "ad gradus et honores . . . promoveri et assumi non posses . . . sine licentia sedis apostolice specialis." The penalties concerned Richard of Lincoln and Nicholas of Autrecourt. See CUP 2: 541 (#1076) and de Rijk, *Nicholas*, 163–64, respectively. Both documents are discussed in Kaluza, *Nicolas*, 122–23.

175. CUP 1: 633 (#522), and 2: #1076.

176. See Pearl Kibre, "Academic Oaths at the University of Paris in the Middle Ages," in *Essays in Medieval Life and Thought. Presented in Honor of Austin Patterson Evans*, ed. John H. Mundy, Richard W. Emery, Benjamin N. Nelson (New York, 1955), 123–37, and Zénon Kaluza, "Le statut du 25 septembre 1339 et l'Ordonnance du 2 septembre 1276," in *Die Philosophie im 14. und 15. Jahrhundert*, ed. Olaf Pluta (Amsterdam, 1988), 350–51, who also draws attention to Gerson's observations concerning the custom of swearing oaths.

177. William Durant, *Speculum iudiciale*, 1: esp. 839–65 (*De appellationibus*), and further X 2.28, and A. Amanien, "Appèl," in *Dictionnaire du droit canonique*, 7 vols. (Paris, 1935–65), 1: 764–807.

178. See CUP 3: 115–16 (#1298).

179. CUP 3: 122 (#1299).

180. CUP 3: 115–16 (#1298).

181. CUP 3: 122–24 (#1300). These are the minutes from the appellate meeting in Avignon.

182. CUP 3: 182 (#1349).

183. CUP 3: 183 (#1350). The list of new errors is edited in CUP 3: 185 (#1352). The errors were first recanted in Avignon, and later in Paris.

184. CUP 3: 183 (#1350), the same letter that, in the introduction, gives an account of the actions of the auditors that had been set on the case.

185. CUP 3: 184–85 (#1351).

186. CUP 3: 183: "Attendentes igitur quod hujusmodi negotium seu causa attentis circumstantiis universis commodius poterit tractari Parisius quam in Romana curia prelibata . . . et in hoc assistentibus cancellario predicto ac magistris in facultate predicta."

187. CUP 3: 496 (#1559).

188. There are no records of the appellate process. The following account of Monzón's appeal is based on CUP 3: 506–12 (#1567). This is a record of the court session that took place on January 27, 1389, in which Monzón was convicted in a contempt of court procedure, and excommunicated, because he fled from Avignon before his appellate case had been decided. Fortunately, the record also provides a sketchy account of the appellate process during the three months prior to Monzón's flight.

189. It seems that only two of d'Ailly's briefs are still extant today. One brief, edited in CUP 3: 502–5 (#1564), is a statement of the facts of the case as d'Ailly understood them. I have used this rich source to reconstruct the earlier stages of the Monzón case. The other brief is the rebuttal of the grounds of Monzón's appeal. It has been edited in Du Plessis, *Collectio*, 1, part 2: 69–74, and was later rewritten as the *Tractatus ex parte universitatis* (see note 87). A copy of Monzón's petition has not been identified yet.

190. CUP 3: 506–12 (#1567). Another official who is mentioned in this document is the pope's fiscal procurator (*procurator fiscalis*). On the canonistic principle that the same person cannot be accuser and judge (*non tanquam idem sit accusator et judex*), the right to prosecute was transferred to the fiscal procurator. See Innocent III, *Qualiter et quando* no. 1. (X 5.1.17), and also note 90. Note, however, that the fiscal procurator had no role in the appellate process. He became involved only when Monzón did not obey the summons to appear in court. Together with the attorneys appointed by the university, he drew up the bill of complaint that led the judges to the contempt of court proceedings against Monzón.

191. These grounds can be inferred from d'Ailly's *Tractatus*. The treatise's purpose is to explain the legitimacy of disciplinary actions of the faculty of theology against Monzón. It is based on the appellee's formal response to the reasons for Monzón's appeal. A fuller discussion of this aspect will be given in Chapter 5.

192. CUP 3: 500–501 (#1562). Another example is provided in CUP 1: #263.

193. Foullechat indicated that he had received advice to appeal. Moreover, his petition suggests that he is not only appealing for himself, but also in the name of his order. See CUP 3: 119 (#1298): "idem frater Dionisius voluit petiitque et requisivit, suo et predicti sui Ordinis nomine," and CUP 3: 123 (#1300): "tamen ipse non bono sed minus sano fretus consilio, dictam revocacionem publicam facere noluerat, sed in vim appellacionis prorumpens . . . appellaverat ad apostolicam sanctaam sedem."

194. CUP 3: #1298, dated November 21, 22, 1364, and #1352, dated April 12, 1369.

195. The record of the contempt of court procedure at the episcopal court is dated August 23, 1387. The brief in which Pierre d'Ailly explains the facts of the case as he understands them is dated May–July 1388. See CUP 3: #1559 and #1564.

196. CUP 3: 508 (#1567): "quod frater Johannes predictus (that is, Monzón) fuerat in dicta albergaria per tres menses et ultra hospitatus et quod de hospitio predicto et curia Romana recesserat, ut ipsa credebat, die tertia mensis Augusti proxime lapsa."

197. CUP 3: #1300.

Chapter 2. The Condemnation of March 7, 1277

1. Doctrinal reactions to Tempier's condemnation were offered by John of Naples (see note 57), Raymond Lull, and Konrad of Megenberg. See P. O. Keicher, *Raymundus und seine Stellung zur arabischen Philosophie. Mit einem Anhang, enthaltend die zum ersten Male veröffentlichte "Declaratio Raymundi per modum dialogi"* (Münster, 1909), and Konrad von Megenberg, *Werke. Ökonomik*, book 3, ed. S. Krüger (Staatsschriften des späteren Mittelalters, vol. 3; Stuttgart, 1984). In addition, mention should be made of an anonymous commentary, discovered and partially edited in Martin Grabmann, "Ein spätmittelalterlicher Pariser Kommentar zur Verurteilung des lateinischen Averroismus durch Bischof Stephan Tempier von Paris (1277) und zu anderen Irrtumslisten" in Martin Grabmann, *Mittelalterliches Geistesleben*, 3 vols. (Munich, 1936), 2: 272–86.

2. Pierre Mandonnet, *Siger de Brabant et l'averroïsme latin au XIIIe siècle*, 2 vols. (Louvain, 1908–11), especially 1: 28–29, 59–63, and 142–95.

3. Fernand van Steenberghen, *Aristotle in the West* (Louvain, 1955), 198–208; *La philosophie au XIIIᵉ siècle*, 2d ed. (Louvain, 1991), 354–59, and 422–26; and *Maître Siger de Brabant* (Louvain, 1977), 149–158. See also John F. Wippel, "The Condemnations of 1270 and 1277 at Paris," *Journal of Medieval and Renaissance Studies* 7 (1977), 173–74, Charles H. Lohr, "The Medieval Interpretation of Aristotle," *CHLMP*, 87–92, and, most recently, John F. Wippel, *Mediaeval Reactions to the Encounter Between Faith and Reason* (Milwaukee, 1995).

4. Fernand van Steenberghen, *Thomas Aquinas and Radical Aristotelianism* (Washington, D.C., 1980), and, more recently Richard C. Dales, *Medieval Discussions of the Eternity of the World* (Leiden, 1990); Luca Bianchi, *Il vescovo e i filosofi. La*

condanna parigina del 1277 e l'evoluzione dell'aristotelismo scolastico (Bergamo, 1990), and Alain de Libera, *Penser au Moyen Âge* (Paris, 1991), 189–245 shed further light on these issues. Still valuable is Wippel, "The Condemnations," 187–201.

5. Pierre Duhem, *Études sur Leonard de Vinci*, 3 vols. (Paris, 1906–13), 2: 411, and 3: vii and 125. See also Pierre Duhem, *Medieval Cosmology*; ed. and transl. Roger Ariew (Chicago, 1985), xxii–xxiii. One of the earliest criticisms of Duhem's thesis, which focused precisely on the articles 39 and 49, was given by Alexandre Koyré, "Le vide et l'espace infini au XIVe siècle," *AHDL* 17 (1949), 45–91. More recently Edward Grant has studied the impact of Tempier's condemnation on the history of medieval science. See his "The Condemnation of 1277, God's Absolute Power, and Physical Thought in the Late Middle Ages," *Viator* 10 (1979), 211–44; "The Effect of the Condemnation of 1277," in *CHLMP*, 537–40; and "Science and Theology in the Middle Ages," in *God and Nature. Historical Essays on the Encounter between Christianity and Science*, ed. David Lindberg and Ronald Numbers (Berkeley, 1986), 49–75. A penetrating discussion of the legacy of Duhem's thesis in the twentieth-century historiography of medieval science is provided by John E. Murdoch, "Pierre Duhem and the History of Late Medieval Science and Philosophy in the Latin West," in *Gli studi di filosofia medievale fra otto e novecento*, ed. Alfonso Maierù and Ruedi Imbach (Rome, 1991), 253–302. For the placing of Grant in the context of the Duhem thesis see Murdoch, "Duhem," 281–283.

6. Mandonnet, *Siger*, especially 1: 191–195, Gilson, *La philosophie au moyen âge*, 2nd. ed. rev. and exp. (Paris, 1947), 559; and van Steenberghen, *Thomas Aquinas*, 75–110. More recently, this interpretation has been taken up in Kurt Flasch, *Aufklärung im Mittelalter? Die Verurteilung von 1277* (Frankfurt, 1989); Roland Hissette, "Note sur le syllabus "antirationaliste" du 7 mars 1277," *Revue Philosophique de Louvain* 88 (1990), 404–16, and also Ludwig Hödl, "'. . . sie reden, als ob es zwei gegensätzliche Wahrheiten gäbe.' Legende und Wirklichkeit der mittelalterlichen Theorie von der doppelten Wahrheit," in *Philosophie im Mittelalter. Entwicklungslinien und Paradigmen*, ed. Jan P. Beckmann, *e.a.* (Hamburg, 1987), 224–29, and 242–43.

7. CUP 1: 534: "Dicunt enim ea esse vera secundum philosophiam, sed non secundum fidem catholicam, quasi sunt duae contrariae veritates, et quasi contra veritatem sacrae Scripturae sit veritas in dictis gentilium damnatorum."

8. Van Steenberghen sets forth this view in several of his publications. See, for instance, *Thomas Aquinas*, 105–9. See also Richard C. Dales, "The Origin of the Doctrine of the Double Truth," *Viator* 15 (1984), 169–79, and Hödl, "'. . . sie reden,'" 225–45.

9. The only other condemnation in the *Collectio errorum* that is anonymous was also issued by Tempier, on December 10, 1270. See CUP 1: 486–87 (#432). Note that the so-called Ockhamist statute of 1340, which appears in the printed tradition of the *Collectio errorum*, is also anonymous. See CUP 1: 505–7 (#1042) and Chapter 3 for a discussion of this censure.

10. This document is more fully discussed in the Selected Bibliography.

11. Note that the 1277 condemnation is one of the very few censures in the *Collectio errorum* that concerned the faculty of arts. This aspect could be considered the third distinctive feature of Tempier's syllabus.

12. Only two medieval manuscripts bear a rubric identifying the holders of the condemned errors. The manuscript Paris, BN lat. 4391, fol. 68 presents the syllabus of 219 errors under the rubric "Contra Segerum et Boetium hereticos." The manuscript Paris BN, lat. 16533 fol. 60 mentions "Principalis assertor istorum articulorum fuit quidam clericus boetius appellatus." See Mandonnet, *Siger*, 2: 220.

13. Roland Hissette, *Enquête sur les 219 articles condamnés à Paris le 7 mars 1277* (Louvain, 1977), 314.

14. This traditional picture goes back to Mandonnet, *Siger*, 2: 214–86 and has been codified in Fernand van Steenberghen, *Maître Siger*, 139–49 and 159–65, though with one important correction, namely the date of the inquisitor's citation of Siger of Brabant. See note 25 below. All the subsequent literature has basically accepted Mandonnet's and van Steenberghen's portrayal of the events. See, for instance, Bianchi, *Vescovo*, 17–18; John F. Wippel, "Thomas Aquinas and the Condemnation of 1277," *The Modern Schoolman* 72 (1995), 237; and François-Xavier Putallaz, *Insolente Liberté. Controverses et condemnations au XIIIe siècle* (Paris, 1995), 51–55, to mention a few of the more recent studies.

15. CUP 1: 541.

16. CUP 1: 543.

17. Jürgen Miethke, "Papst, Ortsbischof und Universität in den Pariser Theologenprozessen des 13. Jahrhunderts," in *Die Auseinandersetzungen an der Pariser Universität im XIII. Jahrhundert*, ed. Albert Zimmermann (Berlin, 1976), 86–87. See also Roland Hissette, "Etienne Tempier et ses condemnations," *RTAM* 47 (1980), 239–42 for a discussion of this thesis.

18. But see Bianchi, *Vescovo*, 206, who draws attention to similar formulas in other university documents and suggests that it may be a standard phrase, or a topos.

19. According to Robert Wielockx, ed., *Aegidii Romani, Apologia* (Florence, 1985), 92 n. 65 correspondence from the papal curia to Paris took about a month to arrive.

20. This letter has been edited in A. Callebaut, "Jean Pecham et l'Augustinisme. Aperçus historiques," *AFH* 18 (1925), 459–60.

21. This suggestion is also made by Miethke, "Papst," 85.

22. Callebaut, "Jean Pecham," 460: "ut receptis eisdem ad discussionem, determinacionem seu reprobationem errorum ipsorum vel etiam ad ordinacionem . . . , nec non et statu eiusdem studii reformando in premissis viderimus faciendam, de fratrum nostrorum consilio procedamus."

23. Wielockx, ed., *Aegidii Romani*, 102 also suggests that *Flumen aquae vivae* may contain echos of the inquiry against Giles of Rome. At the same time, one should keep in mind that such rather vague letters expressing concern over the orthodoxy of teaching at the university had a topical character. Compare, for instance, the opening of *Flumen aquae vivae* to the well-known letter of Pope Clement VI of May 20, 1346, addressed to the masters and scholars in Paris and edited in CUP 2: 587–90 (#1125), which also refers to the theme of *flumen aquae vivae*.

24. Wielockx, ed., *Aegidii Romani*, 77–88 suggests a date after March 7 and before March 28, 1277.

25. Antoine Dondaine, "Le manuel de l'inquisiteur (1230–1330)," *Archivum Fratrum Praedicatorum* 17 (1947), 186–192. Dondaine was the first to re-establish

the correct date of the summons, namely November 23, 1276, not November 24, 1277, as Mandonnet, *Siger*, 1: 255, n. 1 thought. The significance of the correct date is that it places the summons before, not after, the condemnation of March 7, 1277. Dondaine's corrected edition of the inquisitor's citation has been accepted by all scholars, unanimously, who otherwise have remained faithful to Mandonnet's portrayal of the events leading to the censure of March 7, 1277. See also note 14.

26. Dondaine, "Manuel," 187, merely observed that, according to customary inquisitorial proceedings, it was the inquisitor's citation that opened the process. Unfortunately, he did not apply this insight to a reinterpretation of Tempier's censure.

27. The itineraries of the papal court in the years between 1276 and 1284 are summed up in Mandonnet, *Siger*, 276 and van Steenberghen, *Maître Siger*, 163. If one assumes that Siger joined the papal court in 1277, one must also assume that he followed its itineraries to Viterbo, Rome, and Orvieto. See J. M. M. H. Thijssen, "What Really Happened on 7 March 1277? Bishop Tempier's Condemnation and Its Institutional Context," in *Texts and Contexts in Ancient and Medieval Science: Studies on the Occasion of John. E. Murdoch's Seventieth Birthday*, ed. Edith Sylla and Michael McVaugh (Leiden, 1997), 94–95 for a more detailed discussion of the documentary evidence that supposedly supports the thesis that Siger of Brabant filed an appeal at the papal court.

28. This is demonstrated, for instance, in the cases against the theologians Denis of Foullechat and John of Monzón, who both appealed against a sentence. See Chapter 1.

29. Theoretically, Siger could have turned to the pope and asked him, as judge over all major causes, to decide his case. In that scenario, the papal court would not have been an appellate court, but a court of first instance. There is no documentary evidence, however, that Siger took this course, nor is there any trace of a papal judgment in an inquiry against him.

30. In essence, contumacy was considered to be disobedience to an ecclesiastical court. See Chapter 1, note 126.

31. René Gauthier, "Notes sur Siger de Brabant. II. Siger en 1272–1275. Aubry de Reims et la scission des Normands," *RSPT* 68 (1984), 26–28.

32. Gauthier, "Notes," 26.

33. Gauthier, "Notes," 26.

34. CUP 1: 521–30 (#460). See Gauthier, "Notes," 22 and 24. He has convincingly argued that this was a purely administrative conflict, not a doctrinal one.

35. Van Steenberghen, *Maître Siger*, 133, 218, and 221.

36. Louis-Jacques Bataillon, "Bulletin d'histoire des doctrines médiévales: Le treizième siècle (fin)," *RSPT* 65 (1981), 107 has convincingly argued that it is very unlikely that the mad *clericus* who reportedly stabbed Siger of Brabant is identical to Goswin of Chapelle, whose ecclesiastical rank was too high for him to be Siger's servant.

37. Van Steenberghen, *Maître Siger*, 144, and Gauthier, "Notes," 26.

38. Bataillon, "Bulletin," 107 suggested that Siger of Brabant went to Orvieto for matters that concerned his chapter. This suggestion was followed by Gauthier, "Notes," 27.

39. Van Steenberghen, *Maître Siger*, 144 observes: "On ne sait rien des accusa-

tions qui avaient été formulées contre les trois maîtres dénoncés à Simon du Val, ni, dès lors, des griefs qui justifiaient leur citation devant le tribunal de l'inquisiteur."

40. There are no documents to suggest why the suspects were acquitted. Possibly the evidence was inconclusive, or perhaps the Bishop of Liège came to the rescue of his canons and coerced the inquisitor to acquit them.

41. This juridical principle can be found in Gratian's *Decretum,* C.2 q.1 c.14 par.1. John the Teuton offers the following comment in his *Glossa ordinaria* C.2 q.1 c.14 par. 1 "Non potest": "Sive enim quis sit condemnatus, sive absolutus, tamen super eodem crimine saepius agi non potest, ut extra De acusa. De his." He was the first to phrase this general principle, which applied in both accusatorial and inquisitorial proceedings. See Peter Landau, "Ursprünge und Entwickelung des Verbotes doppelter Strafverfolgung wegen desselben Verbrechens in der Geschichte des kanonischen Rechts," *Zeitschrift der Savigny-Stiftung für Rechtsgeschichte* Kan. Abt. 87 (1970), 124–56, esp. 138–52.

42. CUP 1: 542: "Magnarum et gravium personarum crebra zeloque fidei accensa insinuavut relatio, quod nonnulli Parisius studentes in artibus proprie facultatis limites excedentes quosdam manifestos et execrabiles errores, immo potius vanitates et insanias falsas in rotulo seu cedulis, presentibus hiis annexo seu annexis contentos quasi dubitabiles in scolis tractare et disputare presumunt."

43. Tempier distinguishes the important persons who reported the allegations of false teaching (*magnarum et gravium personarum crebra zeloque fidei accensa insinuavit relatio*) from the theologians and other wise men who gave him advice in this matter (*tam doctorum sacrae Scripturae, quam aliorum prudentium virorum communicato consilio*). See CUP 1: 542.

44. "Iidem magistri fuerunt assessores episcopi Stephani in condendo articulos et in concedendo praedictam propositionem. Et ideo cum praedicta magistralis propositio interimat articulum praedicto modo intellectum, si praedicto modo deberet articulus intelligi, illi magistri sibi ipsis contradixissent, omnes etiam XVI magistri qui illam propositionem concesserunt excommunicationis sententiam incurrerent, quae omnia non sunt dicenda." The text is quoted in Wielockx, ed., *Aegidii Romani,* 98 n.6.

45. Henry of Ghent, *Quodlibet II,* ed. Robert Wielockx (Louvain, 1983), 67: "In hoc enim concordabant omnes magistri theologiae congregati super hoc, quorum ego eram unus, unanimiter concedentes quod substantia angeli non est ratio angelum esse in loco secundum substantiam." See also Miethke, "Papst," 86; van Steenberghen, *Maître Siger,* 146–47; Roland Hissette, "Étienne Tempier et ses condemnations," *RTAM* 47 (1980), 234–36.

46. Ernesto Hocedez, "La condamnation de Gilles de Rome," *RTAM* 4 (1932), 56: "Nam nos ipsi tunc eramus Parisiis, et tamquam de re palpata testimonium perhibemus, quod plures de illis articulis transierunt non consilio magistrorum, sed capitositate quorundam paucorum." Hissette, "Etienne Tempier," 238, observes that the "quorundam" refers to the bishop and not to some masters of theology, as some other scholars believed.

47. See, for the latter assessment, Richard Knapwell, *Quaestio disputata de unitate formae,* ed. Francis E. Kelley (Paris, 1982), 12. An exception to the unfavorable views concerning the consistency of the condemnation is Flasch, *Aufklärung,* 56.

48. This new medieval edition is part of the *Collectio errorum in Anglia et Parisiis condemnatorum* and has been printed in Carolus Du Plessis d'Argentré, *Collectio judiciorum de novis erroribus*, 3 vols. (Paris, 1724–36), 1, part 1: 188–200. A modern edition is now available in Henryk Anzulewicz, "Eine weitere Überlieferung der *Collectio errorum in Anglia et Parisius condemnatorum* im *Ms. lat. fol. 456* der Staatsbibliothek Preussischer Kulturbesitz zu Berlin," *Franziskanische Studien* 74 (1992), 375–99. Tempier's original list is edited in CUP 1: 543–55, and reprinted with a German translation and a discussion in Flasch, *Aufklärung*, 99–261. The transmission of Tempier's list of errors is discussed in CUP 1: 556–57, and Roland Hissette, "Une *Tabula super articulis Parisiensibus*," *RTAM* 52 (1985), 171–72.

49. CUP 2: 610–13 (#1147).

50. Mandonnet, *Siger*, 2: 175–91. Hissette, *Enquête*, follows Mandonnet's order and provides on pp. 319–21 a useful concordance of the three different editions of Tempier's articles. Other thematic discussions of the articles are given in Wippel, "The Condemnations," 187–94, and *Mediaeval Reactions*, 19–27.

51. Here follows the beginning of Tempier's introductory letter (CUP 1: 542): "Universis praesentes litteras inspecturis Stephanus, permissione divina Parisiensis ecclesiae minister indignus, salutem in filio virginis gloriiosae. Magnarum et gravium personarum crebra zeloque fidei accensa insinuavut relatio, quod nonnulli Parisius studentes in artibus proprie facultatis limites excedentes quosdam manifestos et execrabiles errores, immo potius vanitates et insanias falsas in rotulo seu cedulis, presentibus hiis annexo seu annexis contentos quasi dubitabiles in scolis tractare et disputare presumunt."

52. See Hissette, *Enquête*, 314–17. Note that in the actual discussion of these articles, Hissette is more careful about claiming whether it is "beyond doubt" that an article is derived from the works of Siger of Brabant or Boethius of Dacia. Moreover, there are hardly any literal quotations or accurate paraphrases among the identified propositions. In some cases, the almost literal similarity goes back to a text of Aristotle or Averroes; see, for example, articles 13, 117, 123, and 129 in Hissette's numbering.

53. Hissette, *Enquête*, 317.

54. Most recently, Calvin G. Normore, "Who Was Condemned in 1277?" *The Modern Schoolman* 72 (1995), 273–81 explores sources from late antiquity and the Islamic world.

55. Wippel, "Thomas Aquinas" argues that Thomas Aquinas's views were targeted in Tempier's condemnation. Roland Hissette, "Saint Tomas et l'intervention épiscopale du 7 mars 1277," in *Studi*, ed. D. Lorenz, O.P. and S. Serafini (Rome, 1995), 204–58 is more cautious. He believes that Tempier's syllabus was only indirectly aimed at Aquinas and that the adherents of the censured views have to be sought primarily in the arts faculty, as Tempier's introductory letter indicates. Note that their disagreement can be resolved if one follows my suggestion and acknowledges that Tempier's introductory letter clearly distinguishes between the propagators of the censured views, who are members of the arts faculty, and the censured views themselves, whose origin is not stated. See further notes 62 and 63.

56. See Roland Hissette, "Albert le Grand et Thomas d'Aquin dans la censure parisienne du 7 mars 1277," in *Studien zur mittelalterlichen Geistesgeschichte und ihren*

Quellen, ed. Albert Zimermann (Berlin, 1982), 229–37 for a discussion of the medieval evidence.

57. Wippel, "Thomas Aquinas," 246.

58. The text of John of Naples has been edited in C. Jellouschek, "Quaestio magistri Ioannis de Neapoli O.Pr.: 'Utrum licite possit doceri Parisius doctrina fratris Thome quantum ad omnes conclusiones eius,'" in *Xenia Thomistica*, ed. S. Szabo (Rome, 1925), 73–104.

59. CUP 2: 281 (#838): "supradictam articulorum condempnatorum et excommunicationis sententiam, quantum tangunt vel tangere asseruntur doctrinam beati Thomae predicti, ex certa scientia tenore presentum totaliter annullamus, articulos ipsos propter hoc non approbando seu etiam reprobando, sed eosdem discussioni scolastice libere relinquendo." Some problems with regard to the transmission of this document are discussed in Anneliese Maier, "Der Widerruf der *articuli Parisienses* (1277) im Jahr 1325," reprinted in Maier, 3: 601–8.

60. Étienne Gilson, *History of Christian Philosophy in the Middle Ages* (New York, 1955), 728 n. 52.

61. See Hissette, "Albert," 226–46 for a survey and discussion of the various interpretations that have been advanced with regard to Thomas's inclusion in Tempier's condemnation of March 7, 1277.

62. Hissette, *Enquête*, 315–16, and Hissette, "Albert," 237–47.

63. Wippel, *Mediaeval Reactions*, 27, and "Thomas Aquinas," 241.

64. It concerned the theses "Quod in homine est tantum una forma substantialis, scilicet anima intellectiva" and "Quod Deus non potest dare esse actu materiae sine forma." The first thesis refers to the so-called doctrine of the unicity of form, which was explicitly condemned at Oxford on March 18, 1277, by Robert Kilwardby, archbishop of Canterbury. For the background see Knapwell, *Quaestio disputata*, esp. 9–32, and James A. Weisheipl, *Friar Thomas d'Aquino. His Life, Thought, and Works, with Corrigenda and Addenda* (Washington, D.C., 1983), 337–41.

65. Van Steenberghen, *Maître Siger*, 147–48.

66. See Wielockx's introduction to *Aegidii Romani*, 75–120 and 215–24 and also Robert Wielockx, "Autour du procès de Thomas d'Aquin," in *Thomas von Aquin. Werk und Wirkung im Licht neurerer Forschungen*, ed. Albert Zimmermann (Berlin, 1988), 413–38.

67. The interruption of Tempier's investigation on the orders of the curia is attested in a letter written by Archbishop John Pecham to the chancellor and regent masters of the University of Oxford on December 7, 1284. Pecham's testimony seems reliable, because from 1276 he was lector at the papal school (*studium palatii*) and he was still at the curia in 1279. This letter has been edited by F. Ehrle, "John Pecham über den Kampf des Augustinismus und Aristotelismus in der zweiten Hälfte des 13. Jahrhunderts," in Franz Ehrle, *Gesammelte Aufsätze zur Englischen Scholastik*, ed. F. Pelster (Rome, 1970), 68 and also in CUP 1: 624–25. See Wielockx, "Autour," 413–14 for a discussion of Pecham's testimony.

68. In my view, Wielockx's portrayal of the inquiries against Thomas Aquinas and Giles of Rome is not very plausible. A different scenario is proposed in J. M. M. H. Thijssen, "1277 Revisited: A New Interpretation of the Doctrinal Investigations of Thomas Aquinas and Giles of Rome," *Vivarium* 35 (1997), 1–29. Independently

of my own study, John F. Wippel, "Bishop Stephen Tempier and Thomas Aquinas: A Separate Process Against Aquinas?" *Freiburger Zeitschrift für Philosophie und Theologie* 44 (1997), 117–36, also questions Wielockx's thesis of a third and separate inquiry against Thomas Aquinas and concludes that the evidence offered in support of this thesis is not convincing.

69. Wielockx, *Aegidii Romani,* 179–223. So Wielockx has observed correctly that the investigation of Giles of Rome included Thomas Aquinas as well. His suggestion that Tempier proceeded against Thomas Aquinas's views a few days after the Giles of Rome investigation is, I believe, unfounded.

70. Thijssen, "1277 Revisited," 10–12, and 26.

71. See note 67: "episcopus Parisiensis Stephanus bonae memorie ad discussionem ipsorum articulorum de consilio magistrorum procedere cogitaret, mandatum fuisse dicitur eidem episcopo, per quosdam Romanae curiae dominos reverendos, ut de facto illarum opinionum supersederet penitus, donec aliud reciperet in mandatis."

72. Wielockx, "Autour," 421 and 427–29. The same suggestion of the presence of "Dominican representations" at the curia was made by Decima L. Douai, *Archbishop Pecham* (Oxford, 1952), 38, though without further elaborating or substantiating this idea.

73. Above, I have indicated how the inquiry that led to the censure of March 7, 1277, probably started. See Thijssen, "1277 Revisited," 29, for the start of the inquiry against Giles of Rome.

74. See note 59.

Chapter 3. False Teaching at the Arts Faculty

1. See, for instance, John E. Murdoch, "*Subtilitates Anglicanae* in Fourteenth-Century Paris. John of Mirecourt and Peter Cheffons," in *Machaut's World: Science and Art in the Fourteenth Century,* ed. M. P. Cosman and B. Chandler (New York, 1978), 51; William J. Courtenay, *Schools and Scholars in Fourteenth-Century England* (Princeton, N.J., 1987), 164; and Gordon Leff, "The 'Trivium' and the Three Philosophies," in *Universities in the Middle Ages,* ed. Hilde De Ridder-Symoens (*A History of the University in Europe,* vol. 1; Cambridge, 1992), 332.

2. In addition to the scholarly literature that will be mentioned in the next notes, the following studies on this subject are most important: Philotheus Boehner, *Collected Articles on Ockham*; ed. Eligius M. Buytaert (St. Bonaventure, N.Y., 1958), 232–67; Neil W. Gilbert, "Richard de Bury and the 'quires of Yesterday's Sophisms,'" in *Philosophy and Humanism. Renaissance Essays in Honor of Paul Oskar Kristeller,* ed. Edward P. Mahoney (Leiden, 1976), 229–57, and "Ockham, Wyclif, and the 'Via Moderna,'" in *Antiqui und Moderni,* ed. Albert Zimmermann (Berlin, 1974), 85–125; Konstanty Michalski, "Les courants philosophiques à Oxford et à Paris pendant le XIVe siècle" (1922); reprinted in Michalski, *La philosophie au XIVe siècle* (Frankfurt, 1969), 1–35.

3. J. M. M. H. Thijssen, "Once Again the Ockhamist Statutes of 1339 and 1340: Some New Perspectives," *Vivarium,* 28 (1990), 145.

4. William J. Courtenay, "Was There an Ockhamist School?" in *Philosophy and Learning. The Universities in the Middle Ages*, ed. Maarten J. F. M. Hoenen, J. H. Josef Schneider, and Georg Wieland (Leiden, 1995), 287.

5. The following brief introduction is based upon Gray C. Boyce, *The English-German Nation in the University of Paris during the Middle Ages* (Bruges, 1927), 34–39; Pearl Kibre, *The Nations in the Mediaeval Universities* (Cambridge, Mass., 1948), 70–75, and 97–103; Olga Weijers, *Terminologie des universités au XIIIe siècle* (Rome, 1987), 199–205; William J. Courtenay, "The Registers of the University of Paris and the Statutes Against the 'Scientia Occamica,'" *Vivarium* 29 (1991), 35–36.

6. Boyce, *English-German Nation*, 13–23, and Courtenay, "Registers," 15–33.

7. See Wiliam J. Courtenay and Katherine H. Tachau, "Ockham, Ockhamists, and the English-German Nation at Paris, 1339–1341," *History of Universities* 2 (1982), 56, for this observation. Note that offenders against the first decree all receive the same penalty, no matter whether they are masters, bachelors or students.

8. CUP 1: 485–86: "Universis presentes litteras inspecturis omnes et singuli magistri quatuor nationum, videlicet Gallicorum, Picardorum, Normanorum et Anglicorum, salutem in Domino sempiternam. A tramite rationis deviare videtur nec Deum habere pre oculis qui que ab antiquis sunt statuta super re licita necnon rationi consona, transgredi non veretur, maxime cum ad hec juramenti vinculo fuerit obligatus. Cum igitur a predecessoribus nostris non irrationabiliter motis circa libros apud nos legendos publice vel occulte certa precesserit ordinatio per nos jurata observari, et quod aliquos libros per ipsos non admissos vel alias consuetos legere non debemus, et istis temporibus nonnulli doctrinam Guillermi dicti Okam (quamvis per ipsos ordinantes admissa non fuerit vel alias consueta, neque per nos seu alios ad quos pertineat examinata, propter quod non videtur suspicione carere), dogmatizare presumpserint publice et occulte super hoc in locis privatis conventicula faciendo: hinc est quod nos nostre salutis memores, considerantes juramentum quod fecimus de dicta ordinatione observanda, statuimus quod nullus decetero predictam doctrinam dogmatizare presumat audiendo vel legendo publice vel occulte, necnon conventicula super dicta doctrina disputanda faciendo vel ipsum in lectura vel disputationibus allegando. Si quis tamen contra premissa vel aliquod premissorum attemptare presumpserit, ipsum per annum privamus, et quod per dictum annum obtinere honorem seu gradum inter nos non valeat nec obtenti actus aliqualiter exercere. Si qui autem contra predicta inventi pertinaces fuerint, in predictis penis volumus perpetue subjacere. . . . . Acta fuerunt hec apud Sanctum Julianum in nostra congregatione facultatis nobis specialiter ad statuendum vocatis anno Domini millesimo trecentesimo tricesimo nono, sabbato post festum beati Mathei apostoli. In quorum testimonium sigilla nostra cum signeto rectoris duximus apponenda."

9. Zénon Kaluza, "Le statut du 25 septembre 1339 et l'ordonnance du 2 septembre 1276," in *Die Philosophie im 14. und 15. Jahrhundert*, ed. Olaf Pluta (Amsterdam, 1988), 343–51. The ordinance is edited in CUP 1: 538–39.

10. Kaluza, "Le statut du 25 septembre," 347–349.

11. Courtenay and Tachau, "Ockham," 71–72 and William J. Courtenay, "The Reception of Ockham's Thought at the University of Paris," in *Preuve et raisons à l'université de Paris. Logique, ontologies et théologie au XIVe siècle*, ed. Zénon Kaluza and Paul Vignaux (Paris, 1984), 44–45. Exact references are given in Thijssen, "Once

Again," 156 n. 58. See further William J. Courtenay, "The Debate Over Ockham's Physical Theories at Paris," in *La nouvelle physique du XIVe siècle*, ed. Stefano Caroti and Pierre Souffrin (Florence, 1997), 50–53.

12. Courtenay, "Registers," 40–41, who follows Du Boulay's conjecture and dates the oath at the end of June 1341. Zénon Kaluza, "Les sciences et leurs langages. Note sur le statut du 29 décembre 1340 et le prétendu statut perdu contre Ockham," in *Filosofia e teologia nel trecento: Studi in ricordo di Eugenio Randi*, ed. Luca Bianchi (Louvain-la-Neuve, 1994), 216–17, however, believes that the oath originated after a meeting of the English-German nation that took place in October 1341 (see below), and was prepared and voted on at that meeting. This would move the date of the oath to the autumn of 1341.

13. See Chapter 1, note 176.

14. CUP 2: 680 (no. 16): "Item, jurabitis quod statuta facta per facultatem artium contra scientiam Okamicam observabitis, neque dictam scientiam et consimiles sustinebitis quoquomodo, sed scientiam Aristotelis et sui Commentatoris Averrois et aliorum commentatorum antiquorum et expositorum dicti Aristotelis, nisi in casibus qui sunt contra fidem. Item, observabitis statutum contentum in altero predictorum duorum statutorum de scientia Okamica, scilicet "quod nullus magister, bachelarius ac scolaris sine licentia magistri disputationes tenentis arguat: quam licentiam sibi non liceat petere verbaliter, sed tantummodo [signative] reverenter." Other university registers that are still extant, such as the Book of the English Nation, have a different version of the oath. The first section and the reference to the "statutes concerning the Ockhamist thought" in the second section have been removed. See CUP 2: 680. The two versions of the oath are discussed by Courtenay, "Registers," 41–42, who indicates that the changes were intentional and occurred sometime between 1355 and 1365.

15. See also Kaluza, "Sciences," 215. Precisely for this reason, the oath reads "statutum *contentum* in altero predictorum duorum statutorum de scientia Ockhamica" instead of the more direct "statutum alterum de scientia Ockhamica." This latter phrasing is excluded because the second decree did not concern Ockham's thought. I think that this interpretation solves the difficulties raised in Courtenay, "Ockhamist School," 287–88.

16. Thijssen, "Once Again," 159–60. The admonition later became a commonplace in certain intellectual circles. See also Courtenay, "Ockhamist School," 288–91, and "Debate," 56–59.

17. Courtenay, "Registers," 44 n. 82.

18. CUP 2: 505–7: "Universis presentes litteras inspecturis omnes et singuli magistri actu regentes Parisius in artium facultate salutem in Domino. Erroribus obviare, quantum potest, unusquisque tenetur, et viam omnimode ad eos precludere, maxime cum ex hiis possit agnitio veritatis occultari. Verum quia ad nostram noviter pervenerit notitiam, quod nonnulli in nostra artium facultate quorundam astutiis perniciosis adherentes, fundati non supra firmam petram, cupientes plus sapere quam oporteat, quedam minus sana nituntur seminare, ex quibus errores intolerabiles nedum circa philosophiam, sed et circa divinam Scripturam, possent contingere in futurum: hinc est, quod huic morbo tam pestifero remediare cupientes eorum fundamenta prophana et errores, prout potuimus, collegimus, statuentes circa illa per hunc modum: . . .

"Si quis autem contra premissa, vel aliquod premissorum attemptare presumpserit, a nostro consortio ex nunc prout ex tunc resecamus et privamus, resecatum et privatum haberi volumus, salvis in omnibus que de doctrina Guillelmi dicti Ockam alias statuimus, que in omnibus et per omnia volumus roboris habere firmitatem. Datum Parisius sub sigillis quatuor nationum videlicet Gallicorum, Picardorum, Normannorum et Anglicorum, unacum signeto rectoris Universitatis Parisiensis, anno Domini MCCCXL, die veneris post Nativitatem Domini."

19. This tradition started with Denifle and Chatelain, the editors of the statute (see CUP 2: 507 n. 2) and was accepted by Ernest A. Moody, "Ockham, Buridan, and Nicholas of Autrecourt: The Parisian Statutes of 1339 and 1340," reprinted in Ernest A. Moody, *Studies in Medieval Philosophy, Science and Logic* (Berkeley, Calif., 1975), 159; Ruprecht Paqué, *Das Pariser Nominalistenstatut* (Berlin, 1970), 12–13; Courtenay and Tachau, "Ockham," 60. Perhaps the passage is a literal quotation from the 1339 statute: "doctrinam Guillermi dicti Okam."

20. Thijssen, "Once Again," 144–45. Moody, "Ockham," 138 and 158–59, because he assumed that the 1340 statute was a vindication of the Ockhamist position, believed that the final clause was added as a warning that the 1340 statute should not be taken as an implicit revocation of the 1339 statute. If the statute of 1340 had been directed against Ockhamists, it would, according to Moody, of itself have been understood as a confirmation of the 1339 statute, in which case special mention of the latter would have been superfluous.

21. Thijssen, "Once Again," 145, and Kaluza, "Sciences," 213.

22. Thijssen, "Once Again," 146, and Courtenay, "Registers," 45. Since we do not know the origin of the rubric, we have no way of knowing whether it really reflected the intention of those who originally drafted the 1340 statute. But this is, of course, true for any of the university documents that have not been preserved as original documents, but only as copies in the university registers.

23. J. M. M. H. Thijssen, "The Crisis Over Ockhamist Hermeneutic and Its Semantic Background: The Methodological Significance of the Censure of December 29, 1340," in *Vestigia, Imagines, Verba: Semiotics and Logic in Medieval Theological Texts (XIIIth–XIVth Century)*, ed. Costantino Marmo (Turnhout, 1997), 371–92. See also Kaluza, "Sciences," 224–242, and further William J. Courtenay, "Force of Words and Figures of Speech: The Crisis over *Virtus sermonis* in the Fourteenth Century," *FS* 44 (1984), 107–28 for a discussion of the history of the expression "virtus sermonis."

24. Important methodological considerations concerning the application of the label "Ockhamist" are given in Courtenay, "Ockhamist School," 266–70.

25. See Boyce, *English-German Nation*, 13–23, who also observes that many important things were not recorded in the proctor's book. In May 1343 a committee of four older masters was appointed to assist the proctor in inspecting and updating the statutes that were copied in the Proctor's Book of the English-German Nation.

26. AUP 1: 52–53: "Item in eadem congregatione ordinatum fuit, quod nullus decetero admitteretur ad aliquos actus legitimos in dicta nacione, nisi prius juraret quod revelaret, si sciret aliquos de secta Occamica ad invicem conspirasse de secta vel opinionibus erroneis fovendis, vel etiam conjuratos esse vel conventicula habere occulta, aliter nisi jure diceret si sciret, ex tunc penam perjurii incurreret. Et hanc ordinacionem voluerunt equivalere statuto."

27. The parallels between oaths and statutes is documented in Courtenay, "Registers," 43 n. 79.

28. For this reason, I disagree with Kaluza, "Sciences," 217, who conjectures that the statute of the English-German nation provides a draft version of the inception oath discussed above. The inception oath clearly refers to the 1339 statute. Kaluza's thesis is also rejected in Courtenay, "Ockhamist School," 286, though for different reasons.

29. AUP 1: 44–45: "Item tempore procuracionis ejusdem sigillatum fuit statutum facultatis contra novas opiniones quorundam, qui vocantur Occhaniste, in domo dicti procuratoris, et puplicatum fuit idem statutum coram universitate apud Predicatores in sermone."

30. Courtenay and Tachau, "Ockham," 57 and 59–60. The entry in the proctor's book was also known to the editors of the CUP and to Paqué, *Das Pariser*, 23–24, but they identified the reference as being to the 1340 statute, and did not recognize the resulting problems.

31. Thijssen, "Once Again," 136–67.

32. Thijssen, "Once Again," 164; Courtenay, "Registers," 48 and "Ockhamist School," 274–75 and 281; and Kaluza, "Sciences," 218–220.

33. Although I have abandoned my previous interpretation (Thijssen, "Once Again," 163–66) of the meaning of *actum* and of the significance of the absence of this term in the statute of 1340, I still believe that the most elegant way to solve the discrepancy in dates is by distinguishing the several stages by which the statute was issued. See also Courtenay, "Registers," 47–48 and "Ockhamist School," 282–83, and Kaluza, "Sciences," 218–20.

34. The *datum* and *actum* are not always explicitly distinguished in the colophon. See A. Giry, *Manuel de diplomatique* (Paris, 1894), esp. 587–89, A. de Boüard, *Manuel de diplomatique française et pontificale* (Paris, 1929), 295–96; and H. Bresslau, *Handbuch der Urkundenlehre für Deutschland und Italien* (Berlin, 1958) 2: 460, 467–68, which also provides the following medieval definition of the difference between *actum* and *datum* (460 n. 1): "Datum quidem inportat solummodo tempus in quo datur littera. Actum autem inportat tempus in quo ea facta sunt super quibus littera datur." According to Courtenay, "Registers," 38–39, *datum* refers to the date of the document, whereas *actum* refers to the place of the meeting, but this is mainly the usage in earlier times.

35. Courtenay, "Registers," 35, and 47–48 and "Ockhamist School," 282–83.

36. See Courtenay, "Registers," 48 and "Ockhamist School," 282. As Courtenay observed, the colophon indicates the delay of approximately five months in the sealing of the 1253 statute that was caused by textual emendations. See CUP 1: 242–44.

37. Kaluza, "Sciences," 219–20. Kaluza believes that the promulgation of the statute is indicated by the term "actum," a position that I also took in "Once Again," 165, but which I now believe to be erroneous. As I mentioned above, *actum* refers to the date of the juridical decisions recorded in the document.

38. AUP 1: 44: "In cujus tempore nichil est factum, quod perfecte ad actum duceretur."

39. AUP 1: 52: "Primo vocatis magistris ad ordinandum etc., quia sigillum procuratoris dicte nacionis fuerat perditum et per dictum procuratorem unum novum factum in forma consimili sicut prius fuit."

40. AUP 1: 43: "Item facta congregacione apud Sanctum Maturinum ad statuendum et ordinandum ordinatum fuit, quod haberemus unam cistam communem cum tribus clavibus, in qua ponatur pecunia nacionis recepta per receptorem nacionis." Here the seal is not explicitly mentioned, but from other evidence it is known that the *cista* or *archa* also contained the seal and other paraphernalia. See the text quoted in note 42, and also AUP 1: xv and xxii; Boyce, *English-German Nation*, 179–80; and Kibre, *The Nations*, 86–87.

41. AUP 1: 43: "Item facta congregacione apud Sanctum Maturinum super statuendo statutum fuit, quod in die eleccionis procuratoris in nacione procurator precedens debet apportare librum et papirum, sigillum cum clavibus, non proponendo obstantia, ne successor in alico valeat prejudicari."

42. AUP 1: 51: "Item in eadem congregatione deliberatum fuit, quod quicunque fieret receptor, juraret fideliter quod de prima pecunia quam reciperet faceret fieri cistam pro nacione cum tribus clavibus, in qua reponeretur sigillum nacionis et pecunia ejusdem cum aliis rebus."

43. CUP 2: #1061.

44. A parallel case seems to have occurred in September 1341, when regent and nonregent masters of the nation met to seal some letter with the nation's seal. Note, however, that at this meeting the participants not only affixed the seal but also made a decree. See AUP 1: 52: "Item vocatis magistris regentibus et non regentibus dicte nacionis ad ordinandum etc. prout moris est, quia littera quedam habebatur sigillata sigillo nacionis predicte."

45. AUP 1: 64–65: "Item convocatis quatuor procuratoribus apud Sanctam Genovesam tribus vicibus sigillate fuerunt VII littere, quatuor Universitatis: una pape, altera magistro Wilhermo de Lumbris due alie duobus cardinalibus; tres alie littere erant supplicatorie pro quibusdam magistris ad suos dyocesanos."

46. The proctor's book records the issuing of two statutes of the faculty of arts in 1339 (AUP 1: 35 refers to the statutes CUP 2: #1023 and #1024); one statute in January 1340 (AUP 1: 40 refers to the statute in CUP 2: #1031); the Ockhamist statute of 1340 (AUP 1: 44–45 refers to CUP 2: #1042); and one statute in 1355 (AUP 1: 188 refers to the statute in CUP 3: #1229).

Chapter 4. Nicholas of Autrecourt and John of Mirecourt

1. See, for instance, Julius R. Weinberg, *Nicolaus of Autrecourt. A Study in 14th Century Thought*, 2d ed. (New York, 1969), 3; Frederick C. Copleston, *A History of Medieval Philosophy* (London, 1972), 260–266; and Armand A. Maurer, *Medieval Philosophy*; 2nd. ed. (Toronto, 1982), 288–91; but also in more specialized studies, such as T. K. Scott, "Nicholas of Autrecourt, Buridan and Ockhamism," *Journal of the History of Philosophy* 9 (1971), 15–41; Ernest A. Moody, "Ockham, Buridan, and Nicholas of Autrecourt: The Parisian Statutes of 1339 and 1340," reprinted in Ernest

A. Moody, *Studies in Medieval Philosophy, Science and Logic* (Berkeley, Calif., 1975), 127–160; and Francesco Bottin, *La scienza degli occamisti* (Rimini, 1982).

2. As far as I am aware, the revisionist approach to the place of Autrecourt and Mirecourt in Ockhamism started with William Courtenay's "John of Mirecourt and Gregory of Rimini on Whether God Can Undo the Past," *RTAM* 39 (1972), 224–56 and 40 (1973), 147–74. This article was reprinted in William J. Courtenay, *Covenant and Causality* (London, 1984). See further Courtenay, "The Reception of Ockham's Thought at the University of Paris," in *Preuve et raisons à l'université de Paris. Logique, ontologies et théologie au XIVe siècle*, ed. Zénon Kaluza and Paul Vignaux (Paris, 1984), 43–64.

3. William J. Courtenay, "Inquiry and Inquisition: Academic Freedom in Medieval Universities," *CH* 58 (1989), 178 and "Erfurt CA 2 127 and the Censured Articles of Mirecourt and Autrecourt," in *Die Bibliotheca Amploniana. Ihre Bedeutung im Spannungsfeld von Aristotelismus, Nominalismus und Humanismus*, ed. Andreas Speer (Berlin, 1995), 348.

4. CUP 2: 505 (#1041).

5. CUP 2: 505: "Cum magistros Nicolaum de Ultricuria licentiatum, et Johannem . . . , Heliam de Corso, Guidonem de Veeli, et Petrum de Monteregali, bacalarios, ac Henricum Anglicum . . . scolarem, in theologia studentes Parisius . . . quatenus eosdem magistros Nicolaum, Johannem, Heliam, Guidonem, Petrum et Henricum" It was quite common for the term "magister" to be further specified, for instance, magister Johannes de Montesono, in sacra theologia magister. Cf. Olga Weijers, *Terminologie des universités au XIIIe siècle* (Rome, 1987), 134.

6. Zénon Kaluza, *Nicolas d'Autrecourt: Ami de la vérité (Histoire littéraire de la France*, vol. 42, part 1; Paris, 1995), 100. Some details, such as the names of the members of the commission that investigated Autrecourt's writings, and dates have been left blank in the draft copy.

7. The document has been edited in Lambert M. de Rijk, ed. and trans., *Nicholas of Autrecourt, His Correspondence with Master Giles and Bernard of Arezzo* (Leiden, 1994), 146–66. It supersedes the edition in CUP 2: 576–587 (#1124). The only extant copy of the *instrumentum* is now kept in the Vatican Secret Archive.

8. In contrast to the official records of the trials against Foullechat and Monzón, which are still extant today in the university archives, this record was already lost in the sixteenth century. See note 43.

9. Kaluza, *Nicolas*, 100–128. The structure of the *instrumentum* is also discussed in de Rijk, *Nicholas*, 139–142.

10. De Rijk, *Nicholas*, 152: "dicto negotio ad memoriam dicti domini nostri Pape reducto."

11. See Kaluza, *Nicolas*, 101 for this chronological reconstruction of Autrecourt's trial, and the sequence of the lists of errors.

12. I owe this suggestion to William Courtenay. See de Rijk, *Nicholas*, 151 par. 5: "Beatissime pater, licet ego, Nicholaus de Ultricuria, superius posita non scripserim manu mea, eoquod littera quam ego scribo inepta est et cum difficultate potest legi, de voluntate ⟨tamen⟩ mea scripta sunt. Et in huiusmodi rei testimonium hanc subscriptionem feci manu mea ac etiam in eadem apposui sigillum quo utor." Passages between angle brackets are additions introduced by the editor of the text.

13. Kaluza, *Nicolas*, 107–14.

14. Kaluza, *Nicolas*, 35–38, 55, 62, 74, and 186.

15. Kaluza, *Nicolas*, 117. The best edition of the still extant letters of Autrecourt to Bernard of Arezzo is de Rijk, *Nicholas*. It supersedes the edition by Josef Lappe, *Nicholaus von Autrecourt, sein Leben, seine Philosophie, seine Schriften* (Münster, 1908), and Nicolaus von Autrecourt, *Briefe*, ed. Ruedi Imbach und Dominik Perler, trans. and with introd. Dominik Perler (Hamburg, 1988). The *Exigit ordo* has been edited in J. R. O'Donnell, "Nicholas of Autrecourt," *MS* 1 (1939), 179–280. The *principium* was probably never written.

16. Kaluza, *Nicolas*, 71 and 116–17.

17. De Rijk, *Nicholas*, 152: "visis et discussis primitus et diligenter attentis ipsis articulis ac responsionibus et declarationibus ipsius magistri Nicolai ad eos subsecutis, necnon et processibus super eisdem alias habitis ac contentis in duabus cedulis per eum traditis, ut prefertur."

18. De Rijk, *Nicholas*, 152–53: "et discussis articulis contra ipsum magistrum ⟨⟨Nicolaum antedictum per eos⟩⟩, ut prediciture, traditis ac etiam assignatis, necnon et ⟨⟨attentis responsionibus et declara⟩⟩tionibus ipsius magistri Nicolai subsecutis ad ipsos, ut predi⟨⟨citur, in tribunali tam⟩⟩ coram ipso domino nostro Clemente papa VIo, cum eum, ut prefer⟨⟨tur, sub oculis su⟩⟩is haberet, quam coram nobis datis, factis, ventilatis et habitis." Note that passages indicated by double angle brackets in the edition have been lost due to damage and are supplied by the editor.

19. The manuscript reads: "visis et diligenter inspectis omnibus et singulis articulis et propositionibus, responsionibus, declarationibus, cedulis et processibus supradictis." De Rijk, *Nicholas*, 162 reads: "declarationibus ⟨contentis in⟩ cedulis et processibus supradictis," but there is no reason to add the conjecture ⟨contentis in⟩.

20. See, for instance, de Rijk, *Nicholas*, 153 (twice): "Ac propositionibus contentis in dicta cedula que incipit 'Ve michi.'"; and also pp. 162–63: "necnon omnes et singulas propositiones predictas contentas in cedula 'Ve michi.'"

21. De Rijk, *Nicholas*, 154: "Deinde p⟨⟨er illos magist⟩⟩ros et prelatos ac doctores discussi fuerunt alii articuli dati et assignati contra ipsum magistrum Nicolaum."

22. This letter is edited in de Rijk, *Nicholas*, 151–52. The manuscript marks this section by the indication "Alia cedula." See de Rijk, *Nicholas*, 140.

23. De Rijk, *Nicholas*, 151–52.

24. Bernard C. Bazán, *e.a.*, *Les questions disputées et les questions quodlibétiques dans les facultés de théologie, de droit et de médecine* (Turnhout, 1985), 103–04. Also Kaluza, *Nicolas*, 114, and 186 has pointed this out.

25. De Rijk, *Nicholas*, 150.

26. De Rijk, *Nicholas*, 153: "Et primitus articulos per dictum magistrum Nicolaum, ut videtur, confessatos in suis responsionibus seu declarationibus. Qui sunt tales."

27. De Rijk, *Nicholas*, 141.

28. Kaluza, *Nicolas*, 63–64.

29. Kaluza, *Nicolas*, 109–10.

30. De Rijk, *Nicholas*, 154: "Deinde p⟨⟨er illos magist⟩⟩ros et prelatos ac doctores discussi fuerunt alii articuli dati et assignati contra ipsum magistrum Nico-

laum. Quorum aliquos simpliciter et aliquos sub forma qua ponuntur, se dixisse negavit."

31. See Kaluza, *Nicolas*, 115–16 for this observation.

32. See note 4.

33. See Chapter 1, and also Thijssen, "Once Again," 157.

34. Kaluza, *Nicolas*, 119–23.

35. Kaluza, *Nicolas*, 121 and 125.

36. The confessed articles and those from "Ve michi" conclude with the statement "revoco tamquam falsum," whereas the other articles conclude with the clause "reputo et assero falsum," or words to that effect. The lists are edited in de Rijk, *Nicholas*, 168–207.

37. De Rijk, *Nicholas*, 166. The *instrumentum* also contains blanks for the names of the witnesses.

38. De Rijk, *Nicholas*, 163: "antedictum magistrum Nicolaum honore magistrali certis ex causis per hanc sententiam apostolica auctoritate privamus eumque ad ascendendum ad magistralem gradum in theologica facultate specialiter tenore presentium inhabilem renuntiamus et indignum, — omnibus et singulis tam presentibus quam futuris ubilibet constitutis ad quos ad magisterium in dicta theologica facultate deputatio, electio, presentatio, promotio seu quevis alia dispositio in quibuscumque studiis et universitatibus pertinent de consuetudine vel de iure, auctoritate predicta districtius inhibentes, ne prefatum magistrum Nicolaum ad hujusmodi magisterii honorem et gradum quoquomodo deputare, promovere, assumere et presentare presumant absque sedis apostolica licentia speciali."

39. Kaluza, *Nicolas*, 122–23 observes that there is no agreement among historians concerning Autrecourt's magisterial degree. He eventually concludes that Autrecourt had received his doctorate before arriving at Avignon, but that Pope Benedict XII was not aware of this fact. See also Kaluza, *Nicolas*, 69.

40. AUP 1: 111, and CUP 2: 505 n. 1, respectively.

41. The dates and events are discussed in Kaluza, *Nicolas*, 124–28.

42. De Rijk, *Nicholas*, 164: "Et quod ipse infra ⟨ ⟩ Parisius se personaliter conferendo, has nostras litteras, seu instrumentum publicum hanc nostram sententiam et ordinationem sic auctoritate apostolica per nos pronuntiatam continens, venerabilibus viris ⟨ ⟩ Cancellario parisiensi ac universitati magistrorum et scolarium Parisius regentium et studentium tradet efficaciter et realiter assignabit."

43. J. M. M. H. Thijssen, "What Really Happened on 7 March 1277? Bishop Tempier's Condemnation and Its Institutional Context," in *Texts and Contexts in Ancient and Medieval Science: Studies on the Occasion of John E. Murdoch's Seventieth Birthday*, ed. Edith Sylla and Michael McVaugh (Leiden, 1997), 113–14. Recall that the still extant copy of the *instrumentum* is a draft version that was kept in the papal archive. See note 7.

44. Here follows the complete text from the entry of the proctor's book. AUP 1: 111: "In cujus procuratione fuerunt acta que secuntur . . . Primo, die sancti Edmundi, scilicet in festo nationis Anglicane, fuit facta congregatio Universitatis, scilicet regencium et non regencium, apud Sanctum Maturinum ad audiendum litteras papales et processus super quibusdam articulis, quos magister Nicholaus de

Ultricuria, bachalarius in teologia, die sancte Katherine proximo sequente in sermone apud Predicatores publice revocavit, aliquos tanquam falsos, et aliquos tanquam falsos, erroneos et hereticos. Et ibidem in sermone ipsos articulos una cum uno tractatu suo secundum mandatum apostolicum idem magister Nicholaus comburebat." Note that the chronicle of events in the proctor's book did not make this distinction between recanted articles and articles that were declared erroneous. It is, however, made in the list that Autrecourt read. See the text cited in note 36.

45. See de Rijk, *Nicholas*, 165.

46. Thijssen, "The 'Semantic' Articles of Autrecourt's Condemnation: New Proposals for an Interpretation of the Articles 1, 30, 31, 35, 57, and 58," *AHDL* 57 (1990), 159 and 163 for allusions by John Buridan and Marsilius of Inghen. Courtenay, "Erfurt," 350–51 has definitively demonstrated that the references in Buridan's and Inghen's texts should, indeed, be understood as references to the condemnation by Cardinal William Curti, and not to that by Cardinal Robert Kilwardby, as I previously believed. Note that this interpretation implies a correction of the 1516 edition of Marsilius of Inghen's text, which reads "auctoritate cardinalis alibi," and not "albi." The latter allusion would, indeed, have been a sure reference to the "White" Cardinal Curti, O. Cist. André of Neufchâteau's citations of Autrecourt's and Mirecourt's condemnations, and a few others as well, are listed in Russell L. Friedman, "Andreas de Novo Castro (fl. 1358) on Divine Omnipotence and the Nature of the Past: I *Sentences*, Distinction Forty-Five, Question Six," *Cahiers de l'Institut du Moyen-Age Grec et Latin* 64 (1994), 103, and 119–28. Other allusions to Autrecourt's prohibition are collected in Kaluza, *Nicolas*, 70 n. 166.

47. F. Stegmüller, "Die Zwei Apologien des Jean de Mirecourt," *RTAM* 5 (1933), 40–78 and 192–204.

48. Stegmüller, "Zwei Apologien," 46: "Ut illi qui sequentia legent, videant propositiones per reverendos magistros meos extractas et intellectum quem habui, et ne in posterum teneant illa, quae magistris praedictis et mihi videntur non tenenda, volo aliqua praemittere, quae super excusatione mea scripsi Reverendo Patri Domino Ebredunensi quorum tenor est in haec verba: Reverendissime Pater: ut legentes vel videntes extractas propositiones de lectura mea melius et clarius intelligere possint mentem meam quam habui et etiam scio contineri expresse in lectura mea, volo per singulas propositiones discurrere."

49. Mirecourt read the *Sentences* in the academic year 1344–45. See Courtenay, "John of Mirecourt," 227–28 and "Erfurt," 343–44.

50. CUP 2: 613.

51. See Chapter 1, notes 33 and 35 for the Dominican and Franciscan legislation.

52. The introductory statement has been edited in Courtenay, "John of Mirecourt's Condemnation: Its Original Form," *RTAM*, 53 (1986), 190–91.

53. Courtenay, "Erfurt," 344 n. 8.

54. The quotation is derived from Kaluza, *Nicolas*, 127 n. 138 (Paris, BN lat. 16408, f.110v): "Pro hiis et similibus advertenda aliqua esse diversimode revocanda et dampnanda, sicut ex articulis multis Parisiensibus antiquis et novis patet, et ex aliquibus dampnatis per aliquos cardinales ad hoc commissos, sicut Atricuria, Mirricuria, Folachat, etc." The cardinal of Autrecourt's trial, of course, is William Curti.

In the appeal stage, the investigation of Foullechat was handled by Cardinal John Dormans. See CUP 2: #1349 and #1350 and Chapter 1.

55. See Stegmüller, "Zwei Apologien," 40, and CUP 2: #950 n. 1 for some biographical details about Pastor, and also Courtenay, "Erfurt," 344.

56. From the Foullechat dossier it appears that it was not unusual for the pope to choose a local delegate. Cardinal Dormans conducted the appellate process in Paris, not in Avignon. See Chapter 1, note 186.

57. On March 29, 1347, Pastor de Serrescuderio was sent as papal *nuntius* to Paris along with Bishop William Lamy. In March 1349, Pastor was still staying in Paris as papal nuncio. I owe this information to William Courtenay. See further Stephanus Baluze, *Vitae paparum Avenionensium*, ed. G. Mollat, 4 vols. (Paris, 1916–22), 4: 78–80, 83, 89, and 90.

58. The charged errors from Mirecourt's commentary on the *Sentences* have been identified by Stegmüller, the editor of Mirecourt's defenses. From time to time, he gives literal quotations from the manuscripts of Mirecourt's commentary. In the footnotes of his edition of Apologia 2, Stegmüller also refers to the corresponding propositions of Apologia 1, whenever they appear on this list. He did not infer, however, any conclusions about the procedure by which Mirecourt's commentary was evaluated. Note, moreover, that the correspondences between Apologia 2 and 1 as indicated in scheme 1 differ in some cases from the correspondences marked by Stegmüller.

59. Stegmüller, "Zwei Apologien," 192: "Isti sunt sensus communes, quod iudicio meo possunt habere propositiones sequente, et qui sunt, quos nunquam credidi nec tenui, et quos etiam quandoque credidi fore veros."

60. Stegmüller, "Zwei Apologien," 195: "Veraciter credo hoc numquam dixisse vel scripsisse; credo tamen quod hoc in sexterno sit repertum propter vitium scriptorum vel propter inadvertentiam meam." Mirecourt suggests that the suspect proposition "Quod peccatum magis est bonum quam malum" should be changed into "Quod magis bonum est peccatum esse quam malum."

61. The list is edited in CUP 2: #1147 and in Franz Ehrle, *I più antichi statuti della Facoltà teologica dell' Università di Bologna* (Bologne, 1932), 68–73. See also Courtenay, "John of Mirecourt," 170–71, for a discussion of Hugolin's rearranged list of Mirecourt's condemnation.

62. The copy preserved in the manuscript BN lat. 15883 (edited by Du Plessis, *Collectio*, 1, part 1: 344–45) also lacks article 23. The same goes for the printed tradition of the articles. The copy preserved in the manuscript Auxerre, Bibl. municipale 243, does not reproduce the articles 18, 22, 23, and 37, whereas the articles 22 and 23 are left out in the list edited by Du Boulay, 4: 298–300. A consequence of these ommissions is that Mirecourt's articles in these copies of the *articuli condemnati Parisius* have received a numbering that is different from the one in Apologia 2 as edited by Stegmüller.

63. Ehrle, *I più*, 68: "Verum quia posteriores articuli, secunda et tertia vice, per quadraginta tres solempnes magistros, post dictam indaginem condempnati, in sua virulentia sunt magis latentes; ego frater Ugolinus de Urbe Veteri, ordinis heremitarum sanct Augustini, memorie dictorum magistrorum indignus discipulus, prout Parisius in actis universitatis theologorum in forma publica reperi, ipsos ar-

ticulos utique noxios, ne nostram Bononie universitatem inficiant, hic inferius annotavi."

64. Articles 4, 6, 7, 8, 30, 32, 39, 40, 41, 42, and 44 of Hugolin's list were not derived from Mirecourt's condemnation, but originated from another list of censured articles.

65. Courtenay, "John of Mirecourt," 191: "aliquos iudicaverimus erroneos, aliquos suspectos ac male sonantes in fide ac etiam in bonis moribus."

66. Courtenay, "Erfurt," 349, has conjectured that Mirecourt may be the author of the vesperies preserved in the manuscript Erfurt, Bibl. Amploniana fol. 127, fols. 51ra–54ra. If true, this would indicate that after his condemnation Mirecourt was, nevertheless, advanced to the *magisterium*.

67. Paul V. Spade, *Peter of Ailly. Concepts and Insolubles* (Dordrecht, 1980), 58.

68. L. M. Eldredge, "Changing Concepts of Church Authority in the Later Fourteenth Century: Peter Ceffons of Clairvaux and William Woodford, O.F.M.," *Revue de l'université d'Ottawa* 48 (1978), 171–73. The text has been edited in Damasus Trapp, "Peter Ceffons of Clairvaux," *RTAM* 24 (1957), 147–48.

Chapter 5. Academic Freedom and Teaching Authority

1. Mary M. McLaughlin, *Intellectual Freedom and Its Limitations in the University of Paris in the Thirteenth and Fourteenth Centuries* (New York, 1977) and "Paris Masters of the Thirteenth and Fourteenth Centuries and Ideas of Intellectual Freedom," *CH* 24 (1955), 195–211; William J. Courtenay, "Inquiry and Inquisition: Academic Freedom in Medieval Universities," *CH* 58 (1989), 168–82; Edward Peters, "*Libertas inquirendi* and the *vitium curiositatis* in Medieval Thought," in *La notion de liberté au moyen âge. Islam, Byzance, Occident*, ed. G. Makdisi, D. Sourdel, and J. Sourdel-Thomine (Paris, 1985), 91–98; David Burr, "Olivi and the Limits of Intellectual Freedom," in *Contemporary Reflections on the Medieval Christian Tradition*, ed. G. H. Shriver (Durham, N.C., 1974), 185–99; and Jürgen Miethke, "Bildungsstand und Freiheitsforderung (12. bis 14. Jahrhundert)," in *Die Abendländische Freiheit vom 10. zum 14. Jahrhundert*, ed. Johannes Fried (Sigmaringen, 1991), esp. 231–40, discuss the dimension of academic freedom in conflicts over academically related orthodoxy and heresy.

2. The distinction between academic freedom from external threat and academic freedom from inner limits upon thought and research is derived from Peters, "*Libertas inquirendi*," 89–90.

3. See Walter P. Metzger, "Academic Freedom and Scientific Freedom," *Daedalus* 107 (1978), 94–95, and Peter Classen, "Libertas scolastica — Scholarenprivilegien — Akademische Freiheit im Mittelalter," in Peter Classen, *Studium und Gesellschaft im Mittelalter*, ed. Johannes Fried (Stuttgart, 1983), 238–41.

4. Metzger, "Academic Freedom," 94–95.

5. Bazán, *Les questions*, 99–123.

6. The same conclusion can be drawn from Mary McLaughlin's *Intellectual Freedom*, the only book-length study on the subject. It appears that none of the

medieval sources discussed by her contains any systematic assertion of the right of freedom of thought and expression. The increase of academic freedom to which McLaughlin alludes concerns the emancipation of philosophy from theology and the expansion of the field of inquiry of theology to encompass virtually every subject, but not the freedom to teach without threat of being censured. See McLaughlin, *Intellectual Freedom*, 170–71 and 313–17, and "Paris Masters," 195–211.

7. Classen, "Libertas scolastica," 255. Peters, *"Libertas inquirendi,"* 89–90 is also sensitive to this aspect. See further the important discussion of medieval academic freedom in Miethke, "Bildungsstand und Freiheitsforderung," 231–40.

8. For details about Godfrey of Fontaines's life and writings see John F. Wippel, *The Metaphysical Thought of Godfrey of Fontaines: A Study in Late Thirteenth Century Philosophy* (Washington, D.C., 1981), xv–xxxv.

9. [Godfrey of Fontaines], *Les Quodlibets V, VI et VII*; ed. M. de Wulf and J. Hoffmans (Louvain, 1914), 402: "Utrum magister in theologia debet dicere contra articulum episcopi si credat oppositum esse verum."

10. Godfrey of Fontaines, *Quodlibet VII*, 404–5.

11. Godfrey of Fontaines, *Quodlibet VII*, 403–4. The quotation is on p. 404: "nam homines non possunt libere tractare veritates quibus eorum intellectus non modicum perficeretur."

12. CUP 2: 281: "sed eosdem discussioni scolastice libere relinquendo." See also Chapter 2, note 59.

13. The text is given in Josef Koch, *Durandus de Sancto Porciano, O.P.* (Münster, 1927), 225–226.

14. This often quoted model of the separation of powers was advocated in the late thirteenth century by the canon Alexander of Roes. See Herbert Grundmann, *Ausgewählte Aufsätze*, 3 vols. (Stuttgart, 1976–78), 3: 275–92. See further Koch, 2: 446 and Stephen C. Ferruolo, "The Paris Statutes of 1215 Reconsidered," *History of Universities* 5 (1985), 11.

15. On the corporate character of the Parisian masters see Gaines Post, "Parisian Masters as a Corporation, 1200–1246," *Speculum* 9 (1934), 421–45 and Pierre Michaud-Quantin, "La conscience d'être membre d'une universitas," in *Beiträge zum Berufsbewusstsein des mittelalterlichen Menschen*, ed. Paul Wilpert (Berlin, 1964), 1–15, and *Universitas. Expressions du mouvement communautaire dans le moyen-âge latin* (Paris, 1970); Gordon Leff, *Paris and Oxford Universities in the Thirteenth and Fourteenth Centuries* (New York, 1968), 27–34; Ferruolo, "Paris Statutes," 1–15; and Jacques Verger, "Teachers," in *Universities in the Middle Ages*, ed. Hilde De Ridder-Symoens (*A History of the University in Europe*, vol. 1; Cambridge, 1992), 144–68.

16. Stephen C. Ferruolo, *The Origins of the University. The Schools of Paris and their Critics, 1100–1215* (Stanford, Calif., 1985), 4–5.

17. The importance of teaching in the professional self-image of the masters is further illustrated by the fact that the two most important confrontations between the masters and the (local) ecclesiastical authorities during the university's early years concerned the license to teach (*licentia docendi*). See P. R. McKeon, "The Status of the University of Paris as 'Parens Scientiarum': An Episode in the Development of Its Autonomy," *Speculum* 39 (1964), 651–75; Leff, *Paris and Oxford Universities*, 27–34;

Astrik L. Gabriel, "The Conflict between the Chancellor and the University of Masters and Students at Paris During the Middle Ages," in *Die Auseinandersetzungen*, ed. Zimmermann, 106–55; Alan E. Bernstein, "Magisterium and License: Corporate Autonomy against Papal Authority in the Medieval University of Paris," *Viator* 9 (1978), 291–309, and *Pierre d'Ailly and the Blanchard Affair* (Leiden, 1978), 1–28. The importance of this episode is especially made clear in Bernstein, "Magisterium," 300–306. See further Leff, *Paris and Oxford Universities*, 34–47.

18. Yves Congar, "Pour une histoire sémantique du terme 'magisterium'" and "Bref historique des formes du 'magistère' et de ses relations avec les docteurs," *RSPT* 60 (1976), 85–112. They have been reprinted in Yves Congar, *Droit ancien et structures ecclésiales* (London, 1982).

19. Congar, "Bref historique," 103–4; Yves Congar, *L'église de saint Augustin à l'époque moderne* (Paris, 1970), 241–48, and M. D. Chenu, *La théologie comme science au XIIIe siècle* (Paris, 1943).

20. Congar, "Bref historique," 102–3, and *L'église*, 241–42. See also Guy Fitch Lytle, "Universities as Religious Authorities in the Later Middle Ages and Reformation," in *Reform and Authority in the Medieval and Reformation Church*, ed. Guy Fitch Lytle (Washington, D.C., 1981), 69–97 for an analysis of how the expertise present in the faculties of theology came, both by conscious assertion and gradual practice, to be accepted in the chain of authority. The terms "master" and "doctor in theology" can be used interchangeably. At Paris "doctor" was perhaps used less frequently. See Olga Weijers, *Terminologie des universités au XIIIe siècle* (Rome, 1987), 142–51, and Verger, "Teachers," 144–48.

21. See, for instance, Constitution 11 of the Fourth Lateran Council (1215) in *Conciliorum oecumenicorum decreti*, ed. J. Alberigo *e.a.*, 3rd ed. (Bologne, 1978), 216. Further sources are provided in Jean Leclercq, "L'idéal du théologien au moyen âge, textes inédites," *Revue des sciences religieuses* 21 (1947), 121–48 and in René Guelluy, "La place des théologiens dans l'église et la société médiévales," in *Miscellanea historica in honorem Alberti de Meyer* (Louvain, 1946), 574–77.

22. See Verger, "Teachers," 161–68 for a more general discussion of the authority of masters and doctors at the medieval university and their place in medieval society.

23. See Stanley Chodorow, *Christian Political Theory and Church Politics in the Mid-Twelfth Century. The Ecclesiology of Gratian's Decretum* (Berkeley, Calif., 1972), 65–96, who also discusses the questions of whether this tradition of dividing sacerdotal power goes back as far as Gratian's *Decretum* and whether the different presbyterial ranks in the hierarchy differ not only in jurisdiction but also in sacramental powers.

24. Congar, "Bref historique," 103–4. See also Jürgen Miethke, "Papst, Ortsbischof und Universität in den Pariser Theologenprozessen des 13. Jahrhunderts," in *Die Auseinandersetzungen an der Pariser Universität im XIII. Jahrhundert*, ed. Albert Zimmermann (Berlin, 1976), 93–94 for a description of the conflict between the future Pope Boniface VIII and Henry of Ghent, which illustrates these two types of power.

25. A lucid discussion of this text is given in Brian Tierney, *Origins of Papal Infallibility, 1150–1350* (Leiden, 1972), 39–45, Chodorow, *Christian Political Theory*,

165–68, and Jan van Laarhoven, "*Magisterium* or *Magisteria*: A Historical Note to a Theological Note," *Jaarboek Thomas Instituut te Utrecht* (1990), 75–94.

26. CUP 3: 280.

27. Congar, *L'église*, 246.

28. CUP 3: 117.

29. Already Koch, 2: 425–26 drew attention to the texts of Godfrey of Fontaines and Servais of Mt. St. Elias.

30. The text has been edited in Roland Hissette, "Une question quodlibétique de Servais du Mont-Saint-Éloi sur le pouvoir doctrinal de l'évèque," *RTAM* 49 (1982), 238–42.

31. See also Hissette, "Question," 235.

32. Hissette, "Question," 238, ll.13–18. The relevant passage from Gratian's *Decretum* I, dist. 80, c.12 (Friedberg, 1: 280) reads as follows: "In illis civitatibus, in quibus olim apud ethnicos primi flamines eorum atque primi legis doctores erant, episcoporum primates, atque patriarchas Beatus Petrus poni praecepit, qui reliquorum episcoporum causas et maiora negotia in fide agitarent."

33. See the *Glossa Ordinaria* on I, dist. 80, c.2: "et expone 'agitare in fide,' id est fideliter." I have used the edition *Decretum Gratiani emendatum et notationibus illustratum una cum glossis* (Paris 1585), col. 480. See also Miethke, "Bildungsstand," n. 60 for the observation that Servais is relying on the *Glossa Ordinaria*.

34. Hissette, "Question," 239: "Dico ergo quod episcopus de iure potest facere statuta in sua dioecesi, ut notatur *De consecratione*, d. III, c. 1, ut et non dicatur quod non est dicendum—et sic fecerunt et faciunt multi episcopi—et ut non fiat quod non est faciendum."

35. Hissette, "Question," 238 ll.7–8: "quia causae fidei pertinent ad solum Papam."; 240 ll. 49–57: "Aut ergo statuitur quod illud quod est dubium inter doctos habeatur pro articulo fidei explicito de novo, ita quod dictum contra hoc erit haeretice dictum et haeresis. Et sic potest facere solus Papa cum concilio."

36. Hissette, "Question," 240 ll. 58–65. Servais quotes from *Ad abolendam*: "singuli episcopi per dioeceses suas cum consilio clericorum, vel clerici ipsi sede vacante cum consilio, si oportuerit, vicinorum episcoporum haereticos iudicaverint, pari vinculo perpetui anathematis innodamus." Both decretals were incorporated in the collection of Pope Gregory IX, as X.5.7.9, and X.5.7.13 respectively. See Friedberg, 2: 780–82 and 787–89.

37. Hissette, "Question," 238 ll.9–12, and ll.89–93. See Friedberg 1: 777 and 970 respectively.

38. Godfrey of Fontaines, *Quodlibet XII*, 100: "Utrum Episcopus Parisiensis peccet in hoc quod omittit corrigere quosdam articulos a praedecessore suo condemnatos." Its date is discussed in Wippel, *Metaphysical Thought*, xvii–xviii.

39. See Chapter 1, notes 160 and 161 for a discussion of the double entendres and the "reversed rhetoric" of this passage.

40. Godfrey of Fontaines, *Quodlibet XII*, 102.

41. Godfrey of Fontaines, *Quodlibet XII*, 103.

42. The reference is to Aristotle, *Nicomachean Ethics*, 1109 b 1–5.

43. A convenient and reliable biography of Ockham in the English language is provided by William J. Courtenay, *Schools and Scholars in Fourteenth-Century En-*

gland (Princeton, N.J., 1987), 194–96, which also mentions all the relevant scholarly literature. See further the introductions to the editions of Ockham's complete theological and philosophical works, the *Opera Philosophica et Theologica* (St. Bonaventure, N.Y., 1967–85). The edition of the *Opera Politica* is still incomplete.

44. Ockham, *Tractatus de quantitate et Tractatus de corpore Christi*, 26*.

45. Ockham, *Tractatus de corpore Christi*, 206 ll. 3–5: "Post praedicta restat ostendere quod non oportet istam opinionem abicere tamquam haereticam, quamvis multi moderni doctores scribentes illam improbent et impugnant."

46. Ockham, *Tractatus de corpore Christi*, 207, ll.15–16: "cum ad solam Romanam Ecclesiam pertineat quaestionem fidei terminare." And further 209, ll. 69–71: "Patet igitur quod cum controversia est inter theologos de aliquo articulo an sit consonus vel dissonus fidei christianae, ad Summum Pontificem est recurrendum."; 209, ll. 79–84: "Videtur igitur ad Romanum Pontificem recurrendum quando quaestio ventilatur de aliquo quod non est expressum in Scripturis canonicis nec est per Romanam Ecclesiam determinatum."

47. See Friedberg, 1: 970: "Quotiens fidei ratio ventilatur, arbitror omnes fratres et coepiscopos nostros non nisi ad Petrum, id est sui nominis et honoris auctorem, debere referre (veluti nunc rettulit vestra dilectio) quod per totum mundum possit ecclesiis omnibus prodesse."

48. Ockham, *Tractatus de corpore Christi*, 209, ll. 61–63. This parallel passage is mentioned in the *Glossa Ordinaria* on C.24 q.1 c.12. See Brian Tierney, *Ockham, the Conciliar Theory and the Canonists* (Philadelphia, 1971) for a more general discussion of Ockham's use of canonistic material.

49. Ockham, *Tractatus de corpore Christi*, 208 ll. 36–51. For the *Glossa Ordinaria* see *Decretum Gratiani una cum glossis*, col. 1722: "Sed dic quod illud intelligendum est, quando tale quid dicunt quod certum est esse heresim. Hic vero ubi dubium est."

50. See note 33.

51. Ockham, *Tractatus de corpore Christi*, 209, ll. 71–79.

52. The theologian John Duns Scotus, however, associated *Ad abolendam* with a bishop's authority to deal with heretical opinions, rather than with heretical persons in his diocese. Along this line, he could argue that the validity of Tempier's condemnation was universal, not just local, and he could refute the argument that Tempier's condemnation "would not cross the sea [i.e., be valid in England] or the diocese." See John Duns Scotus, *Opera Omnia* (Vatican City, 1973), 7: 244–45.

53. Ockham, *Tractatus de corpore Christi*, 209, ll.79–83.

54. Ockham, *Tractatus de corpore Christi*, 213, ll.163–169.

55. Ockham, *Tractatus de corpore Christi*, 211, ll.112–120.

56. The work was planned in three parts, but the second was never written and the third remained unfinished. The treatise *De dogmatibus Johannis XXII*, which in the manuscripts and old prints is usually presented as the second part of the *Dialogus*, does not belong to that work. We have no text of the second part. See Jürgen Miethke, *Ockhams Weg zur Sozialphilosophie* (Berlin, 1969), 87–88 and 92. Like all his other political and polemical works the *Dialogus* was written at the court of Lewis of Bavaria at Munich. Its date and importance are discussed in Miethke, *Ockhams Weg*, 84–85 and 117–18 and Jürgen Miethke, "Ein neues Selbstzeugnis

Ockhams zu seinem *Dialogus*," in *From Ockham to Wyclif*, ed. A. Hudson and M. Wilks (Oxford, 1987), 24.

57. It seems sensible to adopt the methodological principle of Brian Tierney that the attribution of views expressed in the *Dialogus* to Ockham should be substantiated by Ockham's other (political) works. See Tierney, *Origins*, 20.

58. Miethke, "Neues Selbstzeugnis," 27.

59. Ockham's problem of an erring pope had precedents in the canonistic literature, but there erring popes, living in the distant past, were only introduced to examine certain aspects of ecclesiology, whereas Ockham really believed that at his time the church was ruled by a heretic. See Brian Tierney, *Religion, Law and the Growth of Constitutional Thought 1150–1650* (Cambridge, 1983), 15–16 and *Origins*, 33–39 for a discussion of the canonistic material on erring popes.

60. Ockham considered canon law as being placed under theology, and allowed the canonists only to see to it that the ecclesiastical rules were applied properly. See G. H. M. Posthumus Meyjes, "Exponents of Sovereignty: Canonists as seen by Theologians in the Late Middle Ages," in *The Church and Sovereignty c. 590–1918: Essays in Honour of Michael Wilks*, ed. D. Wood (Oxford 1991), 305–8. The fact that Pope John XXII was a canonist, and not a theologian, may well have induced Ockham to include his criticism of the canonists' competence in doctrinal matters in his *Dialogus*.

61. The structure of the first part of the *Dialogus* has been outlined in Wilhelm Kölmel, *Wilhelm Ockham und seine kirchenpolitischen Schriften* (Essen, 1962), 66–86.

62. The main theses of Ockham's ecclesiology are well explained in Miethke, *Ockhams Weg*, 284–99, Tierney, *Origins*, 206–37, McGrade, *The Political Thought of William of Ockham* (Cambridge, 1974), 47–77, John J. Ryan, *The Nature, Structure and Function of the Church in William of Ockham* (Missoula, Mont., 1979), and G. H. M. Posthumus Meyjes, "Het gezag van de theologische doctor in de kerk der middeleeuwen," *Nederlands Archief voor Kerkgeschiedenis* 63 (1983), 113–21.

63. Ockham, I *Dialogus* 2 c.17, fol. 12va: "Hereses implicte damnate dicuntur ille de quibus viris litteratis solummodo in litteris sacris eruditis per subtilem considerationem patet quomodo veritati catholice contente in sacris scripturis vel doctrina expressa universalis ecclesie adversantur."

64. Ockham, I *Dialogus* 2 c.17, fol. 12va: "Est enim notorium quod moderni theologi circa divina opiniones tenent contrarias, quas putant in divinis scripturis fundari, quarum altera in rei veritate scripture divine repugnat, sicut et tenent contrarium opinantes. Unde et eam per scripturam divinam improbare nituntur, sicut in scripturis eorum patet aperte. Et ita in rei veritate altera earum est damnata implicite, cum veritas contraria sit implicite approbata, ex hoc quod doctrina ecclesie, ex qua infertur, noscitur approbata."

65. Ockham, I *Dialogus* 2 c.18, fol. 12vb: "Sed assertio que in rei veritate est heretica, de qua tamen an sit heretica inter doctores opiniones reperiantur contrarie solemniter et explicite condemnare pertinet ad summum pontificem, vel concilium generale, vel ad universalem ecclesiam; igitur ad nullum inferiorem summo pontifice, nec ad collegium inferius summo concilio generali, vel universali ecclesia spectat assertionem huiusmodi tamquam hereticam explicite condemnare."

66. Ockham, I *Dialogus* 2 c.18, fols. 12vb–13ra: "Ex quibus verbis patenter

habetur quod ad sedem beati Petri est questio fidei referenda, et ita nec collegium inferius collegio generalis concilii, nec aliquis episcopus inferior papa potest aliquam heresim, de qua est dubium an sit heresis, condemnare. Et per consequens nullum talem heresim asserentem valet tamquam hereticum condemnare. Irrationabile enim omnino videtur quod episcopus vel inquisitor heretice pravitatis qui sepe sacre scripture imperitus existit, opiniones doctorum theologorum posset tamquam hereticas condemnare." General councils also play a role in Ockham's ecclesiology, as can be gathered from the preceding. I will, however, for the moment not go into Ockham's theory of the relation between pope and council. A general outline of the problematic relation between both authorities is sketched in Tierney, *Origins*, 154–64; see in particular 230–33 for Ockham's opinions.

67. Ockham, I *Dialogus* 2 c.18, fol. 12vb.

68. Ockham, I *Dialogus* 2 c.19, fol. 13ra: "Quamvis ista sententia videatur fortiter esse probata, tamen contra ipsam negantes in mente instantias revolo. Quarum prima est de universitate Parisiensi que multas opiniones multorum, et etiam Thome ipso vivente, tanquam errores excommunicavit et damnavit. Secunda est de duobus archiepiscopis Cantuariensibus, quorum unus erat doctor theologie de ordine fratrum predicatorum, qui fuit postea cardinalis. Secundus erat doctoris theologie fratrum minorum, qui doctrinam fratris Petri Johannis damnavit." Ockham, or this version of the *Dialogus*, seems to conflate Knapwell's condemnation and that of Peter Olivi. For the condemnations by Kilwardby and Pecham see James A. Weisheipl, *Friar Thomas d'Aquino. His Life, Thought, and Works, with Corrigenda and Addenda* (Washington, D.C., 1983), 337–41, and Richard Knapwell, *Quaestio disputata de unitate formae*, ed. Francis E. Kelley (Paris, 1982), 14–32.

69. See the preceding note. As I have indicated in Chapter 2, it is controversial whether the condemnation of 1277 was aimed against views of Thomas Aquinas. Certainly incorrect is Ockham's remark that this condemnation took place during Aquinas's lifetime. Note that Ockham does not mention Tempier.

70. This qualification may well be a pun, for it was not uncommon to characterize statements of alleged academic heretics as being rash. See Chapter 1.

71. Ockham, I *Dialogus* 2 c.19, fol. 13ra: "Cum igitur multorum iudicio inter articulos damnatos Parisius contineantur complures veritates, sequitur quod eadem universitas plures assertiones temerarie condemnavit. Et istius sententie fuerunt illi qui post revocationem dicte sententie quo ad opinionem Thome easdem opiniones Thome prius damnatas nunc Parisius tenent et approbant publice et occulte."

72. Ockham, I *Dialogus* 2 c.21, fols. 13rb/va: "Sunt quidam dicentes quod universitas Parisiensis multas assertiones temerarie excommunicavit, et ideo non quia illas assertiones putant sapere orthodoxam veritatem, sed quia quoquomodo repugnant fidei orthodoxe non apparet."

73. Ockham, I *Dialogus* 2 c.21, fol. 13va: "Alii dicunt quod ideo dicta excommunicatio fuit temeraria reputanda, quia excommunicantes potestatem quam non habebant usurpaverunt. Et ideo iuste fuit sententia postea eadem revocata."

74. Ockham, I *Dialogus* 2 c.21, fol. 13va: "Adhuc est quarta responsio quod episcopus Parisiensis auctoritate apostolice sedis rite eandem tulit sententiam. Damnare autem assertionem hereticam auctoritate apostolice sedis ad inferiorem summo pontifice potest licite pertinere."

75. Ockham, I *Dialogus* 2 c.21, fol. 13va: "Quibusdam videtur quod ferentes aliique revocantes sunt heretici reputandi. Sed qui verius dicant, sciri non potest, nisi precognoscendo an assertiones damnate et postea revocate heretice vel catholice sint censende."

76. Since the Master here only gives one opinion and solves all the objections of the Disciple, it is safe to assume that the Master's opinion reflects Ockham's own position. See also McGrade, *Political Thought*, 18 and 54. Moreover, as we shall see below, the Master's views are consonant with Ockham's discussion elsewhere. The following passages from the *Dialogus* have also been discussed in McGrade, *Political Thought*, 53–61.

77. Ockham, I *Dialogus* 4, especially c.13 and 14, fols. 26rb–27ra. The questions read as follows: (fols. 26rb/va) "ad quem, videlicet spectat errantem corrigere, et qualis debet esse illa correctio que est legitima et sufficiens reputanda." See also McGrade, *Political Thought*, 53–56.

78. Ockham, I *Dialogus* 4 c.14, fol. 26va: "Cupio scire an omnes sciant litterati quod errans correptus a prelato suo vel habente iurisdictionem super ipsum, teneatur errorem suum revocare, licet non fuerit sibi patenter ostensum per eundem quod error suus catholice obviat veritati: Utrum, scilicet ad solam monitionem vel increpationem prelati sui errorem suum debeat revocare."

79. Ockham, I *Dialogus* 4 c.13, fol. 26va: "Quantum ad correctionem dicitur quod illa sola correctio censenda est sufficiens et legitima reputanda qua aperte erranti ostenditur quod assertio sua catholice obviat veritati, ita quod iudicio intelligentium nulla posset tergiversatione negare quin sibi sit sufficienter et aperte ostensum quod error suus catholice veritati repugnat."

80. Ockham, I *Dialogus* 4 c.14, fol. 26vb: "Illi qui in expositione scripture divine, et per consequens in traditione eorum que ad fidem pertinent orthodoxam preferuntur prelatis et iurisdictionem habentibus non tenetur nec debent si erraverint ignoranter opiniones suas tamquam hereticas (licet sint in rei veritate erronee) revocare, quamvis correpti fuerint a prelatis vel aliis, nisi eis patenter fuerit ostensum quod opiniones sue veritati obviant orthodoxe, quia qui maioris auctoritatis est in aliquo nequaquam in hoc minori subiicitur; ergo qui preferuntur prelatis in expositione scripture divine non subiiciuntur eis in hoc. Sed doctores et tractatores scripture divine, et per consequens in traditione illorum que ad fidem pertinent orthodoxam; igitur doctores non tenentur opiniones suas, licet sint erronee revocare, si fuerint a prelatis correpti, nisi probatum fuerit eis evidenter quod eorum opiniones obviant veritati."

81. The text of the preceding note continues as follows, Ockham, I *Dialogus* 4 c.14, fol. 26vb: "Maior est certa. Et minor probatur primo auctoritate Gratiani in Decretis, di. xx, c.i, quia ait. . . . Ex his patenter habetur quod doctores in expositionibus scripture pontificibus preferentur." See also McGrade, *Political Thought*, 55 n. 29. See also the discussion of Gratian's theory at the beginning of this chapter and the literature cited in note 25.

82. Ockham, I *Dialogus* 4 c.14, fol. 26vb: "His verbis ostenditur quod in his que ad fidem pertinent doctores sunt pontificibus preferendi et ita, nisi fuerint ab eis correpti legitime modo preexposito, non tenentur opiniones suas si fuerint erronee revocare."

83. Ockham, I *Dialogus* 4 c.14, fol. 26vb: "Ista ratio videtur dupliciter deficere. Primo, quia Gratianus loquitur de doctoribus ab ecclesia approbatis, sicut de Augustino, Hieronimo et aliis, non modernis similibus doctoris.

84. Ockham, I *Dialogus* 4 c.14, fols. 26vb–27ra: "Ad primam dicunt quod Gratianus non loquitur solummodo de doctoribus ab ecclesia approbatis, sed etiam loquitur de aliis, sicut etiam loquitur de aliis pontificibus quam de illis qui fuerunt temporibus doctorum qui nunc sunt ab ecclesia approbati. Comparat enim in genere statum doctorum ad statum pontificum. . . . .Unde, ut suam intentionem aperte declarent, dicunt quod Gratianus non loquitur de doctoribis prout his diebus nomen doctoris accipitur, sed loquitur de intelligentibus scripture divine tractatoribus, sive magistri, sive discipuli appellentur. Multi enim qui vocantur "discipuli" in expositione scripture divine sunt preferendi magistris. Et ideo sunt etiam pontificibus in huiusmodi preferendi."

85. Ockham, I *Dialogus* 4 c.14, fol. 27ra (continuation of the text of the previous note): "Unde et ratio Gratiani ita concludit de eruditis modernis sicut de antiquis tractatoribus scripturarum, quia eruditi his temporibus scientia ampliori precellunt. Ergo in huiusmodi sunt episcopis et inquisitoribus illiteratis et simplicibus preferendi."

86. Ockham, I *Dialogus* 4 c.14, fol. 27ra: "Et ideo, sicut antiquitus doctores in traditione eorum que spectant ad fidem fuerunt pontificibus preferendi, ita et nunc sunt doctores moderni pontificibus preferendi, dummodo sint doctores propter scientiam excellentem et vitam laudabilem, et non propter munera et preces violentas, vel favores humanos ad magisterium sublimati."

87. This view is expressed in response to a second objection against Ockham's interpretation of *Decretum* dist. 20. Ockham, *Dialogus* 4 c.14, fol. 27ra: "Ad secundam tuam instantiam dicunt quod . . . eadem ratione nec simplices peritorum sequaces tenentur opiniones quas de peritoribus acceperunt aliqualiter revocare, nisi fuerint correpti legitime. Ex quo sequitur quod etiam alii simplices non tenentur (nisi correpti legitime) suas opiniones erroneas revocare, quia omnes simplices consimili iure censeri videntur."

88. See Chapter 1, notes 87 and 189.

89. The first three theses are also discussed in Douglas Taber, Jr., "Pierre d'Ailly and the Teaching Authority of the Theologian," *CH* 59 (1990), 168–72.

90. Pierre d'Ailly, *Tractatus*, 78, quarta conclusio.

91. *Ad abolendam*: "singuli episcopi per dioeceses suas cum consilio clericorum," The decretal was incorporated in the collection of Pope Gregory IX, as X.5.7.9. See Friedberg, 2: 780–82.

92. Pierre d'Ailly, *Tractatus*, 78, quinta conclusio.

93. Pierre d'Ailly, *Tractatus*, 78–79.

94. Pierre d'Ailly, *Tractatus*, 79, sexta conclusio.

95. Pierre d'Ailly, *Tractatus*, 83.

96. Pierre d'Ailly, *Tractatus*, 85.

97. Pierre d'Ailly, *Tractatus*, 85–86, and Taber, "Pierre d'Ailly," 169.

98. Pierre d'Ailly, *Tractatus*, 78 and 80–82. This tendency also appears in other writings by d'Ailly, in other contexts. See Bernstein, *Pierre d'Ailly*, 180–81.

99. See also Taber, "Pierre d'Ailly," 173.

Conclusion

1. See, for instance, Jaroslav Pelikan, *The Christian Tradition*, 5 vols. (Chicago, 1971–89), 1: 3–7 for some methodological observations concerning the place of heresies and condemnations in the history of the development of doctrine.

2. G. R. Evans, *Philosophy and Theology in the Middle Ages* (London, 1993), esp. 10–17, and 35–51.

3. For the expression *salva fide (catholica)* see Peter Classen, "Libertas scolastica — Scholarenprivilegien — Akademische Freiheit im Mittelalter," in Peter Classen, *Studium und Gesellschaft im Mittelalter*, ed. Johannes Fried (Stuttgart, 1983), 256 and 280. The reference to 2 Corinthians 10: 5 "captivare intellectum in obsequium Christi" (or "fidei"), occurs in a number of university documents, precisely in connection with condemnations. See CUP 1: 115, 544, art. 18 (condemnation of 1277); Gerson, 6: 157 and William of Ockham, *Tractatus de quantitate et Tractatus de corpore Christi*, 70–71. Luca Bianchi, "Captivare intellectum in obsequium Christi," *RCSF* 38 (1983), 81–87 discusses the occurrence of this reference in Tempier's condemnation (and in Thomas Aquinas and Bonaventure).

4. The Augustinian and monastic traditions to which this contrast goes back are sketched in Heiko A. Oberman, *Contra vanam curiositatem* (*Theologische Studien*, vol. 113; Zürich, 1974) and Edward Peters, "*Libertas inquirendi* and the *vitium curiositatis* in Medieval Thought," in *La notion de liberté au moyen âge. Islam, Byzance, Occident*, ed. G. Makdisi, D. Sourdel, and J. Sourdel-Thomine (Paris, 1985), 91–98, and William J. Courtenay, "Spirituality and Late Scholasticism," in *Christian Spirituality. High Middle Ages and Reformation*, ed. J. Raitt (New York, 1988), 116–17. See further Stephen C. Ferruolo, *The Origins of the University. The Schools of Paris and Their Critics, 1100–1215* (Stanford, Calif., 1985), 76, 139, 231–235 for the theme of *curiositas* in moral critics of the schools.

5. The theme of vain curiosity in Clement's letter (CUP: #1125) and in some autobiographical reflections of the theologians Thomas Bradwardine and Richard Fitzralph is discussed in William J. Courtenay, "The Reception of Ockham's Thought at the University of Paris," in *Preuve et raisons à l'université de Paris. Logique, ontologies et théologie au XIVe siècle*, ed. Zénon Kaluza and Paul Vignaux (Paris, 1984), 54 and "Spirituality," 115–16, respectively.

6. The background to the theme of "plus sapere quam oportet" is explained in Herbert Grundmann, *Ausgewählte Aufsätze*, 3 vols. (Stuttgart, 1976–78), 417, and Carlo Ginzburg, "High and Low: the Theme of Forbidden Knowledge," *Past & Present* 73 (1976), 28–30.

7. The expression "plus sapere quam oportet" and the themes of curiosity, vainess, inaneness, voidness, and strange doctrines can be found in the following condemnations and letters of ecclesiastical officials: CUP: #59, #473 (the condemnation of 1277), #741, #798, #1042, #1091, #1124, #1125. See also the bull of Eckhart's condemnation in M.-H. Laurent, "Autour du procès de Maitre Eckhart: Les documents des Archives Vaticanes," *Divus Thomas* 39 (1936), 436. For the topic of foreign learning see also Monika Asztalos, "The Faculty of Theology," in *Universities in the Middle Ages*, ed. Hilde De Ridder-Symoens (*A History of the University in Europe*, vol. 1; Cambridge, 1992), 432.

8. The inquiries against the masters of theology William of St. Amour, John of Paris, John of Pouilly, Durand of St. Pourçain, Meister Eckhart, and Thomas Waleys were not initiated in a university context.

9. See William J. Courtenay, *Schools and Scholars in Fourteenth-Century England* (Princeton, N.J., 1987), 47 for this suggestion.

10. CUP 3: 144, and also Asztalos, "Faculty," 418 for similar admonitions in the statutes of the University of Bologna.

11. Gerson, 6: 157,161, 165, 166, and also CUP 2: #798 and 3: 492 (#1559).

12. In addition to the oath mentioned in Chapter 1, which bachelors of theology had to take, it is significant too that the arts faculty issued a statute in 1272 (CUP 2: 499–500) that proscribed bachelors and masters of arts from solving (*determinare*) against faith (*contra fidem*) philosophical questions touching upon faith. Moreover, the statute ordered that henceforth any bachelor of arts wishing to incept as master had to take an oath to observe this and other prescriptions laid down in the same statute. For the text of the oath see CUP 1: 586–87.

13. Gregory the Great, *Pastorale*, II, 4 (PL 77: 30) "Ne igitur incauta locutio simplices pertrahat in errorem." Cf. Luca Bianchi, *Il vescovo e i filosofi. La condanna parigina del 1277 e l'evoluzione dell'aristotelismo scolastico* (Bergamo, 1990) 199 and 206.

14. CUP 4: #1864 and #1868, and Gerson, 10: 30–40.

15. CUP 4: #1988, #1990, and #1999–2017, and Gerson, 10: 164–287.

16. More "conventional" cases of academic heresy within the own faculty were the examinations of the theologians Master John Sarrasin O.P. in 1430 (CUP 4: #2345), master Nicholas Quadrigarii O.E.S.A. in 1443 (CUP 4: #2572), and Master Michael Anglici in 1448 (CUP 4: #2637). The first two were denounced for their teaching during the vesperies. The last one was accused by another theologian, namely Master Michael of Epila, O.P. In the case against John Sarrasin in 1430, the faculty of theology was only asked to participate as an external consultant. The trial took place in the diocese of Rouen at the court of the bishop and the inquisitor. See CUP 4: #2358.

17. For what follows see especially Guy Fitch Lytle, "Universities as Religious Authorities in the Later Middle Ages and Reformation," in *Reform and Authority in the Medieval and Reformation Church*, ed. Guy Fitch Lytle (Washington, D.C., 1981), 82–97, and James K. Farge, *Orthodoxy and Reform in Early Reformation France: The Faculty of Theology of Paris, 1500–1543* (Leiden, 1985), 115–220.

18. See CUP 4: #2369–#2390 for Joan of Arc. The other cases, and many others, are documented in Farge, *Orthodoxy*, 115–220.

Selected Bibliography

SOURCES

Unpublished Sources

The two central collections of unpublished sources for the study of academic censures at the University of Paris are the *Collectio errorum in anglia et parisius condemnatorum*, also sometimes referred to in this study as the Collection of Parisian
Articles, and the Register that the theologian Noël Beda (c. 1470–1536) compiled
of records concerning censures at the University of Paris.

The *Collectio errorum in anglia et parisius condemnatorum* exists in several versions. The short version, which contains the lists of censured views of William of
Auvergne (1241), Bishop Tempier (1270 and 1277), and Robert Kilwardby (1277),
has been preserved in more than thirty medieval manuscripts. The oldest of these
seems to be Paris, BN lat. 15661. During the fourteenth century this collection grew
significantly. The number of copies, however, of this longer *Collectio errorum*, sometimes referred to as the Collection of Novel Articles (*articuli novi, novelli*, or *posteriores*), is far smaller. In addition to the censures of the shorter version, it also includes
the censured views of Nicholas of Autrecourt (1346), John of Mirecourt (1347),
John Guyon (1348), Simon (1351), Guido (Giles of Medonta?) (1354), Louis of
Padua (1362), John of Calore (1363), Denis of Foullechat (1369), and John of
Monzón (1389). The following manuscripts are known: Auxerre, Bibliothèque
municipale 243; Erfurt, B. Amploniana F.179 and Q 151; Munich, Bayrische Staatsbibliothek, Clm 3798, and Clm. 28126; Paris, BN lat. 16553; Rouen, Bibliothèque
municipale 587 (A. 263).

Separately from the manuscript tradition, there exists an early printed tradition of the *Collectio errorum in anglia et parisius condemnatorum*. It is often attached
to the printed editions of Peter the Lombard's *Sentences*, for instance in: Venice:
Vendelinum de Spira, 1477; Venice, 1480; Venice, 1507 (*cum Nic. de Orbellis inter-
pretatione*). It further appears in the following editions of the *Sentences* together with
the commentary by Henry of Gorichem (Gorkum): Nuremberg, 1478, 1499, 1528;
Basel, 1492 [Hain 10197], 1498 [Hain 10198], 1502, 1507, and 1513; Rouen, 1653;
Venice: Simon de Luere, 1506, 1570; Paris: Jean Roigny, 1536, 1550, and Paris: Jean
Petit, 1536. To these latter editions can be added: Basel, 1487 [Hain 10192], 1488
[Hain 10195], 1489 [Hain 10196]. Moreover, the following separate editions of the
Collection of Parisian Articles can be mentioned: *Articuli Parisius condemnati*:
Padua: Mathaeus Cerdonis, c. 1485 [no. 2709]; *Articuli in Anglia et Parisius condem-*

nati: Paris: Antoine Caillant, c. 1483 [no. 2710]; Cologne: Heinrich Quentell, c. 1488, and c. 1490 [nos. 2711 and 2712]. The numbers refer to the *Gesamtkatalog der Wiegendrucke* (Leipzig, 1925–   ).

On October 15, 1523, the faculty of theology approved Noël Beda's suggestion to compile a survey of its pronouncements and judgments. Beda's activities resulted in the production of two Registers, namely the *Liber primus registri [determinationum] facultatis theologie schole Parisiensis in materia fidei et morum incipiens ab anno domini 1284* and the *Liber secundus registri determinationum . . . ab anno domini 1524*, currently preserved in Paris, BN ms. nouv. acq. lat. 1826 and ms. lat. 3381-B, respectively. The first register, which is the only one relevant here, covers the period 1210–1523. Despite its title, the first entry is from 1210, not from 1284. If one were to look in this register at the documents concerning suspect teaching from the thirteenth and fourteenth centuries, one would find that it contains only some records concerning the censures of John of Brescain (1247), Denis of Foullechat (1369), and John of Monzón (1389). The register does not reproduce any documents of the censures of Stephen of Venizy (1241), Nicholas of Autrecourt (1346), John of Mirecourt (1347), John Guyon (1348), Simon (1351), Guido (Giles of Medonta?) (1354), Louis of Padua (1362), or John of Calore (1363). Nor does it contain Bishop Tempier's condemnations of December 10, 1270, and March 7, 1277. The reason is that the archive of the faculty of theology on which Beda relied when drawing up his Register did not have any documents pertaining to these censures. Almost all the original records that were copied in Beda's Register are still extant in the Archive of the University of Paris.

The *Collectio errorum in anglia et parisius condemnatorum* has been little studied. Manuscripts of its shorter version are listed in CUP 1: 556–57, and in Luca Bianchi, *Il vescovo e i filosofi. La condanna parigina del 1277 e l'evoluzione dell'aristotelismo scolastico* (Bergamo, 1990), 207–8 n. 7. See also pp. 25–27 of this study for a brief discussion of the Parisian Articles. This collection is studied and edited in Henryk Anzulewicz, "Eine weitere Überlieferung der *Collectio errorum in Anglia et Parisius condemnatorum* im *Ms. lat. fol. 456* der Staatsbibliothek Preussischer Kulturbesitz zu Berlin," *Franziskanische Studien* 74 (1992), 375–99. A groundbreaking study of the preservation and transmission of academic censures is William J. Courtenay, "The Preservation and Dissemination of Academic Condemnations at the University of Paris in the Middle Ages," in *Les philosophes morales et politiques aux Moyen Age*, ed. C. Bazán, E. Andújar, and L. Sbrocchi, 3 vols. (New York, Ottawa, and Toronto, 1995), 3: 1659–67. Inventories of the longer Collection of Parisian Articles as preserved in the manuscript Auxerre, Bibliothèque municipale 243 and in the early printed tradition are provided in J. M. M. H. Thijssen, "What Really Happened on 7 March 1277? Bishop Tempier's Condemnation and its Institutional Context," in *Texts and Context in Ancient and Medieval Science: Studies on the Occasion of John E. Murdoch's Seventieth Birthday*, ed. Edith Sylla and Michael McVaugh (Leiden, 1997), 108–12. This same article also studies Noël Beda's Register and, on pp. 113–14, provides an inventory of that part of Beda's Register that concerns medieval censures. See also Jules-Alexandre Clerval, *Registre des procès-verbaux de la faculté de théologie de Paris*. 1: 1505–1523 (Paris, 1917), xi–xv, who identified Noël Beda's register as one of the sources used by Du Plessis.

PUBLISHED SOURCES

This section lists the published records that are most pertinent to the study of academic censures at the University of Paris. With few exceptions, studies have not been included. They can be found in the notes and in the list of modern studies below.

The two most important collections of documents are Carolus Du Plessis d'Argentré, *Collectio judiciorum de novis erroribus*, 3 vols. (Paris, 1724–36), and Emile Denifle and Heinrich Chatelain, *Chartularium Universitatis Parisiensis*, 4 vols. (Paris, 1889–91). Also useful, although of a completely different nature, is Heinrich Denzinger, *Enchiridion symbolorum definitionum et declarationum de rebus fidei et morum*, 37th ed. (Freiburg i. Br., 1991), which reproduces a number of medieval documents from older printed editions that are not readily available elsewhere.

The *Chartularium* is not an edition of a medieval chartulary, but rather a collection of miscellaneous documents that are pertinent to the medieval University of Paris, its masters and students, and its officers, arranged in chronological order (1200–1452). Certain documents relevant to academic censures made available in the *Chartularium* are derived from Du Plessis's *Collectio*.

Du Plessis's self-proclaimed goal was to collect the "absurd errors and lies that devastated the Lord's vineyard" (Cant. 2,15), in order to illustrate the truth of the divine oracles "in the same manner as the splendor of the light is more clearly revealed by the shadows." The author claimed that his collection of records was more complete than any of the earlier ones that he used, such as Nicholas Eymeric, O.P., *Directorium Inquisitorum* (c. 1375; first printed in 1503), Bernard of Luxemburg, O.P., *Catalogus Haereticorum* (published in 1522), the *Maxima Bibliotheca Veterum Patrum et aliquorum Scriptorum Ecclesiasticorum* (many editions from the seventeenth century onward), or Bulaeus (Du Boulay), *Historia Universitatis Parisiensis*, 6 vols. (Paris, 1665–73). The *Collectio errorum in anglia et parisius condemnatorum* and Noël Beda's Register were also perused in Du Plessis's *Collectio* and in the *Chartularium*. Other old printed collections that contain relevant documents are E. Martène and U. Durand, *Thesaurus novus anecdotorum*, 5 vols. (Paris, 1717), and E. Baluze and J. D. Mansi, *Miscellanea*, 4 vols. (Lucca, 1761–64).

CENSURES AT THE UNIVERSITY OF PARIS THAT APPEAR IN THE
COLLECTION OF PARISIAN ARTICLES

Stephen of Venizy

On January 13, 1241, a list of ten errors "against theological truth," upheld by Brother Stephen (of Venizy) was condemned by the chancellor and the regent masters of theology of the University of Paris: CUP 1: #128. The case is discussed in William J. Courtenay, "Dominicans and Suspect Opinion in the Thirteenth Century: The Case of Stephen of Venizy, Peter of Tarentaise, and the Articles of 1270 and 1271," *Vivarium* 32 (1994), 186–95.

Condemnation by Stephen Tempier, 1270

On September 10, 1270, Bishop Stephen Tempier condemned thirteen theses: CUP 1: #432.

Condemnation by Stephen Tempier, 1277

On March 7, 1277, Bishop Tempier condemned 219 errors and certain books: CUP 1: #473, reprinted and translated into German in Kurt Flasch, *Aufklärung im Mittelalter? Die Verurteilung von 1277* (Frankfurt, 1989). Tempier's original syllabus of propositions was reorganized during the Middle Ages. This new medieval edition is part of the *Collectio errorum in Anglia et Parisiis condemnatorum* and has been printed in Du Plessis d'Argentré, *Collectio*, 1, part 1: 188–200. A modern edition is now available in Anzulewicz, "Eine weitere Überlieferung," 375–99. At the beginning of the twentieth century Tempier's articles were edited in yet another order by Pierre Mandonnet, *Siger de Brabant et l'averroïsme latin au XIIIe siècle*, 2 vols. (Louvain, 1908–11), 2: 175–91. Roland Hissette, *Enquête sur les 219 articles condamnés à Paris le 7 mars 1277* (Louvain, 1977) reproduces Mandonnet's edition and provides on pp. 319–21 a useful concordance of the three editions of Tempier's articles. A few weeks before the condemnation, Pope John XXI had written a letter to Tempier in which he ordered him to investigate rumors of heresy at the University of Paris: CUP 1: #471. Almost simultaneously with Tempier's condemnation, Pope John XXI wrote a second letter concerning the dissemination of errors at the University of Paris, *Flumen aquae vivae*, which has been edited in A. Callebaut, "Jean Pecham et l'Augustinisme. Aperçus historiques," *AFH* 18 (1925), 459–60. On February 14, 1325, Tempier's condemnation was revoked "as far as it is assumed to concern Thomas Aquinas" by Stephen of Bourret, Bishop of Paris: CUP 2: #838. The textual tradition of this document is discussed in Maier, 3: 601–608. A narrative account and analysis of the events of 1277 is given in Chapter 2.

Prohibition of Six Ockhamist Errors

On December 29, 1340, the arts faculty prohibited six "Ockhamist errors": CUP 2: #1042. See Chapter 3 for a discussion.

Nicholas of Autrecourt

On November 21, 1340, Pope Benedict XII summoned Nicholas of Autrecourt and five other academics from Paris to Avignon: CUP 2: #1041. The report of Autrecourt's trial, including several lists of charged errors, is edited in CUP 2: #1124, is reprinted in Joseph Lappe, *Nicholaus von Autrecourt, sein Leben, seine Philosophie, seine Schriften* (Münster, 1908), 31*–48*, and is reprinted and translated into German in Nicolaus von Autrecourt, *Briefe*, ed. Ruedi Imbach and Dominik Perler, trans. and introd. Dominik Perler (Hamburg, 1988), 75–95. A new critical edition and translation of the material of Autrecourt's trial is provided in Lambert M. de Rijk, *Nicholas of Autrecourt. His Correspondence with Giles and Bernard of Arezzo. A Critical Edition from the Two Parisian Manuscripts, with an Introduction, English Translation, Explanatory Notes and Indexes* (Leiden, 1994), apps. A and B. The fullest account and interpretation of the evidence of Autrecourt's trial is given by Zénon Kaluza, *Nicolas d'Autrecourt: Ami de la vérité* (*Histoire littéraire de la France*, vol. 42, part 1; Paris, 1995), 93–128 . The judicial proceedings against Nicholas of Autrecourt are discussed in Chapter 4.

John of Mirecourt

In 1347 a list of forty errors drawn from the commentary on the *Sentences* of the Cistercian John of Mirecourt was promulgated. The list has been edited in Du Plessis, *Collectio* 1, part 1: 343–345 and CUP 2: #1147. Mirecourt wrote two defenses that have come to be known in the scholarly literature as his Apologies. The first has been edited twice, namely in A. Birkenmajer, *Vermischte Untersuchungen zur Geschichte der mittelalterlichen Philosophie* (Münster, 1922), 113–28, and F. Stegmüller, "Die zwei Apologien des Jean de Mirecourt," *RTAM* 5 (1933), 46–78. An edition of the second defense is provided in Stegmüller, 192–204. William J. Courtenay, in "John of Mirecourt's Condemnation: Its Original Form," *RTAM* 53 (1986), 190–91, edited the introductory statement to the condemnation of Mirecourt's views by the chancellor, Robert de Bardis. The inquiry against John of Mirecourt is discussed in Chapter 4.

John Guyon

On October 12, 1348, John Guyon, O.F.M., recanted five errors: CUP 2: #1158.

Simon

In 1351, Simon, bachelor of theology, recanted the errors derived from his vesperies: CUP 3: #1201.

Guido (Giles of Medonta?)

On May 16, 1354, Guido, O.E.S.A. (Giles of Medonta?), recanted nine errors derived from his teaching, disputations, and collations: CUP 3: #1218.

Louis of Padua

In 1362, Louis of Padua recanted the errors derived from his vesperies: CUP 3: #1270 and A. Combes, *Jean Gerson commentateur dionysien. Pour l'histoire des courants doctrinaux à l'université de Paris à la fin du XIVe siècle*, 2d ed. (Paris, 1973), 644–47.

John of Calore

In 1363, John of Calore recanted the errors derived from his vesperies: CUP 3: #1288.

Denis of Foullechat

Between November 1364 and 1369, certain theses derived from the *principium* by Denis of Foullechat, O.F.M., were examined. Denis appealed to the pope before he finally was made to recant his errors: CUP 3: #1298, #1299, #1300, #1349, #1350, #1351, #1352. A full narrative account and interpretation of Foullechat's trial will be given by Gregory Moule in his forthcoming Ph.D. thesis (University of Wisconsin).

John of Monzón

In 1387, the faculty of theology accused Master John of Monzón, O.P., of having disseminated false teaching concerning the Immaculate Conception during his vesperies and the *resumpta*. Monzón refused to recant the charged errors, and instead appealed at the papal court. Even before the appellate process had come to a conclusion, however, he fled Avignon and appealed again, this time to the papal court of the anti-pope Urban VI in Rome. Monzón's followers were made to recant their views. See CUP 3: #1157–1583. Since the inquiry against Monzón is one of the best-documented cases of academic censure, it has been extensively discussed and analyzed in Chapter 1.

OTHER CENSURES OF ACADEMICS AT PARIS

Master Amalric and the Amalricians

On November 20, 1210, a provincial council in Paris condemned unspecified views of Master Amalric and ten heretics, who in heresiology have come to be known as "Amalricians": CUP 1: #11. The document edited under CUP 1: #12 is not the official list with charges, but part of a chronicle. A fragment of the report of the interrogation of the Amalricians has been preserved, and is edited in M.-T. D'Alverny, "Un fragment du procès des amauriciens," *AHDL* 18 (1950–51), 325–36. A new interpretation of the inquiry against Master Amalric, which can be considered the first academic censure, and that against his followers, which rather belongs in the category of popular heresy, is offered in J. M. M. H. Thijssen, "Master Amalric and the Amalricians: Inquisitorial Procedure and the Supression of Heresy at the University of Paris," *Speculum*, 71 (1996), 43–65.

John of Brescain and Master Raymond

In December 21, 1247, John of Brescain and Master Raymond were forced to recant their erroneous positions. Both were probably theologians, because they are reproved for introducing logic and philosophy in theology: CUP 1: #176.

William of St. Amour

On June 17, 1256, Pope Alexander IV condemned William of St. Amour (and also Odo of Douai and Christian of Beauvais): CUP 1: #288. William had been attacking the mendicants in his treatise *De periculis novissimorum temporum* and in his sermons. The mendicants struck back by denouncing William. In the next two years, William's treatise and excerpts from his sermons became the subject of a doctrinal investigation. William's response to the charges has been preserved and is edited in Edmond Faral, "Les 'Responsiones' de Guillaume de Saint-Amour," *AHDL* 18 (1950–51), 337–94. Other documents relevant to the complicated history of William's accusation, examination, and condemnation are CUP 1: #262, #271, #280, #282, #287, #289, #291, #308, #314, #315, #316, #317, #318, and #321. The public recantation of Christian of Beauvais on August 12, 1257, has been edited in H. Lippens, O.F.M., "Provinciae Franciae O.F.M. Chartularium aliaque documenta saeculi XIII. Documenta ad conventum Rothomagensem spectantia," *AFH* 30 (1937), 59–63. See Jürgen Miethke, "Papst, Ortsbischof und Universität in den Pariser Theologenprozessen des 13. Jahrhunderts," in *Die Auseinandersetzungen an der Pariser Universität im XIII. Jahrhundert*, ed. Albert Zimmermann (Berlin, 1976), 75–81, and Marc Dufeil, *Guillaume de Saint-Amour et la polémique universitaire* (Paris, 1972) for a narrative account and analysis of William of St. Amour's trial.

Giles of Rome

Sometime between March 7 and March 28, 1277, fifty-one charged errors derived from Giles of Rome's commentary on the *Sentences* were examined by Bishop Stephen Tempier. Giles's defense has been edited in *Aegidii Romani, Apologia*, ed. Robert Wielockx (*Opera Omnia*, vol. 3, part 1; Florence, 1985), 49–64. In 1285, Giles was rehabilitated by Pope Honorius IV, in a letter adressed to Ranulph of Houblonnière, bishop of Paris: CUP 1: #522. The letter is an important source for our knowledge of the inquiry against Giles of Rome in 1277. See J. M. M. H. Thijssen, "1277 Revisited: A New Interpretation of the Doctrinal Investigations of Thomas Aquinas and Giles of Rome," *Vivarium* 34 (1997), 1–29, and Chapter 2.

John of Paris

In 1286–87, John of Paris (Quidort) was denounced. The ensuing examination of his commentary on the *Sentences* led to the condemnation of sixteen articles. His apology has been preserved and edited in P. Glorieux, "Un mémoire justificatif de Bernard de Trilia," *Revue des sciences philosophiques et théologiques* 17 (1928), 407–13. In "Bernard de Trilia? ou Jean de Paris?" *Revue des sciences philosophiques et théologiques* 19 (1930), 469–74, Glorieux concluded that the apology, which he had edited a few years before, had indeed been written by John of Paris, and not by Bernard of Trilia as he previously believed.

John of Paris

In 1305–1306, John of Paris, master of theology, was condemned for his position concerning the Eucharist: CUP 2: #656. While his appeal was pending, he died in 1306.

Raymund Lull

Between February 10, 1310, and September 9, 1311, during his stay at Paris, Raymund Lull's *Ars* was examined by the faculty of arts and the chancellor, but no errors were found: CUP 2: #679 and #691.

Brother Bartholomew

In June 1316, Brother Bartholomew, a Cistercian, was forced to recant thirteen articles derived from his commentary on the *Sentences*. The recantation is edited in Konstanty Michalski, "La révocation par Frère Barthélemy, en 1316, de 13 thèses incriminées," in *Aus der Geisteswelt des Mittelalters. Studien und Texte Martin Grabmann zur Vollendung des 60. Lebensjahres*, ed. Albert Lang, Joseph Lechner, and Michael Schmaus (Münster, 1935), 2: 1097.

John of Pouilly

On June 27, 1318, John of Pouilly was cited to Avignon. The papal letter mentioned two errors: CUP 2: #764. The basis for his trial was a list of thirteen suspect propositions that had been sent to the pope by John's enemies among the Franciscan and Dominican orders. The list is edited in Koch 2: 391–93. In July John of Pouilly wrote a *Responsio* against the two charges in the papal letter and the thirteen articles in the list. On October 18, 1319, the commission of investigation derived a new list with nine charges from this *Responsio*. This text has been edited in Koch 2: 413–14. On July 24, 1321 three of the propositions from the new list were condemned by Pope John XXII: CUP 2: #798. On July 27, 1321, John of Pouilly publicly recanted these errors: CUP 2: #799.

John of Jandun and Marsilius of Padua

On April 3, 1327, Pope John XXII in a letter to King Lewis of Bavaria referred to errors of John of Jandun and Marsilius of Padua, which are unspecified in the letter, but which as a matter of fact, were derived from their *Defensor pacis*: CUP 2: #864. On October 23, 1327, Pope John issued the letter *Licet iuxta doctrinam*, in which both academics were condemned as heretics. The papal letter has been printed in Martène and Durand, *Thesaurus*, 2: 704–16. The errors that in John's letter were attributed to John of Jandun and Marsilius of Padua have been published in Denzinger, *Enchiridion*, nos. 941–46. Sometime between September 1 and December 31, 1375, the faculty of theology started an investigation into the French translation of the *Defensor pacis*: Du Plessis, *Collectio*, 1, part 1: 397–400, which also includes quotations from the original 1327 *cedula* of errors. A partial reprint of Du Plessis's edition of the 1375 document (without the list of errors) is provided in CUP 3: #1406.

CENSURES WITHIN THE RELIGIOUS ORDERS

Peter of Tarentaise

The Dominican Peter of Tarentaise was denounced to the minister general of his order, John of Verceil. Between 1265 and 1267, Thomas Aquinas in his capacity as expert theologian wrote a report on theses derived from Tarentaise's commentary on the *Sentences*: Thomas Aquinas, *Responsio ad magistrum Ioannem de Vercellis de 108 articulis* (*Opera Omnia*, ed. Commissio Leonina; Rome, 1979), 42: 277–94. See Courtenay, "Dominicans."

Peter Olivi

In 1283, a list of suspect opinions of Peter Olivi, O.F.M., was sent to the minister general of the Franciscans, Bonagratia of San Giovanni. He assigned a commission of seven Parisian scholars the task of collecting Olivi's erroneous views from his writings. The commission drew up a list (*rotulus*) of false views and added to this another document, the so called *Letter of the Seven Seals*. The latter document is a collection of twenty-two positive statements contradicting Olivi's errors. It is edited in G. Fussenegger, "'Littera septem sigillarum' contra doctrinam Petri Ioannis Olivi edita," *AFH* 47 (1954), 45–53. The list has not been identified yet. Olivi's response to the *Letter of the Seven Seals*, delivered at Avignon in 1283, has been edited in D. Laberge, "Fr. Petri Ioannis Olivi, O.F.M., tria scripta sui ipsius apologetica annorum 1283 et 1285," *AFH* 28 (1935), 126–30. Only sometime between January and May 1285 was Olivi allowed access to his own writings and to the *rotulus* of charged errors. He wrote an *Apologia* to the members of the commission who had censured his opinions. Olivi's 1285 *Apologia* is edited in D. Laberge, "Fr. Petri

Ioannis Olivi, O.F.M., tria scripta sui ipsius apologetica annorum 1283 et 1285," *AFH* 28 (1935), 130–55 and 374–407. In this letter he provides important information concerning the new methods that were used in assessing the orthodoxy of a work. The *Apologia* also reproduces parts of the list of charges. For a narrative account of the events at Olivi's trial and a discussion of the doctrinal issues see the penetrating study by David Burr, *Olivi and Franciscan Poverty. The Origins of the Usus Pauper Controversy* (Philadelphia, 1989).

Durand of St. Pourçain

In 1313, Berengar of Landorra, minister general of the Dominicans, appointed a commission of nine theologians, among whom were the masters Hervaeus Natalis (chairman), Ivo of Caën, John of Parma, and Peter of Palude and the bachelor John of Naples, to examine the commentary on the *Sentences* of the Dominican Durand of St. Pourçain. The reason was that Durand's commentary had been disseminated outside the order without the minister general's permission. The list of ninety-three articles drafted by the commission has been edited in Koch 2: 53–72. Soon afterward, Durand wrote *Excusationes*; the work has not yet been found, but its purport can be reconstructed from Hervaues Natalis's reply, the *Reprobationes excusationum Durandi*. Excerpts of this work have been edited in Josef Koch, *Durandus de Sancto Porciano, O.P.* (Münster, 1927), 222–29. In 1316, Durand's commentary was examined a second time by John of Naples and Peter of Palude, and a list of 235 articles was drawn up. This list has been edited in Koch 2: 72–118.

Peter Olivi

In 1318–20, a commission of eight theologians examined Peter Olivi's *Postille on the Apocalypse* and drew up a list of sixty erroneous articles and gave their votes: CUP 2: #790. The articles themselves are not reproduced in the CUP, nor in Du Plessis's *Collectio*, but in Baluze-Mansi, *Miscellanea*, 2: 258–270, and have been reprinted in Denzinger, *Enchiridion*, nos. 910–916. On February 8, 1326, Pope John XXII condemned Olivi's commentary posthumously. The document, however, has not been discovered yet. The inquiry against Olivi's views is discussed in David Burr, *Olivi's Peaceable Kingdom. A Reading of the Apocalypse Commentary* (Philadelphia, 1993).

William Ockham

In 1324, William Ockham was summoned to Avignon. The results of a preliminary inquest were laid down in a treatise written by John Lutterell, who had brought together and evaluated fifty-six errors taken from Ockham's commentary on the *Sentences*. Lutterell's material was later formalized into the *Libellus contra doctrinam Guillelmi Occam*, edited by Fritz Hoffmann in *Die Schriften des Oforder Kanzlers Iohannes Lutterell. Texte zur Theologie des Vierzehnten Jahrhunderts* (Leipzig, 1959).

The treatise induced Pope John XXII to appoint a commission of theologians to evaluate Ockham's commentary on the *Sentences*. Two reports were produced, designated in the scholarly literature as R and V. Report V was edited for the first time by . A. Pelzer in "Les 51 articles de Guillaume Occam censurés en Avignon, en 1326," *Revue d'histoire ecclésiastique* 18 (1922), 240–70. It was edited a second time in Koch 2: 311–361, together with report R. Records of an earlier inquiry against Ockham, at a provincial chapter in 1323, are edited in Girard J. Etzkorn, "Ockham at a Provincial Chapter, 1323: A Prelude to Avignon," *AFH* 83 (1990), 557–67.

Meister Eckhart

The investigation of Meister Eckhart was started in September 1326 by Henry of Virneburg, the archbishop of Cologne, after Eckhart had been denounced by two fellow Dominicans. The crucial documents of Eckhart's trial are two lists of errors attributed to him, one of forty-nine articles, the other of fifty-nine articles. The latter list was derived from Eckhart's vernacular sermons and was given to him after he had responded to the first list. Both lists, together with Eckhart's defenses, form the *Rechtfertigungsschrift*. This document has been edited twice: by A. Daniels, *Eine lateinische Rechtfertigungsschrift des Meister Eckhart* (Münster i.W., 1923), and by G. Théry, "Édition critique des pièces relatives au procès d'Eckhart contentues dans le manuscrit 33ᵇ de la Bibliothèque de Soest," *AHDL* 1 (1926), 129–268. Historians have generally considered the *Rechtfertigungsschrift* to be a report of the juridical proceedings. This tradition, however, has recently been challenged, with good arguments, by Loris Sturlese. He argues that the *Rechtfertigungsschrift* is a literary product, composed by the first generation of followers of Eckhart at Cologne. Moreover, Sturlese demonstrates that the first list contained only forty-eight articles, instead of forty-nine. See Loris Sturlese, "Die Kölner Eckhartisten. Das Studium generale der deutschen Dominikaner und die Verurteilung der Thesen Meister Eckharts," in *Die Kölner Universität im Mittelalter. Geistige Wurzeln und Soziale Wirklichkeit*, ed. Albert Zimmermann (Berlin and New York, 1989), 192–212. Other documents concerning Eckhart's trial, such as his appeal to Pope John XXII in 1327, his recantation in Cologne (1327), and the condemnation of twenty-eight errors in 1329 in the papal bull *In agro dominico*, have been edited in M.-H. Laurent, "Autour du procès de Maitre Eckhart: Les documents des Archives Vaticanes," *Divus Thomas* 39 (1936) 331–48 and 430–47, and also in Heinrich Denifle, "Acten zum Processe Meister Eckeharts," *Archiv für Litteratur- und Kirchengeschichte des Mittelalters* 2 (1886), 616–40. The report of the experts who investigated Eckhart's opinions at Avignon, the so-called *Votum Avenionense*, has been edited in Franz Pelster, "Ein Gutachten aus dem Eckehart-Prozess in Avignon," in Lang, Lechner, and Schmaus, eds., *Aus der Geisteswelt*, 2: 1099–1124. A new edition of all documents relative to Eckhart's trial is currently being prepared by Loris Sturlese under the title *Acta Echardiana*. The edition is part of the project *Meister Eckhart: Die deutschen und lateinischen Werke*. One volume with documents concerning the examination of Eckhart's views has already appeared: *Die lateinischen Werke*, 5 (Stuttgart, 1988), 197–240. The trial is exhaustively studied in Winfried Trusen, *Der Prozess gegen Meister Eckhart: Vorgeschichte, Verlauf und Folgen* (Paderborn, 1988).

Thomas Waleys and Durand of St. Pourçain

Between 1331 and 1334 the controversy over the Beatific Vision and the investiga-
tion of the views of the Dominicans Thomas Waleys and Durand of St. Pourçain
took place. The documents are edited in CUP 2: #970–#987, #995 and Thomas
Käppeli, O.P., *Le procès contre Thomas Waleys, O.P.* (Rome, 1936), 109–56, 195–239.
In September 1334, when Durand of St. Pourçain died, his views on the Beatific
Vision were still under investigation. The prologue to the expert report by Cardinal
Fournier (Pope Benedict XII) is edited in Maier, 3: 464–79.

STUDIES

In this section I have listed only modern books and articles that relate substantially
to (academic) censures and to the history of the University of Paris and its relations
with the church. The other works that have been cited in this study can be found in
the notes.

Anzulewicz, Henryk. "Eine weitere Überlieferung der *Collectio errorum in Anglia et
    Parisius condemnatorum* im *Ms. lat. fol. 456* der Staatsbibliothek Preussischer
    Kulturbesitz zu Berlin," *Franziskanische Studien* 74 (1992), 375–99.
Asztalos, Monika. "The Faculty of Theology," In *Universities in the Middle Ages*, ed.
    Hilde De Ridder-Symoens, 401–441. *A History of the University in Europe*, vol.
    1. Cambridge, 1992.
Bernstein, Allen E. "Magisterium and License: Corporate Autonomy Against Papal
    Authority in the Medieval University of Paris," *Viator* 9 (1978), 291–309.
——. *Pierre d'Ailly and the Blanchard Affair*. Leiden, 1978.
Bianchi, Luca. "Captivare intellectum in obsequium Christi," *RCSF* 38 (1983), 81–
    87.
——. *Il vescovo e i filosofi: La condanna parigina del 1277 e l'evoluzione dell'aristotelismo
    scolastico*. Bergamo, 1990.
Boyce, Gray C. *The English-German Nation in the University of Paris During the
    Middle Ages*. Bruges, 1927.
Burr, David. "Olivi and the Limits of Intellectual Freedom." In *Contemporary Reflec-
    tions on the Medieval Christian Tradition*, ed. G. H. Shriver, 185–99. Durham,
    N.C., 1974.
——. *The Persecution of Peter Olivi*. Philadelphia, 1976.
——. *Olivi and Franciscan Poverty: The Origins of the Usus Pauper Controversy*. Phila-
    delphia, 1989.
——. *Olivi's Peaceable Kingdom: A Reading of the Apocalypse Commentary*. Phila-
    delphia, 1993.
Bury, John B. *History of Freedom of Thought*. London, 1913.
Classen, Peter. "Libertas scolastica—Scholarenprivilegien—Akademische Freiheit
    im Mittelalter." In Peter Classen, *Studium und Gesellschaft im Mittelalter*, ed.
    Johannes Fried, 238–84. Stuttgart, 1983.

Clerval, Jules-Alexandre. *Registre des procès-verbaux de la faculté de théologie de Paris.* Vol. 1: 1505–23. Paris, 1917.

Congar, Yves. "Aspects ecclésiologiques de la querelle entre mendiants et séculiers dans la seconde moitié du XIIIe siècle et le début du XIVe," *AHDL* 36 (1961), 35–151.

———. "Pour une histoire sémantique du terme 'magisterium,'" *RSPT* 60 (1976), 85–98. Reprinted in Yves Congar, *Droit ancien et structures ecclésiales.* London, 1982.

———. "Bref historique des formes du 'magistère' et de ses relations avec les docteurs," *RSPT* 60 (1976), 99–112. Reprinted in Yves Congar, *Droit ancien et structures ecclésiales.* London, 1982.

Coppens, E. C. "De inquisitoire procedure in het canonieke recht." In *Misdaad, zoen en straf. Aspekten van de middeleeuwse strafrechtsgeschiedenis in de Nederlanden,* ed. H. A. Diederiks and H. W. Roodenburg, 37–47. Hilversum, 1991.

Courtenay, William J. "The Reception of Ockham's Thought at the University of Paris." In *Preuve et raisons à l'université de Paris. Logique, ontologies et théologie au XIVe siècle,* ed. Zénon Kaluza and Paul Vignaux, 43–64. Paris, 1984.

———. *Teaching Careers at the University of Paris in the Thirteenth and Fourteenth Centuries.* Notre Dame, Ind., 1988.

———. "Inquiry and Inquisition: Academic Freedom in Medieval Universities," *CH* 58 (1989), 168–82.

———. "In Search of Nominalism: Two Centuries of Historical Debate," In *Gli studi di filosofia medievale fra otto e novecento,* ed. Ruedi Imbach and Alfonso Maierù, 233–53. Rome, 1991.

———. "The Articles Condemned at Oxford Austin Friars in 1315," in *Via Augustini. Augustine in the Later Middle Ages, Renaissance and Reformation,* ed. Heiko O. Oberman and Frank A. James, III, 5–18. Leiden, 1991.

———. "The Registers of the University of Paris and the Statutes Against the 'Scientia Occamica,'" *Vivarium* 29 (1991), 13–49.

———. "Dominicans and Suspect Opinion in the Thirteenth Century: The Case of Stephen of Venizy, Peter of Tarentaise, and the Articles of 1270 and 1271," *Vivarium* 32 (1994), 186–95.

———. "Erfurt CA 2 127 and the Censured Articles of Mirecourt and Autrecourt." In *Die Bibliotheca Amploniana. Ihre Bedeutung im Spannungsfeld von Aristotelismus, Nominalismus und Humanismus,* ed. Andreas Speer, 341–52. Berlin, 1995.

———. "The Preservation and Dissemination of Academic Condemnations at the University of Paris in the Middle Ages." In *Les philosophies morales et politiques au Moyen Age,* ed. C. Bazán, E. Andújar, and L. Sbrocchi, 3: 1659–67. 3 vols. New York, Ottawa, and Toronto, 1995.

———. "Was There an Ockhamist School?" In *Philosophy and Learning: The Universities in the Middle Ages,* ed. Maarten J. F. M. Hoenen, J. H. Josef Schneider, and Georg Wieland, 263–293. Leiden, 1995.

———. "The Debate Over Ockham's Physical Theories at Paris." In *La nouvelle physique du XIVe siècle,* ed. Stefano Caroti and Pierre Souffrin, 45–65. Florence, 1997.

Courtenay, William J., and Katherine H. Tachau. "Ockham, Ockhamists, and the

English-German Nation at Paris, 1339–1341," *History of Universities* 2 (1982), 53–96.

Dales, Richard C. "The Origin of the Doctrine of the Double Truth," *Viator* 15 (1984), 169–79.

Dufeil, Marc M. *Guillaume de Saint-Amour et la polémique universitaire Parisienne, 1250–1259.* Paris, 1972.

Dykmans, Marc. "A propos de Jean XXII et Benoît XII. La libération de Thomas Waleys," *Archivum Historiae Pontificae* 7 (1969), 115–30.

Eldredge, L. M. "Changing Concepts of Church Authority in the Later Fourteenth Century: Peter Ceffons of Clairvaux and William Woodford, O.F.M.," *Revue de l'université d'Ottawa* 48 (1978), 170–78.

Farge, James K. *Orthodoxy and Reform in Early Reformation France. The Faculty of Theology of Paris, 1500–1543.* Leiden, 1985.

Ferruolo, Stephen C. *The Origins of the University: The Schools of Paris and Their Critics, 1100–1215.* Stanford, Calif., 1985.

———. "The Paris Statutes of 1215 Reconsidered," *History of Universities* 5 (1985), 1–15.

Fitch Lytle, Guy. "Universities as Religious Authorities in the Later Middle Ages and Reformation." In *Reform and Authority in the Medieval and Reformation Church,* ed. Guy Fitch Lytle, 69–97. Washington, D.C., 1981.

Flasch, Kurt. *Aufklärung im Mittelalter? Die Verurteilung von 1277.* Frankfurt, 1989.

Gabriel, Astrik L. "The Conflict Between the Chancellor and the University of Masters and Students at Paris During the Middle Ages." In *Die Auseinandersetzungen an der Pariser Universität im XIII. Jahrhundert,* ed. Albert Zimmermann, 106–55. Berlin, 1976.

Ginzburg, Carlo. "High and Low: The Theme of Forbidden Knowledge," *Past & Present* 73 (1976), 28–41.

Glorieux, P. "L'enseignement au Moyen Age. Techniques et méthodes en usage à la faculté de théologie de Paris au XIIIe siècle," *AHDL* 43 (1968), 65–186.

Grabmann, Martin. "Ein spätmittelalterlicher Pariser Kommentar zur Verurteilung des lateinischen Averroismus durch Bischof Stephan Tempier von Paris (1277) und zu anderen Irrtumslisten." In *Mittelalterliches Geistesleben,* ed. Martin Grabmann, 2: 272–86. 3 vols. Munich, 1936.

Grant, Edward. "The Condemnation of 1277, God's Absolute Power, and Physical Thought in the Late Middle Ages," *Viator* 10 (1979), 211–44.

———. "The Effect of the Condemnation of 1277," in *CHLMP,* 537–40.

Hageneder, Othmar. "Studien zur Dekretale 'Vergentis' (X: V,7,10): Ein Beitrag zur Häretikergesetzgebung Innocenz' III," *Zeitschrift der Savigny-Stiftung,* Kan. Abt. 49 (1963), 138–63.

———. "Der Häresiebegriff bei den Juristen des 12. und 13. Jahrhunderts." In *The Concept of Heresy,* ed. W. Lourdaux and D. Verhelst, 42–104. Louvain, 1976.

Häring, Nikolaus M. "Die ersten Konflikte zwischen der Universität von Paris und der kirchlichen Lehrautorität." In *Die Auseinandersetzungen an der Pariser Universität im XIII. Jahrhundert,* ed. Albert Zimmermann, 38–52. Berlin, 1976.

Hissette, Roland. *Enquête sur les 219 articles condamnés à Paris le 7 mars 1277.* Louvain, 1977.

———. "Etienne Tempier et ses condemnations," *RTAM* 47 (1980), 231–70.

———. "Albert le Grand et Thomas d'Aquin dans la censure parisienne du 7 mars 1277." In *Studien zur mittelalterlichen Geistesgeschichte und ihren Quellen*, ed. Albert Zimmermann, 229–237. Berlin, 1982.

———. "Une question quodlibétique de Servais du Mont-Saint-Éloi sur le pouvoir doctrinal de l'évêque," *RTAM* 49 (1982), 238–42.

———. "Une *Tabula super articulis Parisiensibus*," *RTAM* 52 (1985), 171–72.

———. "Note sur le syllabus 'antirationaliste' du 7 mars 1277," *Revue Philosophique de Louvain* 88 (1990), 404–16.

Hocedez, Ernesto. "La condamnation de Gilles de Rome," *RTAM* 4 (1932), 34–58.

Hödl, Ludwig "'. . . sie reden, als ob es zwei gegensätzliche Wahrheiten gäbe.' Legende und Wirklichkeit der mittelalterlichen Theorie von der doppelten Wahrheit." In *Philosophie im Mittelalter. Entwicklungslinien und Paradigmen*, ed. Jan P. Beckmann, *e.a.*, 225–45. Hamburg, 1987.

Kaluza, Zénon. *Les querelles doctrinales à Paris. Nominalistes et réalistes aux confins de XIVe et XVe siècles.* Bergamo, 1988.

———. "Le statut du 25 septembre 1339 et l'Ordonnance du 2 septembre 1276." In *Die Philosophie im 14. und 15. Jahrhundert*, ed. Olaf Pluta, 343–51. Amsterdam, 1988.

———. "Les sciences et leurs langages. Note sur le statut du 29 décembre 1340 et le prétendu statut perdu contre Ockham." In *Filosofia e teologia nel trecento. Studi in ricordo di Eugenio Randi*, ed. Luca Bianchi, 197–258. Louvain-la-Neuve, 1994.

———. *Nicolas d'Autrecourt. Ami de la vérité. Histoire littéraire de la France*, vol. 42, fasc. 1. Paris, 1995.

Käppeli, Thomas. *Le procès contre Thomas Waleys, O.P.* Rome, 1936.

Kelly, H. Ansgar. "Inquisition and the Prosecution of Heresy: Misconceptions and Abuses," *CH* 58 (1989), 439–51.

———. "Inquisitorial Due Process and the Status of Secret Crimes." In *Proceedings of the Eighth International Congress of Medieval Canon Law*, ed. Stanley Chodorow, 407–427. Vatican City, 1992.

Kibre, Pearl. *The Nations in the Mediaeval Universities.* Cambridge, Mass., 1948.

———. "Academic Oaths at the University of Paris in the Middle Ages." In *Essays in Medieval Life and Thought: Presented in Honor of Austin Patterson Evans*, ed. John H. Mundy, Robert W. Emery, and Benjamin N. Nelson, 123–37. New York, 1955.

Koch, Josef. *Durandus de Sancto Porciano, O.P.* Münster, 1927.

———. *Kleine Schriften.* 2 vols. Rome, 1973.

Lambert, Malcolm D. *Medieval Heresy: Popular Movements from Bogomil to Hus.* London, 1977.

Leff, Gordon. *Paris and Oxford Universities in the Thirteenth and Fourteenth Centuries.* New York, 1968.

———. "The 'Trivium' and the Three Philosophies." In *Universities in the Middle Ages*, ed. Hilde De Ridder-Symoens, 307–37. *A History of the University in Europe*, vol 1. Cambridge, 1992.

Lourdaux, W. and Verhelst, D., eds. *The Concept of Heresy.* Louvain, 1976.

Mandonnet, Pierre. *Siger de Brabant et l'averroïsme latin au XIIIe siècle.* 2 vols. Louvain, 1908–11.

McGinn, Bernard. "Eckhart's Condemnation Reconsidered," *The Thomist* 44 (1980), 390–414.

McGrade, Arthur S. *The Political Thought of William of Ockham.* Cambridge, 1974.

McKeon, P. R. "The Status of the University of Paris as 'Parens Scientiarum': An Episode in the Development of Its Autonomy," *Speculum* 39 (1964), 651–75.

McLaughlin, Mary M. "Paris Masters of the Thirteenth and Fourteenth Centuries and Ideas of Intellectual Freedom," *CH* 24 (1955), 195–211.

——. *Intellectual Freedom and Its Limitations in the University of Paris in the Thirteenth and Fourteenth Centuries.* New York, 1977.

Metzger, Walter P. "Academic Freedom and Scientific Freedom," *Daedalus* 107 (1978), 93–115.

Michalski, Konstanty. "La révocation par Frère Barthélemy, en 1316, de 13 thèses incriminées." In *Aus der Geisteswelt des Mittelalters. Studien und Texte Martin Grabmann zur Vollendung des 60. Lebensjahres,* ed. Albert Lang, Joseph Lechner, and Michael Schmaus, 2: 1091–1098. Münster, 1935.

Michaud-Quantin, Pierre. "La conscience d'être membre d'une universitas." In *Beiträge zum Berufsbewusstsein des mittelalterlichen Menschen,* ed. Paul Wilpert, 1–15. Berlin, 1964.

——. *Universitas. Expressions du mouvement communautaire dans le moyen-âge latin.* Paris, 1970.

Miethke, Jürgen. "Theologenprozesse in der ersten Phase ihrer institutionellen Ausbildung: Die Verfahren gegen Peter Abaelard und Gilbert von Poitiers," *Viator* 6 (1975), 87–117.

——. "Papst, Ortsbischof und Universität in den Pariser Theologenprozessen des 13. Jahrhunderts." In *Die Auseinandersetzungen an der Pariser Universität im XIII. Jahrhundert,* ed. Albert Zimmermann, 52–95. Berlin, 1976.

——. "Bildungsstand und Freiheitsforderung (12. bis 14. Jahrhundert)." In *Die Abendländische Freiheit vom 10. zum 14. Jahrhundert,* ed. Johannes Fried, 221–47. Sigmaringen, 1991.

Moody, Ernest A. "Ockham, Buridan, and Nicholas of Autrecourt: The Parisian Statutes of 1339 and 1340," *FS* 7 (1947), 113–146. Reprinted in Ernest A. Moody, *Studies in Medieval Philosophy, Science and Logic,* 127–60. Berkeley, Calif., 1975.

Moore, R. I. "Heresy as disease." in *The Concept of Heresy,* ed. W. Lourdaux and D. Verhelst, 1–12. Louvain, 1976.

Nardi, Paolo. "Relations with Authority." In *Universities in the Middle Ages,* ed. Hilde De Ridder-Symoens, 77–108. *A History of the University in Europe. vol 1.* Cambridge, 1992.

Oberman, Heiko A. *Contra vanam curiositatem.* Zürich, 1974.

Paqué, Ruprecht. *Das Pariser Nominalistenstatut.* Berlin, 1970.

Peters, Edward, ed. *Heresy and Authority in Medieval Europe: Documents in Translation.* Philadelphia, 1980.

Peters, Edward. "*Libertas inquirendi* and the *vitium curiositatis* in Medieval Thought." In *La notion de liberté au moyen âge. Islam, Byzance, Occident,* ed. G. Makdisi, D. Sourdel, and J. Sourdel-Thomine, 91–98. Paris, 1985.

——. *Inquisition.* New York, 1988.

——. "Transgressing the Limits Set by the Fathers: Authority and Impious Exegesis in Medieval Thought." In *Christendom and Its Discontents: Exclusion, Persecution, and Rebellion, 1000–1500,* ed. Scott L. Waugh and Peter D. Diehl, 338–62. Cambridge, 1996.

Post, Gaines. "Parisian Masters as a Corporation, 1200–1246," *Speculum* 9 (1934), 421–45.

Posthumus Meyjes, G. H. M. "Het gezag van de theologische doctor in de kerk der middeleeuwen," *Nederlands Archief voor Kerkgeschiedenis* 63 (1983), 113–21.

Putallaz, François-Xavier. *Insolente Liberté. Controverses et condemnations au XIIIe siècle.* Paris, 1995.

Russell, Jeffrey B. *Dissent and Order in the Middle Ages: The Search for Legitimate Authority.* New York, 1992.

Ryan, John J. *The Nature, Structure and Function of the Church in William of Ockham.* Missoula, Mont., 1979.

Southern, Richard W. "The Changing Role of Universities in Medieval Europe," *Historical Research* 60 (1987), 133–46.

Swanson, R. N. *Universities, Academics and the Great Schism.* Cambridge, 1979.

Tedeschi, John. *The Prosecution of Heresy. Collected Studies on the Inquisition in Early Modern Italy.* Binghamton, N.Y., 1991.

Thijssen, J. M. M. H. "Once Again the Ockhamist Statutes of 1339 and 1340: Some New Perspectives," *Vivarium,* 28 (1990), 136–67.

——. "The 'Semantic' Articles of Autrecourt's Condemnation. New Proposals for an Interpretation of the Articles 1, 30, 31, 35, 57, and 58," *AHDL* 57 (1990), 155–75.

——. "Academic Heresy and Intellectual Freedom at the University of Paris, 1200–1378." In *Centres of Learning in Pre-Modern Europe and the Near East,* ed. Jan-Willem Drijvers and A. A. MacDonald, 217–28. Leiden, 1995.

——. "Master Amalric and the Amalricians: Inquisitorial Procedure and the Suppression of Heresy at the University of Paris," *Speculum,* 71 (1996), 43–65.

——. "1277 Revisited: A New Interpretation of the Doctrinal Investigations of Thomas Aquinas and Giles of Rome," *Vivarium* 34 (1997), 1–29.

——. "What Really Happened on 7 March 1277? Bishop Tempier's Condemnation and Its Institutional Context." In *Texts and Contexts in Ancient and Medieval Science. Studies on the Occasion of John E. Murdoch's Seventieth Birthday,* ed. Edith Sylla and Michael McVaugh, 84–114. Leiden, 1997.

——. "The Crisis Over Ockhamist Hermeneutic and Its Semantic Background: The Methodological Significance of the Censure of December 29, 1340." In *Vestigia, Imagines, Verba. Semiotics and Logic in Medieval Theological Texts (XIIth–XIVth Century),* ed. Costantino Marmo, 371–92. Turnhout, 1997.

Tierney, Brian. *Ockham, the Conciliar Theory and the Canonists.* Philadelphia, 1971.

——. *Origins of Papal Infallibility, 1150–1350.* Leiden, 1972.

Trapp, Damasus. "Peter Ceffons of Clairvaux," *RTAM* 24 (1957), 101–54.

Trusen, Winfried. "Der Inquisitionsprozess: Seine historischen Grundlagen und frühen Formen," *Zeitschrift der Savigny-Stiftung für Rechtsgeschichte,* Kan. Abt. 105 (1988), 168–230.

———. *Der Prozess gegen Meister Eckhart: Vorgeschichte, Verlauf und Folgen.* Paderborn, 1988.

Ullmann, Walter. "Some Medieval Principles of Criminal Procedure," *Juridical Review* 59 (1947), 1–28. Reprinted in Walter Ullmann, *Jurisprudence in the Middle Ages.* London, 1980.

Van Laarhoven, Jan. "*Magisterium* or *Magisteria*: A Historical Note to a Theological Note," *Jaarboek Thomas Instituut te Utrecht* (1990), 75–94.

Van Steenberghen, Fernand. *Maître Siger de Brabant.* Louvain, 1977.

———. *Thomas Aquinas and Radical Aristotelianism.* Washington, D.C., 1980.

Verbeke, Gerard. "Philosophy and Heresy: Some Conflicts Between Reason and Faith." In *The Concept of Heresy,* ed. W. Lourdaux and D. Verhelst, 72–198. Louvain, 1976.

Verger, Jacques. "Teachers." In *Universities in the Middle Ages,* ed. Hilde De Ridder-Symoens, 144–68. *A History of the University in Europe.* vol 1. Cambridge, 1992.

Walther, Helmut G. "Häresie und päpstliche Politik: Ketzerbegriff und Ketzergesetzgebung in der Übergangsphase von der Dekretistik zur Dekretalistik." In *The Concept of Heresy,* ed. W. Lourdaux and D. Verhelst, 104–44. Louvain, 1976.

Weijers, Olga. *Terminologie des universités au XIIIe siècle.* Rome, 1987.

Wielockx, Robert. "Autour du procès de Thomas d'Aquin." In *Thomas von Aquin. Werk und Wirkung im Licht neurerer Forschungen,* ed. A. Zimmermann, 413–38. Berlin, 1988.

Wippel, John F. "The Condemnations of 1270 and 1277 at Paris," *Journal of Medieval and Renaissance Studies* 7 (1977), 169–201.

———. *Mediaeval Reactions to the Encounter Between Faith and Reason.* Milwaukee, 1995.

———. "Thomas Aquinas and the Condemnation of 1277," *The Modern Schoolman* 72 (1995), 233–72.

———. "Bishop Stephen Tempier and Thomas Aquinas: A Separate Process Against Aquinas?" *Freiburger Zeitschrift für Philosophie und Theologie,* 44 (1997), 117–36.

Index